© 2022 Oregon Parks and Recreation Department
725 Summer Street NE Suite C Salem Oregon 97301

ISBN: 978-0-578-39104-5 (Paperback)

All photos courtesy OPRD except where noted.
Copyediting and photo captions by Jean Thompson, OPRD.
Additional review by Christy Sweet, OPRD Historian.

"So the Future Will Have a Place":
The First Century of Oregon State Parks

MARIN AURAND AND MARC CARPENTER

Table of Contents

In 2022, the Oregon Parks and Recreation Commission consisted of seven members, appointed by the Governor and confirmed by the Senate, to set policy and adopt rules for the agency. The Commission also promotes Oregon's outdoor recreation policy and has specific authority to acquire property and set fees for the use of park facilities. Commissioners serve four-year terms. As specified by state law, the Commission has a representative from each of Oregon's congressional districts, plus representatives of the areas east of the Cascade Mountains and west of the summit of the Coast Range.

Members

Jennifer H. Allen, Chair
Congressional District 1

Steve Grasty
Congressional District 2

Jonathan Blasher
Congressional District 3

Elizabeth Hill
Congressional District 4

Victoria Berger
Congressional District 5

Lisa Dawson
East of the Cascades

Doug Deur
West of the Coast Range

Staff

Steve Shipsey, Assistant Attorney General
Lisa Sumption, Director
Denise Warburton, Executive Assistant to the Director and Commission

Foreword

This book tells the story of Oregon's State Parks from the vantage point of 2021, chronicling the challenges that have faced the Parks system over the past 100 years and celebrating the individuals – leaders, staff, volunteers, and members of the public – who have stepped up along the way to support, protect and defend what is now the nation's premier State Parks system. The narrative also acknowledges where Oregon State Parks have fallen short, where we have perpetuated inequity and injustice by excluding – or simply not fully welcoming – staff and visitors on the basis of race, gender, ability, and other "differences."

As you will read in the final chapter, "the purpose in studying history is not to judge our predecessors, but to critique ourselves and our own leap from aspiration to service" (p. 177). As this book goes to print, the Oregon State Parks system continues to face significant challenges. Climate change is no longer a future threat, it has arrived: megafires and sea level rise threaten some of our most treasured landscapes. Demands on our Parks continue to grow, outpacing the resources available to maintain and sustain them. We still have a long way to go to make certain our Parks evolve and adapt to these challenges, while making sure we are truly welcoming to all visitors.

What this book makes clear, however, is that facing challenges with courage and an innovative spirit is a through-line in the history of Oregon's State Parks. The successes of the past century can be credited to people coming together to solve problems, bound by a shared love for our Parks and a commitment to their enduring legacy. We invite you to work with us to create a more socially equitable, ecologically resilient, and economically vibrant State Parks system, so that the future will have a place.

Oregon State Parks and Recreation Commission
July, 2021

Tub Springs 1927

Introduction

So the Future Will Have a Place

In 1933, Sam Boardman, the first Superintendent of Oregon State Parks, wrote an S.O.S. There was a scenic area along the Oregon Coast that was about to be sold, and Boardman's hands were tied. It was the middle of the Great Depression, and Boardman couldn't afford to buy the land on behalf of the state. Only four years into his tenure, he was frustrated by what felt like an endless uphill battle to secure the natural beauties of Oregon. If people did not act quickly, he feared, all of the state's greatest treasures would be gobbled up by development, and nothing would remain to be preserved and protected. He had to move forward with his feet on the ground and his eyes on eternity:

> *From the day I took up this work I have walked in the dust, but never have I let my vision be obscure of the future. The scar of the event of any one day must not be carried to a tomorrow. The future is the hope of mankind. Can't we lay the keel so the future will have a place?*

This kind of S.O.S would be called by every park administrator that would follow. Calls for more money, more land, more protections, and more help were sometimes answered, but were largely ignored by the general public until a point of crisis. Boardman cast himself as the lone crusader for Oregon Parks, but he was one of a chorus of men and women who rallied for the cause of scenic spaces for more than 100 years. Boardman's simple call to "lay the keel" was in response to the roiling waters of political machinations, funding shortages, cultural shifts, and national tragedies. The fortunes of the Oregon State Parks system ebbed and flowed with times, but there was always some storm on the horizon. Parks staff, leaders, and supporters fought to keep the system shipshape with every gale. But while Oregon's state park system has sometimes foundered, somehow, despite disaster, parks people have kept it from sinking.

This is a history of what became the *Oregon State Parks and Recreation Department*. Our focus is on how the system was conceived, grown, threatened, shaped, and reshaped as times and expectations changed. Our story takes us to moments of plucky idealism and catastrophic shortsightedness, from the department's shaky start as an adjunct of state highway system to its development as a full-fledged agency charged with over 113,000 acres of public lands and counting, along with a broad portfolio of tasks, divisions, and duties variously connected to an evolving mission. This story is also a story of shifts in mindset over nature and government, over travel and tourism, over preservation and use, over who parks are for and how they should be. Parks were shaped by the people, and the people were shaped, willingly or unwillingly, by the times. Whatever the era, the parks relied, at the end of the day, on the people working daily "in the dust."

Our story begins with a view of the ocean, automobile travel, Good Roads, and tourism. It follows economic booms and busts, changing needs and demographics, and the whims of politicians, volunteers, and bureaucrats. As parks grew, conceptions of nature, preservation, history, and recreation shifted. Protections were put in place, money was given and taken away, and the role of parks in the statewide governmental system was challenged and debated at the highest levels and, eventually, the ballot. The one constant has been the need to adapt, sometimes reluctantly, to these shifting sands. Adaptation and struggle are central themes of the book. There was always a crisis brewing for Oregon state parks. That the system exists at all—much less that it has gained the successes it has—is a testament to hard work of those who loved parks enough to fight against the tides.

That hard work includes the labors of those who have shaped the history of Oregon State Parks before us. Elisabeth Walton Potter, the first professional Park Historian, collected the materials that form the backbone of the Oregon State Parks and Recreation archive. The thousands and thousands of pages of material in this archive date back to earliest moments of park creation and cover more than could ever be captured in a single text. The digital extensions of the archive added by Katherine Schutt after Walton stepped down were vital to the last few chapters of this book. Sam Boardman, W. A. Langille, Chet Armstrong, Thomas R. Cox, Lawrence Merriam, Dave Talbot, and others all dedicated time and resources to writing on the history of Oregon state parks. Many more sat down with Potter, Merriam, or Schutt to tell their stories. This book could not exist without them.

But every book, and every collection, has limitations. The loudest voices in the archive are from the top. We have many sources from Sam Boardman and Dave Talbot, quite possibly the two loudest men in the history of the park system. But we have much less from the park advocates, opponents, and folks on the ground whose remembrances were not preserved in this same way. Our archival record, and thus our book, is quiet—at times silent—on the lives, feelings, and struggles of the everyday park workers who were instrumental in the foundation and upkeep of parks. We bring out those aspects where we can, but the story of life on the ground in Oregon state parks we leave for future historians.

We have also deliberately written a history of the Oregon state park *system* rather than of individual parks. It would take thousands of pages to do justice to the hundreds of parks and recreation areas we might have talked about—even if we focused just on the 256 in the current system and not the parks that were once were dreamed of or have yet to be. We mention specific parks when the story leads us to them, but frequent or absent mentions of a particular park does not mean that we were gauging importance or picking favorites. Dave Talbot, the longest-serving Superintendent in the first hundred years of Oregon parks, was once asked if there was a park that was his personal favorite. His response?

"No. It is like picking out which of your kids you like best. It is just not possible. They all have their own individual personalities.... All of Oregon is a park."

When we were commissioned to write this book, we were given a significant amount of free rein in what we should cover and how we should cover it. We were told to keep it grounded and keep it interesting—which have tried, at least, to do. And we were instructed to tell the story "warts and all," which has helped us with those goals. Early on, as we looked through the records, we noticed the theme of persevering through crisis. Some crises parks faced with the rest of the state or the nation; others were unique to the parks system. There was no Golden Age for Oregon state parks. The challenges have changed and shifted over the decades, but they have never disappeared.

Most of this book was written in 2020. Oregon State Parks and Recreation was, like so many other institutions, buffeted by the blows of disaster throughout the months we were writing. Planned interviews and events evaporated. Many of the people who originally met with us to bring this book into being had to leave the department. The future remains uncertain in so many ways, big and small.

At previous turning points in the history of the Oregon parks system, staff and legislatures looked to the public for guidance. Parks were designed to be for the people, and parks will only survive if the people fight for them. Rather than adjuncts of a distant bureaucratic machine, parks are parts of communities. The greatest failures of the Oregon state park system have come from times in which the parks system falls out of step with the people it is designed to serve. The greatest successes have come from building a shared vision, for the present *and* the future, with an invested public.

Parks have often been framed as a legacy, something that lives on after we die. Sam Boardman once wrote, "We can take nothing. We can leave much." And generations of hard work by parks people has left us much. But the work is never done. The fight to give the future a place, a park, a legacy—that fight continues, for everyone who works at Oregon State Parks, and everyone who cares about them.

Bradley State Wayside, 1920s

CHAPTER 1

Abundantly Blessed with a Thousand and One Wonders:
The Road to Oregon's State Park System
(1913 - 1929)

It all started with a beach, or so the story goes. Fresh off his successful campaign for governor the year before, Oswald West acquired a stretch of land just south of Cannon Beach near Haystack Rock in 1911, braced by the forest on one side and the ocean on the other. Newly sensitized to the beauty of the coast and fearing the encroachment of unsightly development, West purportedly resolved to do something to protect the beach as a public good—in keeping with his ethos of public ownership and government conservation. As workers were preparing to finish his beachfront home in early 1913, the governor gave his biennial message to the legislature, as usual laying out an ambitious agenda he hoped they might pursue. Among the 40-plus proposals for the "greater development of the State and the increased prosperity of her people" was an item labeled "Good Roads"—a standard part of governors' messages throughout the decade, addressing the desirability of building roads for these new "automobiles" that seemed to be increasingly popular. After noting that the recent election had shown that the voters did not want any costly expansion of the roadways, West proposed that "[t]he ocean beach from the Columbia River to the north to the California State line on the south should be declared a public highway." In a legislative session otherwise marked by contention between the governor and the state legislature, this part of the governor's raft of proposals passed easily, with no recorded dissension or debate. On February 13, 1913, it became Oregon law that the tideline of (nearly) all Oregon beaches was "a public highway and shall forever remain open as such to the public."[1]

Most histories of the public parks and public recreation in Oregon begin with this law, and for good reason. Oregon beaches are a foundational part of

---

1 Kay Weeks, "Oswald West Coastal Retreat," *Working on the Past in Local Historic Districts*, U.S. National-al Park Service **(www.nps.gov/tps/education/workingonthepast/index.htm)**; "Oswald West, Governor of Oregon, to the Twenty-Seventh Legislative Assembly," (Salem: Willis S. Duniway, State Printer, 1913), pp. 3, 12; *State of Oregon... General Laws* (Salem: State Printing Department, 1913), Chapters 47, 80. A small portion of tideland had already been sold to private interests, and was thus exempted from this law.

Oregonian identity, and the public character of those beaches is one of the distinguishing traits of the state. But while it has become legendary, there is little evidence that many people saw the first beach bill as significant at the time. Unlike the public debates, furor, and celebration over beach legislation in the 1960s, this first law was passed with minimal attention. It is possible that Oswald West, as he claimed much later in the 1940s, knew precisely what he was doing when he maneuvered this secretly massive public land bill through the legislature. But it was a milestone whose full weight would not be felt for decades.[2]

Milestones are built on minutiae. Oswald West's proclamation mattered because it became law. It became law because the Oregon legislature was already primed to support it. Two days before Governor West enshrined Oregon beaches as public highways, the Oregon Legislature met jointly in special night session to hear from experts in the Good Roads movement. As they had for years, these activists extolled the value of preserving nature along roadsides of all sorts—and the economic prosperity that would bring. Two years before the proclamation, West's acquisition of picturesque property south of Cannon Beach helped set his devotion to coastal preservation in motion. Four decades before that, in 1871, Oregon's first public parks were created in Portland and Sodaville. In rural and urban Oregon, then, there was interest in developing public lands for recreation long before there were state laws to that effect. From the centuries and millennia before Euro-American arrival to the present day, Indigenous people and communities in what became Oregon have commemorated places of especial beauty and significance in the land they shape through reciprocal relationships. Every history has a tail that stretches beyond the horizon.[3]

The significance of the first milestones that built the Oregon state park system, such as West's public beach bill, are clearer in retrospect than they were at the time. State parks were auxiliary to highways in the 1921 and 1925 laws that laid the groundwork for the system. Subsumed in larger debates about public lands and public roads, surrounded by other conservationist causes and alternative opportunities for outdoor recreation, Oregon State Parks only slowly developed its own identity. But the activists and administrators who laid the foundations for Oregon state parks shaped the blueprint of the system for decades to come, in ways they may not have foreseen. Amidst a broad sympathy for nature and recreation in Oregon (a sympathy that did not always extend to the budget), amongst a broad array of park organizations, Oregon State Parks only slowly found a place.

---

2 Oswald West, "Seashore Conservation," *Oregon Daily Journal* Aug 8, 1949; Kathryn A. Straton, *Oregon's Beaches: A Birthright Preserved* (Oregon State Parks and Recreation, 1977).

3 For the meeting with Good Roads advocates, see *Journal of the Legislative Assembly... of the State of Oregon... 1913* (Eugene: The Guard Printing Company, 1913), pp. 555 – 556.

The Whole Country ... a Park:
Indigenous Peoples and the Land They Made

Native people have savored and celebrated their cultures' connection to the land since time immemorial. Long before Euro-American invaders imposed their own geography on what they called Oregon, Indigenous people and nations have identified spaces of especial beauty, cultural relevance, and/or spiritual power, including celebrated locales like Wy-am (Celilo Falls) and Gii-was (Crater Lake). Native identity shaped and was shaped by ties to the land, as it continues to be for many Indigenous people in Oregon today. Use did not preclude reverence. Indeed, agricultural, gathering, fishing, and hunting practices were seen as a way of fulfilling a reciprocal relationship with the land. Some spaces, like Wy-am (Celilo Falls), were meeting grounds—local fishers had special rights over the waters, but a multitude of Native peoples and nations met there to trade, socialize, and negotiate. Other spaces, like Gii-was (Crater Lake), were reserved largely for sacred activity, considered places of heightened spiritual hazard, power, and opportunity. But all spaces in the region were, and are, Native land, inextricably woven into Indigenous life and identity. Colonialism, invasion, and the incalculable Indigenous deaths inflicted by both have strained but not severed these connections. The relationship between Native people and communities and their homeland continues.[4]

Euro-American settlers in early Oregon, too, got much of their recreation outdoors. Hunting and berry-picking served pleasurable as well as practical purposes. While the word "hike" remained a term of contempt in the nineteenth century, early Oregonians nonetheless went on long walks, stargazed, and sometimes even climbed mountains for pleasure. Cookouts and clambakes could mark special occasions, or become them. In later years, some early Euro-American emigrants to Oregon recalled a love of wilderness as one of the things that drew them to the nascent state. John Minto, one of these early emigrants, attributed his move west to Oregon in part to his "love of nature... the fields and the woods—the streams and the seashore."[5]

Love of nature was a shared idea; "Oregon wilderness" was (and is) an unnatural concept. The natural landscapes extolled by Euro-American

---

4 Douglas Deur, "A Most Sacred Place: The Significance of Crater Lake among the Indians of Southern Oregon," *Oregon Historical Quarterly* 103 (2002): pp. 18 – 49; David Lewis, "Four Deaths: The Near Destruction of Western Oregon Tribes and Native Lifeways, Removal to Reservation, and Erasure from History," *Oregon Historical Quarterly* 115 (2014): pp. 414 – 437; Katrine Barber, *In Defense of Wy-Am: Native White Alliances and the Struggle for Celilo Village* (Seattle: University of Washington Press, 2018); Special Issue: Remembering Celilo Falls, *Oregon Historical Quarterly* 108 (2007).

5 Cox, *The Park Builders*, 5 – 6; Rev. Robert Forby, *The Vocabulary of East Anglia...*, v. 2 (London: J.B. Nicholas and Son, 1830): p. 158; Inez Eugenia Adams Parker, "Early Recollections of Oregon Pioneer Life," Folder: Inez M. Parker, Box M – Rei, Diaries and Reminiscences, Mss 1509, Oregon Historical Society Special Collections, Portland, OR; Earl Pomeroy, *In Search of the Golden West: The Tourist in Western America* (New York: Alfred A. Knopf, 1957), pp. 40 – 41 and 114 – 118; John Minto to George Himes, n.d. [likely 1900s], Folder 4, Box 1, John Minto Papers, Mss 752, Oregon Historical Society Special Collections.

conservationists were not untouched by human hands. Native communities had formed relationships with the land, and altered it, for generations. This was clearest in areas where Indigenous communities practiced the cultivation and alteration of the environment through the use of fire. Controlled burns were a tool used to promote the growth of useful plant species and animals suitable for hunting. As a result of these burns, Euro-American colonizers had found much of the Willamette Valley as a "whole country for miles together [brought to] the conditions of a park" when they first arrived. Many who lamented changes in the forests and fields likely didn't realize that they had played a part in destroying the existing "conditions of a park" in the Willamette Valley and elsewhere. Mass deaths of Indigenous peoples from invasion, disease, and wars brought the controlled burns they used nearly to a stop in the 1850s. American administration virtually halted the remaining Indigenous practices of controlled burns in Oregon until the twenty-first century. Later attempts to preserve or recreate "wilderness" in parklands and forestlands have sometimes stumbled in part because Indigenous knowledge and action had been a critical part of the purported "wilderness"; only recently has the scientific consensus begun to recognize that the controlled burns used by Indigenous communities can still play a vital role in land management. There is a hope in many Indigenous communities that other persisting reciprocal relationships of the land will also receive broader recognition.[6]

Nature's Special Gifts:
State Parks Before the Creation of a Park System

While the language and concept of nature changes over time, reverence of some sort has deep and recurrent roots. What was new in the parks movements was less a sense of nature's worth than a sense that nature needed to be preserved for the public good. One forerunner of this sentiment in Oregon was Thomas S. Summers, a settler who created what is sometimes purported to be the first public park in Oregon, Sodaville Springs, in 1871. "[N]ature's special gifts," he piously proclaimed, "are not intended for private exploitation." The park proper centered on a natural mineral spring, whose pungent water was believed to have curative effects. Summers's park, like many that followed, was designed with the hope of mixing public good and private interest. The famed

---

6 Robert Boyd, "Strategies of Indian Burning in the Willamette Valley," in *Indians, Fire, and the Land in the Pacific Northwest*, ed. Robert Boyd (Corvallis: Oregon State University Press, 1999): pp. 94 – 138; Leland Gilsen, "Willamette Valley Pyroculture," *Current Archaeological Happenings in Oregon* 17 (1992): pp. 9 – 11; H.S. Lyman, "Reminiscences of F. X. Matthieu," *Quarterly of the Oregon Historical Society* 1 (1900): pp. 73 – 104, esp. 88; Megan K. Walsh, Cathy Whitlock, and Patrick J. Bartlein, "1200 years of fire and vegetation history in the Willamette Valley, Oregon and Washington, reconstructed using high-resolution macroscopic charcoal and pollen analysis," *Palaeogeography, Palaeoclimatology, Palaeoecology* 297 (2010): pp. 273 – 289; William Cronon, "The Trouble with Wilderness; Or, Getting Back to the Wrong Nature," *Uncommon Ground: Rethinking the Human Place in Nature*, William Cronon, ed. (New York: W. W. Norton, 1995): pp. 69 – 90.

Sodaville Springs its immediate environs he *did* reserve for public good—while reserving the area surrounding the new park for himself. The draw of these medicinal springs drove the development of Sodaville, which had some success as a resort town, particularly in the 1890s. The bet had paid off. Summers, who had fought a lengthy legal battle for title to Sodaville Springs before making them a public park, proclaimed that he did so "for the benefits to arise therefrom to the public *and* to myself." Parks were a public good, but from the get-go many also hoped they would draw both locals and tourists to the beauties of Oregon. And in Sodaville as in grander and more famous projects, the energies of boosters turned first to the unique and the extraordinary.[7]

Few sites are more extraordinary than Crater Lake, made a national park in 1902 but known as a natural wonder for millennia before that. As photographs made the deep, clear, and strikingly blue lake nationally famous, tourists flocked as best they could to the remote regions of southern Oregon. The fight to turn the site into a "National Park for the pleasure and instruction of the people" was long but relatively frictionless. Early highway enthusiasts often invoked the breathtaking, famous, and remote lake when they called for more and better roads. For audiences that did not see highways as (just) an economic necessity for shipping, the call for means to convey visitors to Crater Lake could be a useful way to begin a call for good roads. As time wore on, they began to argue for beautiful roadways generally, not just for connection to a few extraordinary sites. This involved a push for parks, attacks on garish gas stations, a call for billboard regulation or elimination, and similar measures to make driving on highways an aesthetically pleasing experience.[8]

In the 1900s and 1910s, a number of Oregon cities embraced the "city beautiful" movement, which envisioned aesthetic spaces and natural places within urban landscapes as a key to social uplift and mental health. There needed to be parks and reserves for the citizenry, not just for the preservation of a few extraordinary spaces. The most visible and extensive of the Oregon "city beautiful" efforts was in Portland, which by 1911 had created an integrated system of city parks, as part of a grand plan that at its peak included an urban population of millions commuting by train, trolley, and some day (one planner dreamed) flying cars. The backbone of Portland's city beautiful movement remains as the

---

7 At the request of Thomas Summers, Sodaville Mineral Springs Park was put under the jurisdiction of the state of Oregon in 1891, but was not made a part of the state parks system until 1947. The site was deeded back to the community in 1975; the famed springwater is no longer potable. Cox, *The Park Builders*, 6 – 7, 180; Jennifer Moody, "Memories Spring Eternal in Sodaville," *Corvallis Gazette-Times* July 12, 2014; *Journal of the Senate... of the State of Oregon, 1891* (Salem: Frank C. Baker, 1891), 204 [emphasis mine]; Thomas A. Chambers, *Drinking the Waters: Creating an American Leisure Class at Nineteenth-Century Mineral Springs* (Washington, D.C.: Smithsonian Institutions, 2002).

8 Douglas Deur, "A Most Sacred Place"; Erik Weiselberg, "He All But Made the Mountains: William Gladstone Steel, Mountain Climbing, and the Establishment of Crater Lake National Park," *Oregon Historical Quarterly* 103 (2002): pp. 50 – 75; Sharon M. Howe, "Photography and the Making of Crater Lake National Park," *Oregon Historical Quarterly* 103 (2002): pp. 76 – 97; Hugh Myron Hoyt, Jr., "The Good Roads Movement in Oregon, 1900 – 1920," PhD diss., (University of Oregon, 1966).

nucleus of the Portland Parks System. Indeed, many city centers in Oregon beyond Portland are still shaped by parks conceived in this era.[9]

Even in these early years, the preservation movement encompassed history as well as nature, often rolled together under the mantle of heritage. Joseph N. Teal, a business-minded mainstay among the preservationists in Portland, also funded several statues across Oregon meant to forever immortalize a celebration of Euro-American conquest onto the landscape. Washington Park, acquired by the city of Portland in 1871, seemed a natural place to house the permanent monuments to history created for the 1905 Lewis and Clark Exposition. Among state parks, Champoeg, particularly, was an early example of the move to preserve history and nature as intertwined.[10]

Located just south of present-day Newberg, Champoeg was an Anchuyuk Kalapuya village that became a blended community with retired Hudson's Bay fur traders in the late 1820s. The site gained fame as the location of an 1843 settler meeting that organized a provisional local structure of American governance in what became Oregon—and later became the site of one of the first parks funded by the state. In the decades after statehood, when the movement to create and commemorate a heroic pioneer history for Oregon was gathering steam, Champoeg was one of the earliest to be memorialized. In 1901, the Oregon Legislature funded the erection of a monumental granite obelisk near the supposed site of the 1843 meeting (choosing from among the possibilities the location better viewed by passing boats on the Willamette River). In 1905, the Legislature purchased the lands surrounding the memorial, and in 1913 made it a state-funded park—though Champoeg did not become a part of the official Oregon State Parks system until 1943, one hundred years after the events it celebrated.[11]

"Provisional Government Park," as Champoeg was drably titled from 1913 to 1943, was primarily a venue for event planning and historical interpretation. Interested parties disagreed on many things—state officials, the Daughters of the American Revolution, Indian War veterans, and citizens' boards clashed on

---

9 The sources on visions of Portland as a future hub for flying cars are tragically scanty—see Carl Abbott, "Greater Portland: Experiments with Professional Planning, 1905 – 1925," *Pacific Northwest Quarterly* 76 (1985): pp. 12 – 21, esp. 12; John Fahey, "A.L. White, Champion of Urban Beauty," *Pacific Northwest Quarterly* 72 (1981): pp. 170 – 179; William Wyckoff with William Cronon, *How to Read the American West: A Field Guide* (Seattle: University of Washington Press, 2014), 296 – 297; Robert D. Russell, Jr., "Unrealized Visions: Medford and the City Beautiful Movement," *Oregon Historical Quarterly* 102 (2001): pp. 196 – 209; Cox, *The Park Builders*, 9 – 10.

10 Jeffrey Uecker, "Picturing the Corps of Discovery: The Lewis and Clark Expedition in American Art," *Oregon Historical Quarterly* 103 (2002): pp. 452 – 479; Marc James Carpenter, "Reconsidering *The Pioneer*, One Hundred Years Later," report submitted to the Oregon Parks and Recreation Department, June 27, 2019, **https://www.oregon.gov/oprd/OH/Documents/Fellow2019MarcCarpenterReconsideringThe%20Pioneer.pdf**.

11 David G. Lewis, "The Kalapuya Village of Champoeg," *Quartux* June 25, 2016; Melinda Marie Jetté, *At the Hearth of the Crossed Races: A French-Indian Community in Nineteenth-Century Oregon, 1812 – 1859* (Corvallis: Oregon State University Press, 2015); J. Neilson Barry, "Champoeg Park," *Oregon Historical Quarterly* 40:4 (1939), pp. 336 – 342; Katrine Barber, " We Were at Our Journey's End': Settler Sovereignty Formation in Oregon," *Oregon Historical Quarterly* 120:4 (2019): 382 – 411.

many aspects of Champoeg as they strove to collaborate towards its success. But all promoted the cultivation of native plants as a constituent part of the park, from caretaker Albert Tozier's efforts at artful landscaping to the Daughters of the American Revolution's fundraising campaign for a native plant arboretum on the site. Nature, all sides seemed to agree, should be a part of history—and history should be a part of preservation.[12]

Scenic Roads and Automobile Pleasure Drives:
The Drive for Good Roads

The government decree preserving Oregon beaches as public highways in 1913 also works as a marker because it points to the long connection between highways and parks in Oregon. Also formed in 1913, Oregon State Highway Commission (and its successors) managed Oregon state parks from their slow inception in 1921 through the end of the 1980s. Even after the inauguration of an independent Oregon Parks and Recreation Department in 1990, roads and parks in Oregon have remained closely linked.[13]

From the beginning, the connection between highways and parks was pragmatic but purposeful. In the 1910s, automobiles were transforming from playthings of the rich to the mainstay of the middle class. At the same time, trucks were increasingly seen as the best way to transport goods to and from rural areas. The push for public roads thus had a wide range of supporters. Those who linked roads to parks hoped to draw on that support. When the Oregon state parks system began in earnest in 1921, highways were already seen as a constituent part of state government in Oregon. Growing the parks system under

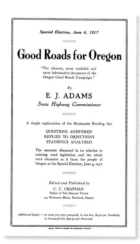

"The whole road situation as it faces the people of Oregon . . ."

---

12 John Hussey, *Champoeg: Place of Transition; A Disputed History* (Portland: Oregon Historical Society, 1967), esp. 270 and 274.

13 Merriam, Jr., *Oregon's Highway Park System 1921 – 1989*, pp. 17 – 19.

the mantle of the highways department seemed safer at the time than subjecting parks to the whims of changing legislatures. But there was also a feeling of natural connection between highways and parks among many of the boosters of the park system and the citizens of Oregon. Highways in Oregon were viewed by many as a means to experience the beauty of nature. Tourism and Good Roads movements were mutually reinforcing. Those hoping to promote tourism at places of remote scenic beauty needed good roads to take visitors there; those hoping to promote the building of roads needed a wholesome cause and a set of destinations for those roads to lead to. Crater Lake, they hoped, was only the beginning.

Highway boosters were a fractious group, within and beyond the local, state, and national Good Roads movements. Muddy roads that had worked well enough for horses were dangerous or impossible for automobiles. In a time before shock absorbers, even technically passable roads were deeply unpleasant to drive along—particularly at the high speeds enabled by these new vehicles. Farmers who wanted to build up rural roads sometimes clashed with the automaker consortiums that funded Good Roads activism, who argued against spending on roads that "began nowhere and ended nowhere" rather than on more options for urban drivers. Paving companies, the other major corporate force behind Good Roads, simply wanted to maximize road production everywhere. And although the leadership of Oregon Good Roads movements in the 1900s and 1910s tended to be corporate-backed, many of those who pounded the proverbial pavement for the movement were motivated by regional pride, aesthetic concerns, and even conservation. Good Roads activists were a critical component of the early parks movement, for local and national as well as state parks. After the passage of federal funding for state highways in 1916 and especially after the road-building boom that followed World War I, such activists were increasingly at the forefront of the Oregon Good Roads movement. The paving and automobile industries had achieved their objectives. It was the local activists who cared where roads were built, what their aesthetic qualities were, and whether nature was preserved as a part of the journey—or amidst a set of possible destinations.[14]

The creation of the Columbia River Highway from 1912 to 1916 was both a template and a threat for Good Roads activists and park-builders. For preservationists, the Columbia River Highway was a triumph. Designed with nature conservation and aesthetics in mind, the winding road provided (and provides) breathtaking vistas and views of natural wonder along the Columbia. Portland magnate Simon Benson, who had thrown his support and land behind the Columbia River Highway just as he had behind Portland Parks, got almost precisely what he wanted: the highway connected Portland to points east but

14 Hal S. Barron, "And the Crooked Shall Be Made Straight: Public Road Administration and the Decline of Localism in the Rural North, 1870 – 1930, *Journal of Social History* 26 (1992): pp. 81 – 103, esp. 94; C. H. Claudy, "Federal Aid in Fighting Mud," *Scientific American* 116 (1917): pp. 14 – 15; Preston Lerner, "Innovations in Driving: Shock Absorbers," *Popular Science* Sept 19, 2012.

This 1915 road was typical of the era: technically passable, "deeply unpleasant to drive along."

more importantly connected well-heeled automobilists near and far to the beauties of nature. Benson's case for the restorative leisure such a highway would offer won the day, and taxes and bonds paved the Columbia River Highway.[15]

But this made the Columbia River Highway—and perhaps highways and parks more generally—a class issue. Labor unions and farmers' groups objected to the use of state monies to pay for what they saw as a "speedway for the idle rich." Why should they pay for the restorative leisure of the aristocratic automobilists, for "scenic roads and automobile pleasure drives," when farmers still needed to get goods to market and laborers still needed land of their own? Many questioned the use of any land for non-productive purposes, or the building of roads for anything but utilitarian concerns. Good Roads enthusiasts and park boosters took note. Later efforts for parks and beautification in Oregon were especially sensitive to the issue of taxes, and to the need to build broad public support.[16]

---

15 Ronald J. Fahl, "S. C. Lancaster and the Columbia River Highway: Engineer as Conservationist," *Oregon Historical Quarterly* 74 (1973): pp. 101 – 144; William G. Robbins, "Town and Country in Oregon: A Conflicted Legacy," *Oregon Historical Quarterly* 110 (2009): pp. 52 – 73, esp. 65.

16 Lawrence M. Lipin, "'Cast Aside the Automobile Enthusiast': Class Conflict, Tax Policy, and the Preservation of Nature in Progressive-Era Oregon," *Oregon Historical Quarterly* 107 (2006): pp. 166 – 195.

Engineered to showcase the magnificent natural features of the Gorge, the winding beauty of the Columbia River Highway is breathtaking to this day.

Highways largely faded as a class issue in the 1920s. In part, this was because of a change in how highways were paid for. Wanting to avoid a class-based backlash like the one that sparked during the construction of the Columbia River Gorge Highway, the state legislature hiked up automobile license fees in 1917. When it became clear in 1918 that a highway system extensive enough to serve urban and rural Oregonians needed more funding than such fees could bear, Good Roads activists and the legislators they had elected pushed for something more extensive. Progressive Oregonians had famously attempted all sorts of novel taxation schemes in the 1900s and 1910s. In 1919, the Oregon legislature passed the first gasoline tax in the country. Much more money was still needed for highways—bonds would still be used, federal monies still sought. But with the day-to-day expenses of the Oregon state highway system now paid through automobile fees and gasoline taxes—in other words, by those who used the roads—there were fewer calls of conspiracy.[17]

But support for the rapidly expanding highway system boomed largely because automobiles were moving from a luxury good to a middle-class desire, and trucks from a useful transport option to a rural necessity. Automobile leisure, seen as a diversion of the well-to-do in the 1910s, became a middle-class aspiration in the 1920s. Office workers increasingly saw the car as a necessity; unions in the 1920s and beyond included outdoor recreation as part of the good life they hoped to enable. Between 1910 and 1920, Oregonians acquired more automobiles per capita than most of the rest of the country—there was 1 registered automobile for every 7 residents in 1920, one of the highest rates at the time (though still not as high as California). Most Oregonians now saw a pleasurable

---

17 R. Rudy Higgens-Evenson, "Financing a Second Era of Internal Improvements: Transportation and Tax Reform, 1890 – 1929, *Social Science History* 26 (2002): pp. 623 – 651, esp. 636 – 640; John Chynoweth Burnham, "The Gasoline Tax and the Automobile Revolution," *Mississippi Valley Historical Review* 48 (1961): pp. 435 – 459, esp. 438 – 440.

drive along the Columbia Gorge Highway as a wholesome recreational activity that both middle- and upper-class families could enjoy. Parks were a part of this leisure. When Oregon state parks were first established as an entity in 1921, the core of their mandate was to create and conserve the restorative leisure of nature for those driving and stopping along the good roads of Oregon.[18]

This 1939 ad campaign presages the postwar boom years, when leisure time and automobiles turned into tourism dollars.

Attractions and Scenic Beauties:
Oregon State Parks Start Small

What marks 1921 as a beginning of the Oregon state parks system is a law passed on February 28 to "to empower the highway commission to acquire rights of way along state highways for the maintenance and preservation of scenic beauties along such highways." Like the beach bill of 1913, the act enabling Oregon state parks was passed by the legislature with majority support and little debate. It gave the highway department significant power to acquire lands within three hundred feet of state highways, "for the maintenance and preservation of the roadbed" or to "aid in the maintenance and preservation of the attractions and the scenic beauties thereof." Although it was correctly presumed that such lands would typically be acquired through purchase or donation, the act bestowed the state highway commission with the power of eminent domain where necessary. "[I]n the name of the people of the state of Oregon," the highway commission would now manage a system of "attractions and scenic beauties" in the state—at least if they were next to the road.[19]

---

18 Peter J. Hugill, "Good Roads and the Automobile in the United States 1880 – 1929," *Geographical Review* 72 (1982): pp. 327 – 349, statistics on 340; Higgens-Evenson, "Financing a Second Era of Internal Improvements," esp. 636 – 640; Lawrence M. Lipin, *Workers and the Wild: Conservation, Consumerism, and Labor in Oregon, 1910 – 1930* (Urbana: University of Illinois Press, 2007), chap. 3.

19 Sam A. Kozer, compiler, *State of Oregon Constitutional Amendments... Together with the General Laws...* (Salem: State Printing Department, 1921), Chapter 343 [S.B. 365], quotations from 654; "To Beautify Roads," *Oregon Voter* 24 (1921), 586.

This law was the scaled-down version of a more ambitious plan pursued by Oregon Governor Benjamin Olcott, who had assumed office after the death of Governor Withycombe in 1919. Like his good friend and political mentor Oswald West before him, Olcott's breakthrough moment for preservation came from the Oregon coast. Dismayed by land logged bare right up to the Cannon Beach-Seaside road, Olcott issued a public call in 1920 for maintenance and preservation of roadside beauty. Riding on years of local activism and a national movement for nature cultivation and preservation, Olcott was able to garner widespread support for his proclamation of "the patriotic and civic duty" of every Oregonian "to preserve our wonderful natural surroundings."[20]

Olcott's original proposal to the legislature was a grab-bag of preservationist goals, including not only scenic beautification but also a broader mandate for state parks and the billboard ban sought by the Good Roads movement. The slimmed-down law that passed was correctly seen as an "opening wedge"; state parks and other preservation efforts could be built from core legislation protecting highways. The highway commission began slowly acquiring and creating roadside parks and attractions almost as soon at the law was passed—though parks were not a priority for most highway engineers. The first such acquisition to be framed as a distinct space, Sarah Helmick State Park, was donated in 1922.[21]

The State Highway Commission was given official authorization to acquire and supervise "parks, parking places, camp sites, public squares and recreation grounds" in 1925, almost precisely the powers originally sought in 1921. Importantly, this new mandate also came with at least some funds from the new gasoline tax. Olcott had been roundly defeated in the election of 1922, in significant part because he had openly opposed the briefly ascendant Oregon Ku Klux Klan, and left the state shortly afterwards. But the "wedge" of legislation he had gotten through in 1921 continued to expand in 1925 and beyond, helped along by a decentralized movement of preservationists within and beyond the government.[22]

---

20 Cox, *The Park Builders*, 36 – 41, quotation from 36.

21 Merriam, Jr., *Oregon's Highway Park System 1921 – 1989*; Virginia Nesbit, "Sarah Helmick and Helmick Park," *Quarterly of the Oregon Historical Society* 26:4 (1925): 444 – 447.

22 Merriam, Jr., *Oregon's Highway Park System 1921 – 1989*, 20; Cox, *The Park Builders*, 41 – 46; Eckard V. Toy, "The Ku Klux Klan in Oregon," *Experiences in the Promised Land: Essays in Pacific Northwest History*, G. Thomas Edwards and Carlos A. Schwantes, eds. (Seattle: University of Washington, 1986): pp. 269 – 286; Arthur H. Bone and Walter M. Pierce, *Oregon Cattleman/Governor/Congressman: Memoirs and Times of Walter M. Pierce* (Portland: Oregon Historical Society, 1981), esp. 186 – 221; Robert R. McCoy, "The Paradox of Oregon's Progressive Politics: The Political Career of Walter Marcus Pierce," *Oregon Historical Quarterly* 110 (2009): pp. 390 – 419.

Speak of the Beauties of Oregon:
Robert W. Sawyer and the Spark of Conservation

A key figure among those pushing for state parks was Robert W. Sawyer, a newspaperman and jurist with a longstanding interest in nature preservation and a finger on Oregon's political pulse. A blue-blooded Harvard-trained lawyer who had worked for Louis Brandeis in private practice, Sawyer abandoned his old life (and his first marriage) in 1910 to elope with his neighbor's wife for points west. Remarried and reinvented, Sawyer wandered through a number of temporary jobs. Moving to Bend for the health of his new family in 1912—he wanted to try his hand at outdoor labor and his new wife Mary hoped the dry climate would help her tuberculosis—Sawyer was briefly a lumber sorter in a sawmill. Finding it "rather hard work" for not much pay, within months he wrote his way into the newspaper business, becoming the owner and editor of the *Bend Bulletin* by 1917 and remaining at the helm until 1953. He eventually returned to law, appointed and then elected as Deschutes County judge from 1920 to 1927, when he left to join the Highway Commission. Though in many respects a small-government conservative, Sawyer pushed for government conservation *and* development of Oregon land and resources, and the enablement of both through good roads connecting the east, the valley, and the coast of the state to rest of the country.[23]

Like most activists, Sawyer had a conversion story. In 1919, he had a chance visit with two titans of the burgeoning conservation movement, Director of the National Park Service Stephen T. Mather and renowned naturalist (and eugenicist) Madison Grant. The two men were touring the West Coast, admiring spaces of natural beauty and warning of their fragility. With Sawyer as with many other audiences, they focused on economic potential. Natural beauty was a precious resource, they argued, that could bring tourists, profit, and prestige to remote stretches of Oregon. Sawyer, his interest in preservation already kindled by Good Roads rhetoric, "caught the spark and set to work."[24]

Sawyer saw conservation and park creation as part of a broader system of land use and regional development. Beautiful highways leading to majestic parks would encourage travel and bring tourists across the state. Known as a booster of lumber interests, Sawyer was less liable than many to raise the hackles of industry when he pushed for trees along highways and selected spaces for parks.

---

23 The work in the sawmill was built up as a quasi-mystical origin story in later years; Sawyer edited out his reflections on the hardness of the work and the paucity of the pay before sending his own miniature biography to *Oregon Voter* editor C. C. Chapman. John Francis Sprague, *Sprague's Journal of Maine History* 1 (Dover, ME: John Francis Sprague, 1913): p. 286; "Lawyer Elopes with Partner's Wife," *Boston Post* Oct 28, 1910, found in "Mary Crane, 1886," People of Brookline, **BrooklineHistoricalSociety.org**; Robert Sawyer to C. C. Chapman, July 8, 1930, Folder: "C. C. Chapman," Box 5, Robert W. Sawyer Papers, Ax 100, Special Collections & University Archives, University of Oregon Libraries, Eugene, OR; Cox, *The Park Builders*, 32 – 33.

24 Cox, *The Park Builders*, 33; Thomas R. Cox, "The Crusade to Save Oregon's Scenery," *Pacific Historical Review* 37 (1968): pp. 179 – 199.

As an activist, Sawyer preferred soft power over hard votes. In the 1920s, the Oregon public voiced loud support for parks—but also pushed to cut government expenses and services. Sawyer thus pursued what historian Thomas Cox has called "conservation through subterfuge," doing much of his work behind the scenes, seeking to limit public debate over particular park acquisitions or park budgets.[25]

This cautious approach to funding distinguished Oregon among the national state parks movement(s). While the passage of the 1921 legislation enabling Oregon state parks became law only a month after the first meeting of the National Conference on State Parks in Iowa, this timing reflected general growth of interest in parks rather than a specific cause and effect. Over the course of the 1920s, the national state parks movement came to push for independent state parks agencies or departments of conservation, to better pursue park priorities independent of other concerns. Charles G. Sauers, a famed Indiana park builder, was sent to Oregon by the National Conference of State Parks in the fall of 1927 to build support for just such an independent agency. He pointed not only to his own state, but to the successes of leaders in the state parks movement like California and New York. Yet within a few months, Sauers changed his tune. Sawyer, who had just resigned his judgeship to take a position on the Highway Commission that summer, had rallied his allies and defeated the idea behind the scenes. They brought Sauers around to their way of thinking— Oregon, he came to agree, needed to go a different way.[26]

Sawyer wanted to keep parks funding away from legislative battles. The highway department got its basic operating funds without going through appropriations, instead getting paid directly by gas taxes and vehicle fees. Although there was broad support for state parks, their focus on recreation made them seem like a luxury. If state parks remained under the mantle of highways, Sawyer argued, they would be less prone to attack from legislators hunting for cost-saving measures. Moreover, Sawyer and many others saw highways and parks as naturally aligned: both could enable recreation, evoke beauty, and promote travel to places of natural beauty and/or historical import.[27]

Preserving and commemorating history had been imagined as part of the highway-and-park system since before the creation of a formal department. The park at Champoeg had been sited and built with the traffic of the day—steamboats—in mind. In the 1910s and 1920s, the caretakers and boosters of Champoeg hoped to loop Willamette Valley highways close enough to Provisional Government Park to draw in visitors using newer forms of transportation. The

---

25 Cox, *The Park Builders*, chap 4.

26 Rebecca Conard, "National Conference on State Parks: Reflections on Organizational Genealogy," *The George Wright Forum* 14:4 (1997): pp. 28 – 43; Cox, *The Park Builders*, 47 – 49.

27 *Ibid*, 52 – 53; Jno. D. Guthrie to Robert W. Sawyer, Sept. 5, 1932, Folder 2, Box 1, Robert W. Sawyer Papers. Oregon might have pursued state parks by different means than the national movement, but shared the national underlying philosophy of an emphasis on recreation wedded to the creation of a "virile and universal… effort of wild conservation." "The First National Park Conference," *Iowa Conservation* 5:1 (Jan/ March 1921), p. 9.

Roosevelt Highway in southern Oregon was built to loop near Table Rock, the engineers having hoped to lure motorists to see famous sites from the official portion of the Rogue River War(s) of the 1850s in addition to the glories of nature. One highwater mark of the era was the new Old Oregon Trail Highway, planned as a historical equivalent to the Columbia River Gorge Highway. The dedication of the highway in 1923 took place at what is now Emigrant Springs State Heritage Area. The event drew between twenty and thirty thousand people, including President Warren Harding. The dedication celebrated the recreated "Road that Won an Empire," and memorialized the hardships Euro-American emigrants to Oregon had suffered when they traveled across the continent to seize Native land in the Pacific Northwest. Although the gloss of the past articulated at the time was profoundly problematic, the notion of history as part of what parks should preserve and present has deep roots. Many early park figures, including Sawyer, saw historical sites as part of the scope of the organization.28

Sawyer paired the subtlety of his political approach with a broad public appeal for parks, framing them as matters of civic virtue. He strove for a core of experts kept afloat by a raft of volunteers. Voluntarism extended to land acquisitions. Many of the state parks of the 1920s were built thanks to donations, carefully solicited and widely praised by Sawyer and like-minded conservationists. Through the contacts and prowess he had built up as a respected newsman, Sawyer was able to keep the state parks and other conservation measures in the public eye, not only through his own newspaper but through a broad network of everyday activists. "Speak of the beauties of Oregon," he advised one such activist nervously about to go on the radio for the first time, then "refer to the state highway system." Sawyer's quiet work in the halls of political power only worked because of a groundswell of popular support—one that he had helped foster.29

Sawyer saw volunteering as essential for citizenship, and vital to the park system. Recruiting volunteers was both a way to conserve the scant resources allowed to parks and to build public investment in them. When pursuing new land for parks, Sawyer pushed for professionals, but also for the involvement of the citizenry. Sawyer was unable to fund a formal site survey as the state parks department in California had done, but he did throw his weight behind fellow journalist Eric Allen's scheme to use the Boy Scouts, proposing that each troop in the state survey the public land nearest them use their training and mark "all those spots in their territory where they like to camp or picnic and which they think ought to be open to them as long as they live and ought to be open to future generations of boys for camping and picnicking [sic]." Although there

---

28 Aileen Wilson, "The Amazing Journey: The Roosevelt Highway," *Oregon Motorist* June 1928, pp. 13 – 14, 30; Florence Leach, "The Old Oregon Trail: The Road That Won an Empire," *Oregon Motorist* Jan. 1925, pp. 12 – 13; Chelsea K. Vaughn, "'The Road That Won an Empire': Commemoration, Commercialization, and Auto Tourism at the 'Top o' Blue Mountains,'" *Oregon Historical Quarterly* 115 (2014): pp. 6 – 37; Robert W. Sawyer to Burt Brown Barker, June 25, 1935, Folder 33, Box 1, Robert W. Sawyer Papers.

29 Robert W. Sawyer to Mrs. Jack Murphy, Feb 2, 1931, Folder 2, Box 3, Robert W. Sawyer Papers.

is little evidence that enough troops participated to have an effect, and in fact Sawyer was no longer in the Highway Commission when it was implemented, Allen's call to the Boy Scouts got to the heart of Sawyer's approach to conservation: volunteers who with their special skills were preserving for the public that which was precious to them, and educating themselves at the same time.[30]

Women's organizations were an especially critical part of the loose coalition of interest groups that pushed for state parks. Public campaigns drew much of their leadership and their rank-and-file from majority-women garden clubs and nature clubs. Jessie Honeyman, a well-connected Good Roads activist and park promoter, was the most famous of the women who led volunteer public relations campaigns for parks and good roads in the 1920s and 1930s. Later the namesake of Jessie M. Honeyman State Park, she rallied club women to write their legislators, fundraised, and coordinated public programs to talks, newspaper articles, and radio. The subtle legislative achievements of Sawyer and ilk were only possible because the issues they pushed for had been made relevant to legislators by activists like Honeyman.[31]

12 Acres of Wilderness for Every Oregonian:
The Progress of Parks at the Beginning of a New Era

Keeping parks tied to highways might have helped preserve the nascent system when legislative fights over taxes grew bitter, but this relationship also meant that parks were dependent on highway policymakers who might have other priorities. Despite the technically broad powers granted to the Highway Department in 1921 and the more robust and explicit language passed in 1925, the state park system grew slowly and haphazardly for most of the 1920s. Highway engineers might care about aesthetics, but many viewed parks as a comparatively low priority. In his first year with the Highway Commission, in 1927, Sawyer and his compatriot Henry B. Van Duzer doubled the meager landholdings the state park system had managed to acquire. But Sawyer worried that such progress was temporary, likely to last only as long as he and his allies sat on the commission. What would keep the parks a priority if some new commission saw highways solely as a means of transportation? In places where adequate provision for parks had not been made, Sawyer warned, "The good road built to bring the tourist to the scenery has [already] taken the scenery away." How could the future of parks be secured?[32]

---

30 Merriam, Jr., *Oregon's Highway Park System 1921 – 1989*, 22 – 23; Eric Allen to J.C. Ainsworth, c/o Robert Sawyer, Nov. 3 1932, Folder 12, Box 1, Robert W. Sawyer Papers; Eric Allen, "Boy Scout Survey" [undated], *ibid*.

31 "Garden Clubs and Roadside Beauty in Oregon," *The American Magazine of Art* 24 (1932): p. 228; Gail E. Evans, "Promoting Tourism and Development at Crater Lake: The Art of Grace Russell Fountain and Mabel Russell Lowther," *Oregon Historical Quarterly* 116 (2015): pp. 310 – 343.

32 Robert W. Sawyer, "Why Oregon Needs State Parks," *Oregon Motorist* May 1930, pp. 5 – 7.

Increasing government funding seemed unlikely. Governor Isaac L. Patterson, who appointed Sawyer shortly after he came to office in 1927, was a vocal supporter of roads and parks. But like many other legislators, his support did not necessarily extend to the budget. Rebuffing Sawyer's request for highway funding specially reserved for parks, Patterson preached expansion in the same breath as fiscal restraint. He framed the leaders of the state parks movement, New York and California, as spendthrift, noting that Oregon was constructing its system at a fraction of the cost. Nature and history needed to be preserved for the citizens of Oregon, Patterson argued, but "with the least expenditure possible."[33]

Patterson, Sawyer, and others discussing parks at the time often evoked the vast stretches of federal forest land when they discussed the benefits and beauties of Oregon. Patterson thought state parks could be run with the least expenditure possible because "the huge area of national forests [in Oregon] afford a wilderness area that is unsurpassed in scenic or recreational facilities…. every man, woman and child could have 12 acres allotted to him [sic] as a private park for his individual use if that should prove desirable." Sawyer used the same notion, revised up to 13 acres a head, to call for popular support for a national bill to swap railroad grant lands next to highways for timberlands further from the public eye. The state parks system was not created in a vacuum; it existed alongside local parks, National Parks, National Forests, and for a time state-owned parks managed separately (like Champoeg). Tied to highways by purpose as well as name, the system was only slowly developing an ethos or identity.[34]

Sawyer's most consequential act on the Highway Commission seemed trifling at the time. From the beginning he had argued that the highway department needed a dedicated parks superintendent. In the summer of 1929, his colleagues relented—though they insisted on hiring from within, and assumed that the job (first labeled "Parks Engineer") would be a temporary expedient to deal with new land acquisitions. Sam Boardman, selected to be Oregon's first State Parks Superintendent, instead served for 21 years. By some mix of luck and guile, Sawyer had, by getting this position created, established the continuity of support from within the government he desired. And just in time. In December of 1929, Governor Patterson died suddenly, and within six months the new governor had dismissed Sawyer from his post.[35]

When Albin W. Norblad ascended to the governor's office in 1929, he seemed like a natural ally for Sawyer and the rest of the Highway Commission. Like Sawyer, a conservation-minded conservative, Norblad had made his political bones in Astoria, campaigning on good roads, tourism, lumbering, and

---

33 Governor Isaac L. Patterson, "Oregon's State Parks," *Oregon Motorist* Aug. 1928, pp. 5 – 6, 19.

34 Patterson, "Oregon's State Parks," 6; Sawyer, "Why Oregon Needs State Parks," 7; Jno. D. Guthrie, "Thirteen Million Acres of Recreation," *Oregon Motorist* Aug 1931, pp. 9 – 11, 19.

35 Cox, *The Park Builders*, 54 – 56; Stephen R. Mark, *Preserving the Living Past: John C. Merriam's Legacy in the State and National Parks* (Berkeley: University of California Press, 2005): pp. 87 – 88;

fishing. An early supporter of the Roosevelt Highway who led the charge to rename it the Oregon Coast Highway (U.S. 101), he spoke often about the natural beauty of Oregon generally and the coast specifically. "Nowhere else in the world," he proclaimed on multiple occasions, "can you find... such a general lavish display of old mother nature as that presented and reached by the Oregon Coast Highway. It takes you along a panorama which unfolds to you nature's choicest gems." As he pronounced in his 1930 Fourth of July address:

> Oregon, the promised land... [has] 1001 wonders. There
> are the marble halls — Crater Lake — Wallowa Lake
> in the Alps of America, our unsurpassed beaches—the
> splendid fishing streams, the snow clad mountain peaks,
> the great forests—wonderful highways—all this and more
> constitutes our Oregon.

Highways, to Norblad as to Sawyer, were (if well-constructed) central to the nature and draw of the state.[36]

But Norblad was unable to win even his own party's nomination for governor in 1930—and many believed his dismissal of Sawyer was a big part of the reason. Ascending to office in an election year, Norblad was campaigning as soon as he was governing—and Fred J. Brady, a major figure in his campaign, was also a lobbyist for the "black top gang," a construction company consortium with an interest in highway contracts. Norblad, when he removed Sawyer from the Highway Commission, accused him of creating a "lack of harmony" in the department. Norblad's political foes, and Sawyer's fellow newspapermen, suspected instead that the new governor was in pocket of the "black top gang," and planned to replace the whole Highway Commission with compromised cronies. Many at the time believed this scandal was the most critical of the factors that cost Norblad his party's nomination—though they were divided over whether his intent had, in fact, been corrupt. Both Norblad and Sawyer would continue their advocacy for good roads, business-minded nature conservation, and Oregon State whether or not they were in public office.[37]

In 1931, just after Norblad departed, the state parks department (led by Sam Boardman) named a new acquisition near Bend "Robert W. Sawyer Park." In 1933, Sawyer came back, appointed to the newly created State

---

36   Irl S. McSherry for Albin W. Norblad, "Fourth of July Address," July 4, 1930, Folder: Official Papers of the Governor's Office, Box 1, Albin Walter Norblad Papers, Ax 680, Special Collections & University Archives, University of Oregon Libraries;; Albin W. Norblad, "Oregon Coast Highway," (n.d. but likely 1931), Folder: "Speeches," *ibid*; Albin Walter Norblad, "Roadside Survey," July 31, 1930, *ibid*.

37   Hugh Currin, "Albin W. Norblad's Administration," June 12, 1931, p. 11, Folder: Official Papers of the Governor's Office, Albin Walter Norblad Papers; *Oregon Journal* April 27, 1930, p. 11; "Vigorous Protest on Removal of Sawyer Voiced," *Eugene Guard* May 28, 1930; Sawyer to Chapman, July 8, 1930. Albin W. Norblad played a key role the creation of Fort Stevens State Park. See "Fort Stevens: In the Beginning," *FYI* 209 (Sept 12, 1997), Oregon Parks and Recreation Digital Archive.

Parks Commission. Sawyer had secured foundational funding for state parks, and set in motion the man, Sam Boardman, who would define the system for decades. The two remained close—though they would occasionally good-naturedly tussle over who thought of what in the early days of the park system. Sawyer continued to lobby for good parks and good roads into the 1950s.[38]

Fitness, Proportion, and Harmony:
The Meaning of "Public" in Oregon State Parks

At the national and the state levels, parks struggle with the dual mandate to serve the public in the present and to preserve for the public of the future. There is a fundamental tension between the mandate of preservation and the dictates of recreation. Then as now, navigating the two required what Jessie Honeyman called "[f]itness, proportion and harmony": recognizing the need for a middle ground, adapting to changing tastes of recreation, and making it harmonious and minimally destructive to the nature, heritage, and beauty the parks were charged with protecting on behalf of the public.[39]

But who counted as "the public" would continue to shift. By the 1920s, the target audience for state parks in Oregon had moved from rich White men (and their families) to rich *and middle-class* White men *and women* (and their families). Native people were seldom consulted on their homelands, and along with other people of color were not considered a potential partner or constituency for the parks for decades to come. Even the Indigenous place-names that remained attached to parks have often been replaced or effaced to make room for the names of donors or other honorees, as when the grounds of the Suislaw-derived Camp Woahink became Jessie M. Honeyman Memorial Park. Honeyman deserved to be honored in some way, and there is no reason to think this erasure was intentionally malicious. Rather, the racial assumptions of the early park system were so ingrained that they passed without significant notice for most of the twentieth century.[40]

The Oregon state parks system was created at a time when much of Oregon embraced White supremacy, and visions of the parks and intended guests reflected those beliefs. Support for White supremacy crossed party lines and class lines. In the same 1921 message in which he laid out the new plan for highways and parks, Republican Governor Olcott proudly asserted that "in Oregon the pioneer blood flows more purely and in a more undiluted stream than in any other state

---

38 Cox, *The Park Builders*, 56; Samuel H. Boardman to Robert Sawyer, May 15, 1933, Folder 10, Box 3, Robert W. Sawyer Papers.

39 Honeyman quotation from "Garden Clubs and Roadside Beauty in Oregon," 228.

40 William A. Langille, "Jessie M. Honeyman Memorial State Park," July 8, 1941, Folder: Inventory of Park Articles, Box: Samuel H. Boardman Papers, Oregon State Parks and Recreation Collection, Oregon State Parks and Recreation, Salem, OR; Patty Wheat Philips, "Revisiting Woahink and Cleawox," Shichil's Blog July 10, 2015; Natchee Blu Barnd, "A Lot to Ask of a Name: White Spaces and Indian Symbols," Oregon Humanities Aug 30, 2018.

in the Union," from the "little band of men [that] voted at Champoeg" onward. Olcott proclaimed that Oregonians should "preserve our land and our resources for the people of our own race and nationality." His 1922 opponent Walter Pierce, elected with Klan support, fought even harder for White supremacist legislation. Such opinions were mainstream and uncontroversial among Euro-Americans in the state and much of the nation at the time. Unusually, Governor Norblad in 1930 preached racial harmony, welcoming Filipinos to the state (and encouraging them to visit the parks!) and at one point announcing from the governor's office to Oregonians that despite what "many of your best friends" feel, "colored people [are] [s]ome of our finest citizens." This was progress at the end of a Klan-infested decade, likely reflecting in part the modest successes of the Oregon NAACP in the era. But a speech proclaiming to skeptical White Oregonians that Black people were, in fact, people—that they were productive citizens rather than "passive" invaders—also marked how far Oregon had to go. The state as a whole, and the parks specifically, are still working and struggling to reckon with the legacy of White supremacy as they push for a more equitable state, and to shape parks for a more inclusive sense of the public (see Chapter 7).[41]

Forever Remain Open to the Public:
The Many Beginnings of Oregon State Parks

When did Oregon State Parks begin? One could make plausible arguments about the assumption of state control over Sodaville in 1891, or over Champoeg in 1905. The beginning has been placed at 1921, when the first legislation for Oregon state parks went through; at 1922, when Sarah Helmick State Park became the first part of the new system; even at 1925, when the legislation laying aside more specific powers and responsibilities for parks was established. The date has at times been 1929, the year "Father of State Parks" Sam Boardman was appointed. Until the "Father," the logic goes, how could the parks system be said to have been born?[42]

This chapter opens in 1913, another popular date for the origin of the Oregon State Parks system, when Oswald West proclaimed beaches as public highways, Oregon's government first took over the finances at Champoeg, and the Highway Department that would run state parks for decades was first

41 *Message of Ben W. Olcott to the Thirty-First Legislative Assembly, Jan. 10 1921* (Salem: State Printing Department, 1921), p. 17; McCoy, "The Paradox of Oregon's Progressive Politics"; Albin Walter Norblad, "Colored People," April 27, 1930, Folder: Official Papers of the Governor's Office, Albin Walter Norblad Papers; Irl S. McSherry for Albin W. Norblad, "Rizal Day Celebration," Dec 30, 1930, *ibid*; Kimberley Mangun, *A Force for Change: Beatrice Morrow Cannady and the Struggle for Civil Rights in Oregon, 1912 – 1936* (Corvallis: Oregon State University Press, 2010); Alec Weis *et al*, "Applying a Lens of Racial Equity to Our Parks," *Parks & Recreation* 53 (2018), 36+.

42 Elisabeth Walton Potter to Craig Tutor, cc Jim Lockwood and James Hamrick [email], Dec 1 1999, Folder: Tracing the Origins of OPRD, Box: Park History, Oregon Parks and Recreation Collection; Oregon Parks and Recreation Department, *Centennial Horizon: Shaping the Future of Oregon's Parks, Recreation, Conservation and Preservation* (Salem: Oregon State Parks, 2008).

established. But in truth, there is no one single origin for Oregon State Parks. All of these dates are potentially valid, because each marks an important step toward what the system would come to be. The goal, the mission, and the imagined future of what became Oregon Parks and Recreation has changed many times over the years. New changes may even suggest new dates of origin, in the years to come.

None of those involved in the proclamation of public beaches as highways seems to have appreciated the full importance of the largely ceremonial action. It was only decades later in the McCall era, when the ethos of public beaches was ingrained enough in Oregon to charge a movement, that this act was retroactively recognized as momentous. The same was true of state parks—the pragmatic choices and fleeting decisions that defined their earliest iteration shaped what they would be for the rest of the century, quite beyond what the early activists and administrators might have envisioned. The choices made today are no different.

Sam Boardman, Silver Falls State Park, 1940s

CHAPTER 2

A Magnificent Beggar:
Samuel Boardman and the Formation of Oregon State Parks (1929 - 1950)

The important thing was to make it a park. When Sam Boardman fought, wheedled, and speechified for the acquisition of the 12 miles of craggy Curry County coastline that would one day bear his name, what mattered to him was that the land and its beauties be preserved. For a while, he thought that the land might be the heart of a broad new National Park, showing the glory of the Oregon Coast. But its eventual fate as a state park also served. As the land donations that made the park a reality were beginning to be finalized in 1949, Boardman could console himself that he had saved another stretch of precious trees and scenic views. When he retired in 1950, the still-growing Samuel H. Boardman State Park (later Scenic Corridor) was named after him—surely a salve, though Boardman died just a few years later in 1953.

In 1970, Alfred "Cap" Collier, a longtime member of the State Parks Advisory Committee and founder of Collier Memorial State Park, spoke at a dedication event for the still-growing Boardman park. He summed up his longtime friend as a "magnificent beggar," who asked nothing for himself but who went begging for the people of Oregon." During Sam Boardman's 21-year tenure as the first State Parks Superintendent, the Oregon State Park system swelled from 6,444 acres of park lands to over 57,000 acres. More than 18,000 acres of that land were donated. Even more than they had been in the 1920s, donations were a critical part of building the state park system under Sam Boardman. One of his greatest assets was his ability to convince others that the preservation of land for future generations could be a powerful means of building a legacy. Boardman's time as head of State Parks would coincide with a population boom in Oregon and in the whole United States, a rise in leisure travel aided by rapidly expanding highway systems, and two of the most famous tragedies of the twentieth century: The Great Depression and World War II. Boardman weathered a turbulent era of growth and change with his signature brand of amiable stubbornness and an unwavering love of scenic spaces.[43]

---

43 "Park Dedication: Moment to Remember," *Medford Tribune*, August 16, 1976, Folder: Retirement, Box: Samuel H. Boardman Papers, Oregon State Parks and Recreation Collection, Oregon State Parks and Recreation, Salem, OR.

As the "magnificent beggar" secured scenic vistas and park lands, he also fought to create an ethos and legacy that he hoped would guide the state park system and its caretakers for the next 100 years. The Boardman ethos would emphasize reverent protection and preservation of the land over engagement and recreation. When Boardman was appointed, most of the Highway Department, which remained in charge of state parks, viewed scenic waysides and timber as an afterthought. Careful work from Robert Sawyer, Henry B. Van Duzer, Jessie M. Honeyman, and others had laid the groundwork for state parks, and had quietly crafted the patchwork system that Boardman inherited in 1929. When Boardman left office in 1950, the number of parks in Oregon had expanded from 46 to 151, and the state parks system had developed its own profile—with the lyrical, larger-than-life Boardman at the center of the frame. For better or worse, Boardman ran the parks as an extension of himself, rarely ceding control to anyone, and resisting the attempts of his superiors in government to dictate park procedures. As Marshall Newport Dana, a famed editor and longtime friend, would write on the eve of Boardman's retirement: "other states have state parks superintendents. Oregon has Sam Boardman."[44]

If I Had a Third Arm, I Would Use It Only to Doff My Hat to Each Tree I Met: Sam Boardman's Long Love of Trees

Samuel Boardman was born in Lowell, Massachusetts in 1874 and lived in Wisconsin and Colorado before coming to Oregon in 1904. Previously a civil engineer on various construction projects, his early years in Oregon were spent as a homesteader in an arid portion of Eastern Oregon that now bears his name. Irrigation came too late to the area to make Boardman's land profitable, and he felt he had to abandon homesteading for an engineering job with Oregon Highways. Although his early professional life was dedicated to the exacting work of a civil engineer, Boardman was also "born with a New Englander's affection for trees." Before he worked for the Highway Department, he planted and cultivated trees in Eastern Oregon. In the 1920s, he was one of only a handful of highway engineers who made beautification projects along roadways a priority. This yen for trees was emotional as well as aesthetic; as Boardman once wrote, "If I had a third arm, I would use it only to doff my hat to each tree I met. The stateliness, the serenity of a tree is the vitamin for troubled minds." Boardman's love of scenic landscapes was echoed in larger scenic conservation movements, particularly the environmentally-focused members of the Good Roads movement, but with Boardman it manifested first as a confluence of engineer pragmatism and settler romanticism. He saw the natural environment of arid Eastern Oregon as an incomplete landscape, and he toiled to replicate the shaded environment of his

---

44 "Biography – Subject: Samuel H. Boardman," June 15, 1950, Folder: Retirement, Box: Samuel H. Boardman Papers; *Statesman Journal* Jan 27, 1953, 1 – 2; "The Oregon-Boardman State Park System," *Oregon Journal,* June 5, 1950, Folder: Retirement, Box: Samuel H. Boardman Papers.

These Russian olive and locust trees along Highway 30 between The Dalles and Ontario may have been planted by Boardman himself. That the non-native species grew at all in arid eastern Oregon speaks to Boardman's dogged nature: among other care and feeding, he surrounded some saplings with cacti to deter jackrabbits.

childhood home in New England on the high desert he had moved to. But he was also passionate about preserving existing trees and forests. Boardman and his wife Anna Belle both donated their time and money to the Save-the-Redwoods League, with the Boardman family sponsoring several redwood groves over the years. [45]

Working under the Highway Commission in the 1920s, Boardman set to work planting trees along Highway 30, the "Old Oregon Trail." The initial plan for the highway had focused on its history (discussed in Chapter 1). Boardman hoped to make it beautiful as well as historical. He dreamed of replacing the arid desert highlands with verdant tree-lined drive. The *Oregon Journal* described his somewhat madcap planting technique. "With what he called a highway hoopie, two barrels of water, a bucket, and an assortment of trees, Boardman started planting the most likely places along the highway from The Dalles to Ontario." Around particularly vulnerable trees, he would plant a ring of cacti, saying "I am strictly averse to having the rabbit girdle my trees in any manner, but I'll be damned if I am going to let them sit down to do it." His hope was to create

---

45 "Biography – Subject: Samuel H. Boardman," June 15, 1950; John Clark Hunt, "Boardman Pushed Oregon Parks," *Oregon Journal*, Aug. 21, 1962, pp. 1- 2, Folder: Retirement, Box: Samuel H. Boardman Papers; Thomas R. Cox, *The Park Builders: A History of State Parks in the Pacific Northwest* (Seattle: University of Washington Press, 1988), 79, 82; Samuel H. Boardman Grove, Angeline Boardman Kirk Grove, Walter W. Boardman Memorial Grove, **https://www.savetheredwoods.org/donate/dedicate-a-redwood-grove-or-tree/dedicated-groves/**.

shaded resting spots for travelers and also increase the bird life in the quiet arid landscape. This was alteration, not preservation; Boardman's love of nature was for most of his life reserved for green spaces, not brown ones. But his attitude matched that of the other park builders of the 1910s and 1920s. It was this dogged determination to enhance the landscape that would attract the attention of Robert Sawyer and other park advocates later in the decade. [46]

In 1936, seven years after Boardman became Park Superintendent, the tree planting program in Eastern Oregon was officially halted, as the "[r]esults obtained [did] not appear to justify further expenditures in additional tree plantings." Mourning the loss of his dream, Boardman wrote to his fellow engineer and conservationist R.H. (Sam) Baldock, comparing his tree-planting campaign to the early issues and criticism Baldock had faced while experimenting with a design for oiled roads (which was eventually widely adopted). Seeming to speak half of the highway department and half of himself, Boardman mourned "[h]ow difficult we find it to consider the pace of the snail; to believe and trust in things that are skeptical, to a certain extent, to our analytical minds." But even in his disappointment he tried to evoke the necessity of conservation for posterity. In the same letter to Baldock, Boardman reflected on the importance of highways and (especially) parks as a means of "building an edifice that will honor you long after you are gone." The shape of that imagined edifice changed over time for many people. By the 1930s, reflecting broader changes in conservation movement, Robert Sawyer had changed his views on the cultivation of non-native timber. As he wrote to Boardman:

> *Years ago I shared the somewhat common belief that tree planting was a desirable thing to undertake on any highway. In recent years my opinion has entirely changed and I think now that tree planting almost anywhere along the highway is a mistake... As I remember, you were largely responsible for this planting and at the time I thought well of it. Now, however, it is my feeling that since the trees are not native and since their presence produces an incongruous effect in the desert setting they are quite out of place.*

Boardman, however, remained unconvinced. [47]

The shifting sands of conservation work was never more apparent than in Boardman's relationship with landscape alterations. As an engineer, Boardman believed firmly that land could be enhanced through trees and non-native wildlife. When he assumed his role as Park Superintendent, he urged all workers to protect the land as it was, rather than alter it for the comfort of the visitor—

---

46 Hunt, "Boardman Pushed Oregon Parks."

47 Samuel H. Boardman to R. H. Baldock, Aug 4, 1936, Folder: Correspondence, Box: Samuel H. Boardman Papers; *Highway Research News* 34 (1969), pp. 10 – 11; Robert W. Sawyer to Sam Boardman, May 18, 1939, Folder 10, Box 3, Robert W. Sawyer Papers, Ax 100, Special Collections and University Archives, University of Oregon Libraries, Eugene, OR.

but remained willing to alter environments whose "nature" he did not recognize. In his retirement, Boardman looked fondly on the work of planting trees as a means of communing with the landscape and focusing an eye on the future environmental health of Oregon. [48]

Boardman's early dedication to trees never wavered, and was mirrored in his later dedication to the state park system as a whole. In the 1950s as he had in the 1920s, Boardman wrote: "Plant a tree and be a part of your continuity of tomorrow. Leave something of yourself in the planting of a tree that may speak for you when your lips have been stilled." He used this notion of scenic beauty living on for generations as a way to raise money, acquire land, and inspire those who worked in parks. Boardman wrote, "one of the greatest friends of mankind is the tree. Talk about the dog being man's best friend – there is no comparison. I know what trees will do – fight for you, never give up – for I lived with them in the desert." [49]

The Job Was Waiting for Him:
The Legend of Sam Boardman

By the time Boardman retired, his name was synonymous with Oregon state parks. In a retrospective published in 1962, the *Oregon Journal* wrote of Boardman's 1929 appointment to the role of what became Parks Superintendent that it was as though "the job was waiting for him." Boardman's own reflections, as was his wont, leaned towards the lyrical. In 1947, at arguably the height of his fame, he wrote (in third person):

> *Through a pass of the Cascades some eighteen years ago,*
> *a native of Eastern Oregon sagebrush land entered... an*
> *enchanted land so picturesque that the visitor stood bewildered*
> *by its beauty. The visitor had been appointed State Park*
> *Superintendent. His billet—a park system for the state. To*
> *develop one in the valley of Shangri-La...*

Reality, as usual, failed to live up to Boardman's prose. His appointment was less cosmically inspired than it seemed in reminiscences. When Boardman got the call to a meeting in Salem on August 6, 1929, he was working on a road-oiling crew with the Highway Department in Southwestern Oregon. There can be little doubt that he was awestruck by the beauty of the valley as he drove to the capital (this was a man who tipped his hat to trees). But Boardman was also worried that that he might be reassigned to some other onerous task—or even a desk job. He was pleasantly surprised by his appointment to head the

---

48 Samuel H. Boardman to R. H. Baldock, Aug 4, 1936, Folder: Correspondence, Samuel H. Boardman Papers; *Highway Research News* 34 (1969), pp. 10 – 11; Robert W. Sawyer to Sam Boardman, May 18, 1939, Folder 10, Box 3, Robert W. Sawyer Papers, Ax 100, Special Collections & University Archives, University of Oregon Libraries, Eugene, OR.

49 Samuel Boardman to Charles Sprague, May 1, 1950, Folder: Correspondence, Box: Samuel H. Boardman Papers; "Guest Editorial: Sam Boardman," *Oregon Journal*, July 20, 1950, *ibid*.

newly conceived State Parks program, effective immediately. But his initial title was Park Engineer, not Superintendent, and many on the Highway Commission assumed his job would be temporary. Destiny would require a lot of help. [50]

In the 1950s, as both men were facing retirement, Samuel Boardman and Robert Sawyer discussed this pivotal moment in 1929. Looking to solidify their legacies, each commented on the early need for a parks program. Sawyer wrote:

> ... while Mr. Van Duzer [chairman of the Oregon Highway
> Commission in 1929] in the end was, as you say, very
> enthusiastic about parks, he was not at all enthusiastic when I
> first brought up in the Commission the proposal that we create
> the office to which you were later appointed... It was only after
> you were appointed to the position and with your personality
> and superb performance that Van became enthusiastic.

Indeed, Robert Sawyer had been adamant that the park system needed a Superintendent in charge of parks, arguing strongly against management by commission or committee, which many on the Highway Commission had favored. Boardman agreed that his own role in the park system was made possible only after the hard work of Judge Sawyer to secure a position. He wrote, "I know only too well that you were the yeast that raised the Park Department into being.... Yours was the only move at the time to acquire a park system." In fact, of course, both men had relied on the labor and support of many others, for popular support and practical application of their park plans. Like Sawyer had in the 1920s, Boardman would face an uphill battle for funding and recognition throughout his career. Unlike Sawyer, he would be able to do so from a stable position within the government—a position that he would steadily expand through his own tenacity and temerity. [51]

When Boardman was made head of the Park system, it consisted of 46 parks totaling 6,444 acres. Many of these areas had been obtained under the 1921 law that authorized the Highway Commission to acquire rights of way within 300 feet of the center line of the roadway. This law enabled the construction of roadside rest areas and waysides, which still made up the majority of the 46 parks that Boardman inherited in 1929. The law had been expanded in 1925, allowing for the preservation of scenic spaces and recreation grounds in addition to road waysides. The Oregon state park system had been increasing its holdings since Sawyer had joined the Highway Commission in 1927. Indeed, over half of what Boardman inherited came from the few years Sawyer and Van

---

50 Hunt, "Boardman Pushed Oregon Parks"; Samuel H. Boardman, "The Birth of a Park System: Our Scenic Beauty," in "Oregon State Park System: A Brief History," Samuel H. Boardman *et al*, *Oregon Historical Quarterly* 55 (1954): pp.– 179 – 233, esp. 181; Cox, *The Park Builders*, –54 – 55, 80.

51 Sawyer to Boardman, February 13, 1952, Folder 10, Box 3, Robert W. Sawyer Papers; A "State Parks Commission" was created in 1929, but met only once. See Lawrence C. Merriam, *Oregon's Highway Park System 1921 – 1989: An Administrative History* (Salem: Oregon Parks and Recreation Department, 1992), p. 21; Boardman to Sawyer, February 19, 1952, Folder 10, Box 3, Robert W. Sawyer Papers; Cox, *The Park Builders*, 82.

Duzer had worked together at the end of the 1920s (see Chapter 1). From this growing foundation Boardman spurred an explosion of growth, increasing more than eightfold the land under the management of Oregon state parks. Boardman shifted from a strategy of conservation by subterfuge to a larger-than-life call for preservation, using the role of Parks Superintendent as a sort of bully pulpit to preach the value of nature. [52]

Boardman leapt into action as soon as he was appointed. After his official assignment was granted, he got to work, reading up on old correspondence and visiting acreage already under Highway control. By Thursday of that week, Boardman was driving through Bend in a borrowed car to confer with Robert Sawyer on the most immediate preservation needs in the state of Oregon. He never stopped moving, logging thousands of miles on his state-issued cars over the years. His only mandate was passed down from the short-lived State Park Commission of 1929, which had declared that their goal was to "create and develop for the people of the State of Oregon a state parks system, to acquire and protect timbered strips on the borders of the state highways… and to preserve the natural beauty of the state"—language clearly influenced by the wording of the 1925 law. Boardman latched onto this last notion, "to preserve the natural beauty of the state," and that mandate would serve as a guidepost for him over the next 21 years. [53]

Keep That Which Is Placed in Your Care in Its Natural State: Developing a Park Ethos

Sam Boardman's legacy had two key facets. First, his was an era of acquisition. The state park system grew at an unprecedented rate during his tenure. Second, Sam Boardman worked to create an ethos that would guide how Oregon state parks would be acquired and managed. He saw his role as that of a protector of Oregon lands. Just as he had seen growing trees in the desert as a sacred duty, Boardman believed that it was his generation's responsibility to protect Oregon from development so that future generations could enjoy natural spaces. This vision did not preclude visitors, but Boardman wanted those who visited state parks to treat nature with the same reverence that he did. Insufficiently solemn recreation he would try to curtail where possible; conservation would be the first priority. Boardman's greatest strength in this goal was his prolific letter writing, his humorous memos, and his clear and unwavering belief that the natural landscape would act as a curative for modern life—that the "answers to a distressed world" could "be found in the God-given sermonettes of a park system."[54]

---

52   "Biography – Subject: Samuel H. Boardman," June 15, 1950.

53   Cox, *The Park Builders*, 85 and 83.

54   Boardman, "The Birth of a Park System: Our Scenic Beauty," 182.

Key to Boardman's park philosophy was the desire to maintain the "wild" characteristics of the verdant landscape. This desire only grew as he became more enmeshed in his role, and he regretted actions that had marred the landscapes under his control. Early in his parks career, Boardman instructed his caretakers to cut a trail at Latourell Falls (in Guy W. Talbot State Park). He thought this would give park visitors a nice walk between the falls. But once the trail had been created he lamented that he had ruined Latourell Falls. In his attempt at display:

> *The very foundation upon which depended the beauty of the*
> *entire picture has a great gash across it. The aesthetic sense of*
> *the individual curdled before reaching the beauty spot.... From*
> *then on, I became the protector of the blade of grass, the flower*
> *on the sward, the fern, the shrub, the tree, the forest.*[55]

He remembered this lesson for the rest of his years in state parks and regularly taught those coming after him to have the same respect for a park's natural state.

Boardman's notions of land preservation ran contrary to the views of many Oregonians who saw land as a means of profit, rather than a sacred space. In rural Oregon, landowners and communities sometimes resented the governmental encroachment that came with most early conservation initiatives. Rural and urban business interests often supported conservation as a means of promoting tourism, and thus prioritized development with conservation

Crazy stunts, like pushing old cars over the falls, slowly disappeared, as the core parcels of today's Silver Falls State Park came to the state, piece by piece.

---

55 Boardman, "Guy W. Talbot and George Joseph State Parks," in "Oregon State Park System: A Brief History," 196 – 198, esp. 198.

areas that would maximize profit. How the land was meant to be used, and by whom, was a contentious debate in Oregon, and Boardman's role placed him in the center of this controversy. Sawyer was first and foremost a booster of rural economic growth, and from that vantage point was still able to coax some support for conservation from those constituencies. Boardman more often alienated them. He had a visceral negative reaction against development, which he would maintain all his life, and that made him less willing to compromise than Sawyer. Boardman saw the damage that the development and commercialization of scenic locations caused, and he vowed to halt their spread.[56]

Boardman's fight against uncouth commercialization of nature came to a head several times at Silver Falls (eventually Silver Falls State Park). Perhaps the most egregious misuse of the natural world for recreation (in Boardman's view) occurred in Silver Falls before the state purchased any land. The property owner, D.E Geiser, would stage stunts as a means of cashing in on the waterfall attraction. As Boardman later recalled:

> [Geiser] built a low dam just above the lip of the South Falls, got a chap with an enclosed canoe ["Daredevil Al" Fausset]. Ran a wire through a ring on the bow of the canoe, anchored the wire to the bottom of the pool, a 184-foot drop. The voyager got into the padded canoe, the dam was pulled. The canoe failed to follow the wire, but turned sideways. The voyager was fished out with a set of broken ribs. The canoe demolished. Mr. Geiser couldn't get any more human guinea-pigs, so he built a track in the bottom of the creek, sent ancient cars over the brink for the plunge. These were Fourth of July stunts and drew very well. I believe the entrance fee was twenty-five cents.

Acquiring the land from Geiser drew such extravagant stunts to a close, but Boardman still had to deal with what he called "pestiferous" property owners if he wanted to expand the park and make it the place of reverence he imagined. An unregistered concessionaire who advertised his trailside ice cream by means of a "bell with a resonance likened unto a bullmoose calling to its mate" was bad enough. A man named Fred Volz ran a honky-tonk next to the state picnic area, only 100 feet from the South Falls, was even worse. Bullmoose bells and honky-tonk music, Boardman believed, ruined the quiet introspection visitors—at least the *right* kind of visitors—expected. And Boardman was willing to play hardball, and to threaten with the power of eminent domain granted in 1921 but unused for parks until his tenure. The man with the ice cream bell was tractable, but Fred Volz initially rejected all offers. When Volz refused to sell at market price, Boardman later claimed, the streets around Volz's business were vacated. When he still didn't budge, his property was condemned. On the verge of a trial, Volz relented,

---

56 Lawrence M. Lipin, *Workers and the Wild: Conservation, Consumerism, and Labor in Oregon, 1910 – 1930* (Urbana: University of Illinois, 2007).

the honky-tonk closed, and the sonic landscape of Silver Falls would no longer be mixed with the sound of hawking wares or raucous music.[57]

Boardman entertained correspondents with stories of many such encounters, from noise of vendors to the sudden sighting, on his first visit to what is now the Devil's Punchbowl State Natural Area, of "a roly-poly brown bear" loosely chained to one of the park trees. Later in his career, when camping in parks was being debated, Boardman recalled these early encounters with crass commercialism. He could see no clear dividing line between a trod-upon campsite and a bear chained to a tree.[58]

To combat the human tendency to commodify the landscape, Boardman tried to fashion parks staff in his own image. He regularly sent out grand letters to caretakers expounding on the proper deference that should be shown to natural lands. The caretakers, those men who lived on park grounds and were in charge of all aspects of park upkeep, Boardman viewed as the most important among the staff to be imbued with his philosophy. In 1938, caretakers made $80 dollars each month—at the time enough to support a modest living, but an insufficient wage with which to feed a family. For this rate they were the sole interpreters, rangers, maintenance men, and engineers for their parks. A caretaker at Cape Lookout in 1938 wrote of the type of work he was responsible for:

> *The cleaning and grading and the bucking of the numerous windfalls was all done with hand tools. We used rope block and tackle (hand pulled rigging) to remove the sections of the windfalls blocking the route. We worked six days a week 8 hours a day for $.50 (fifty cents) an hour and we were all glad to have a job. The only deduction from our monthly pay check was one cent per day for accident insurance. There was no overtime pay.*

When advocating a pay raise for caretakers three years later, Boardman detailed what was expected of them:

> *A man should be qualified enough to pass on to the visitor information about the flora and forest cover of the park under his supervision. He should have personal qualifications wherein he can meet the visitor with courtesy and a park friendship. He should wear a uniform where he would be distinguishable to patrons of the park looking for information. A uniform on an*

---

57 Boardman, "Silver Creek State Park," in "Oregon State Park System: A Brief History," 210 - 218, esp. 213; See also Jeff Brekas, "The Daredevil Al Story," *Trail's End: News from Silver Falls* (Summer 1995); J. M. Devers to R. H. Baldock, Nov. 21, 1932, Folder: Correspondence, Box: Samuel H. Boardman Papers; Zeb Larson, "Silver Falls State Park and the Early Environmental Movement," *Oregon Historical Quarterly* 112 (2011): pp. 34 – 57. As was typical for men of his generation and position, Boardman's classism could stray into racism—as in his reflexive assumption that "native hunters" were especially likely to set fires, and thus should be presumptively surveilled. See "Boardman to J. C. Ainsworth," Nov. 24, 1936, Folder: Correspondence, Box: Samuel H. Boardman Papers.

58 Samuel Boardman to Hon. J.M Dever, May 21, 1932, Folder: Correspondence, Box: Samuel H. Boardman Papers.

officer has a tendency to keep the peace. I just haven't had the
nerve to ask these caretakers to buy a suit out of the salary they
are getting. On peak days I have no method of policing the
parks. If I could get a higher type of man, a trustworthy man,
I could have him made a deputy sheriff and secure at least a
semblance of the law for emergency cases.

First and foremost, Boardman taught his caretakers not to alter the landscape unless it was absolutely necessary to do so. He wrote to all caretakers:

It is better to let the fern in a pathway brush against the hem
of a skirt then to "citify" it with breadth and clearance. Within
the fern is a touch of friendliness and understanding that is so
often missing in a handclap. Keep that which is placed in your
care in its natural state.

Boardman preached reverence of nature above all else, and so expected his caretakers to act as the front line against those that would despoil his parks. This did not indicate an opposition to visitors, but rather a belief that those visitors would be best served by making friends with trees and enjoying the touch of ferns. He wrote, "The saving grace of a synthetical people lies in the naturalness of a hinterland, which in your case is the park under your supervision." Prioritizing nature over convenience, he thought, would be the best way to serve visitors.[59]

A large portion of Boardman's correspondence with his caretakers centered on the swift removal of graffiti, usually in the form of hearts and initials etched into trees. He wrote, "you will find the wayfarer who would design his initials upon the bark of a tree. To such, kindly refer them to the inner partition of a privy where their posterity inspirations will have the setting that their mental abilities rate." Boardman would always favor the destruction of the man-made, the park bathrooms, over damage to trees. He offered similar advice to The Pacific Telephone Company battling its own version of vandalism, noting sarcastically that some of the best American literature can be found carved into bathroom stalls,

You cannot deter the actions of a knife point in the hands of
youth, but you can direct it…. The Country privy is a national
institution. More poet laureates have secured the fundamentals
of their profession from country privies than obtained in later
years from the curriculum of English universities… You may
evolve levity from the foregoing. I was never more serious in
my life. If I desired to create levity, I wouldn't be writing this in
my office. I would have breezed it from a privy.

---

59   Records of Employment Sent to Personnel Director, Nov. 5, 1938, Folder: Retirement, Box: Samuel H. Boardman Papers; Cape Lookout Photographs, Envelope 51, Folder: Cape Lookout, Box: Cape Lookout, Oregon State Parks and Recreation Collection; Boardman to R.H. Baldock, March 11, 1941, Folder: Correspondence, Box: Samuel H. Boardman Papers; Samuel Boardman to Park Caretakers, May 22, 1936, *ibid*; Samuel Boardman to All Caretakers of Oregon Parks, May 22, 1936, *ibid*.

Boardman's care for parks did not prevent him from a few well-intentioned jokes at the expense of the public he was preserving the lands for. Especially if they dared to desecrate his trees.[60]

Boardman's desire to focus on the conservation of greenery in the parks did not necessarily overwhelm his practical side. When he forbade cars from driving right up to Silver Falls (an act for which he never stopped getting complaints), he rerouted them to a donated parking lot, rather than banning them from the area outright. Boardman's pursuit of primordial perfection was leavened, when it had to be, by his perception of the possible—though he often dreamed impossible dreams.[61]

A Way for You to Keep Your Name Green Forever: Park Creation at a Time of Desperation

When Sam Boardman was made head of parks in August of 1929, the world economy was already edging towards freefall—though few would notice until the stock market crash that October. Like nearly everyone else, Boardman had difficulty grasping the present or planning the future as the Great Depression set in. Writing to the recently ousted Sawyer in 1931, Boardman worried that "all Highway work is of an uncertain nature these days. My particular work seems to set upon a quick sand foundation. No one seems to really know where they are at." Boardman nonetheless pushed for an ambitious program of acquisition. With little land and less money, with parks still seen as an extravagance by many, Boardman spent the 1930s crisscrossing the state, justifying the need for parks not only to the Highway Commission but also to Oregonians themselves.[62]

Funding from the gas tax was not enough to support Boardman's plans for expansion. The tax had been enacted in 1919 to support highways, and the park system had to compete with other highway priorities. Stretched thin before the Great Depression, highway budgets now had to deal with even more expenses—including new state highways projects that employed hundreds of jobless men with families. Highway Commissioner Henry Van Duzer was sympathetic to parks, but was reluctant to give them priority.[63]

---

60 Samuel Boardman to All Caretakers of Oregon Parks, May 22, 1936, Folder: Correspondence, Box: Samuel H. Boardman Papers; Samuel Boardman to General Manager, The Pacific Telephone & Telegraph Co., Feb 1, 1952, "Samuel 'Sam' H. Boardman, Oregon State Superintendent of Parks 1929 - 1951: Essays, Humorous Letters, Editorials and Published Articles 1922 to Present Times," Samuel Boardman Papers Digital Collection, Oregon State Parks and Recreation Collection, Salem, OR [hereafter "Boardman Articles 1922 to Present Times"].

61 "Boardman, "Silver Creek State Park," 211.

62 Samuel H. Boardman to Robert W. Sawyer, May 25, 1931, Folder 10, Box 3, Robert W. Sawyer Papers.

63 ODOT History Committee, "Oregon on the Move," (Salem: Oregon Department of Transportation, 2013), Oregon State Parks and Recreation Digital Collection; Hugh Currin, "Albin Walter Norblad's Administration," June 12, 1931, Folder: Official Papers of the Governor's Office, Albin Walter Norblad Papers, Ax 680, Special Collections & University Archives, University of Oregon Libraries, Eugene, OR.

Public support was fragile. Once the hard times hit, state parks seemed like a luxury. Some still saw the forests and beaches as boundless, and were thus skeptical of the need for special protections parks could provide. Others put development ahead of tourism. While funds from the Highway Commission for acquisition remained sparse, Boardman saw in the tragedy of the Great Depression an opportunity to purchase land for a song from landowners suddenly in need of cash. There might not be much money for parks, but as land prices plummeted, more people were willing to sell on the cheap.[64]

Boardman's preferred method, however, was to wheedle, cajole, or sweet-talk donations of land or dollars from the movers and shakers of the time. Donations had been the mainstay of park acquisition since before the Oregon park system had existed, as far back as Sodaville in the 1890s, but Boardman was unusually successful—and audacious. E.R Jackman, retired from Oregon State's Extension Service, recalled Boardman's approach to land donations.

> [He would say] you've got a lot of money, but you're going to die in a couple days, and no one will remember you. I have a way for you to keep your name green forever, and I'll even pay for it. All you have to do is give us a little land.

There were reportedly 99 gifts of land for parks during Boardman's tenure, and many more sales below market value. Boardman's offer of immortality was appealing. [65]

Sometimes Boardman's sharp wit could turn cruel. In 1936, Sam Boardman wrote to R.H Baldock bemoaning his latest struggles to acquire a land donation from an Oregonian. In this instance, it was former Highway Commissioner Carl Washburne, who had been Baldock's boss from 1932 to 1935. Boardman characterized a three-hour meeting in which he had attempted to coax Washburne into a donation as a "diatribe of dithering diarrhea," one that, once over, propelled Boardman straight to the liquor store. "He [Washburne] reiterated again and again. I can't think of half of the prattle. The phone would ring. People wanted to see him. It was the day before Christmas. I took it for three hours. He never wriggled up to the point, if any, until I turned the knob of the door." Given Boardman's own famed loquaciousness—he talked so much during Highway Commission meetings that even allies like Sawyer suggested that he instead send his reports in writing—complaints about Washburne's "prattle" are especially striking. The land Boardman was asking for did eventually become Carl G. Washburne Memorial Park—in 1962, after both men were dead.[66]

---

64 Joel Havemann, "He Gave Us Our Parks," *The Sunday Oregonian,* Jan 2, 1966, Folder: Correspondence, Box: Samuel H. Boardman Papers.

65 Joel Havemann, "He Gave Us Our Parks."; Samuel H. Boardman Monument Dedication Program, Aug 7, 1970, Folder: Monument Dedication, 1970, Box: Samuel H. Boardman Papers; Lawrence C. Merriam, "Oregon Parks and the Evolution of Forest Policy," March 2, 1987, p. 1, unfiled, Oregon Parks and Recreation Collections.

66 Samuel Boardman to R.H Baldock, Dec. 28, 1936, Folder: Correspondence, Box: Samuel H. Boardman Papers; Cox, *The Park Builders,* 83.

Many of Boardman's early acquisitions centered on the Oregon Coast along Highway 101, already widely seen in Oregon as a wonder of aesthetics and a magnet for tourists (see Chapter 1). But where businessmen, boosters, and even some of his fellow conservationists praised the draw of the Oregon Coast Highway's "1001 wonders," Boardman feared what might follow the tourists. He looked to the East Coast and southwards to see the type of damage that he wanted to avoid, disparaging the New Jersey and California coasts alike as ravaged by commercialization:

> *Today the Atlantic coast is shacked from end to end. There is no place where the air is washed clean, no place that is free from the ugly design of the hand of man, where one can stand in silence in the midst of the soul building of our Maker. The shore line of California is "hot-dogged" and "beer-parloured."*

Boardman saw Oregon beaches as the single most important area for acquisition, not only for coastal communities, but for the state as a whole. And time was of the essence, as he wrote in 1936:

> *Already shacks and signs are beginning to show their ugliness. It seems to me one of the outstanding acquisitions to be made in the State today. There is no scenic road in the world today to compare with it. Its preservation consists mainly of land alone. The opportunity in its preservation is before us. How to put it over is still to be worked out. Its preservation means as much to Ontario, Bend, Boardman as it does to any coastal area.*

The coast had long spurred conservationist thinking, since at least Governor Oswald West in 1913. But Boardman's plans included more than the beaches—particularly since the stated reason for the preservation of the tideland, to serve as a public highway, had been superseded by U.S. 101. Pointing to the high costs paid for public shores in other states, Boardman spent much of his time and energy trying to preserve as much of the coast as possible parkland under his control—the beaches, the birds, the views, and (of course) the trees. This devotion also revealed his priorities. In ignoring Eastern Oregon for the first decade of his superintendency, Boardman furthered the alienation some rural communities felt towards the emergent state parks system and revealed his disaffection for deserts and similar spaces (though he slowly came around in the 1940s).[67]

Boardman didn't battle alone, although his outsized personality sometimes made it look that way. Private citizens continued to play a vital role in advocating for the park system. One newspaper noted:

---

67 Samuel Boardman to Mr. J.C Ainsworth, June 30, 1936, Folder: Correspondence, Box: Samuel H. Boardman Papers; Boardman to Sawyer, September 16, 1936, Folder 10, Box 3, Robert W. Sawyer Papers; Samuel Boardman to Mr. J.C Ainsworth, June 30, 1936, Folder: Correspondence, Box: Samuel H. Boardman Papers.

Sam has had some valiant helpers in the long struggle to make the people of Oregon appreciate their scenic values. We remember particularly the three ladies whom we have sometimes called the three musketeers: the late Jessie Honeyman, Mrs. Rockey and Mrs. C.S Jackson. Many is the time we have seen then move into battle with Mr. Boardman to persuade reluctant legislative committees to enact necessary and protective laws and to supply indispensable appropriations.

More than a "valiant helper," Jessie Honeyman had been fighting her own state-wide battles for preservation before Boardman had even been appointed. Her work with the Good Roads movement and Garden Clubs had helped to spur public support and parks legislation in the 1920s, reflected in the laws giving garden clubs an advisory role in beautification with native plants in parks and along roadsides. Already well-versed in Good Roads activism, Honeyman established the Oregon Roadside Council in 1931, which was affiliated with the National Roadside Council. This organization shared Boardman's vision of preservation, but focused more minutely on protecting roadside timber and prohibiting billboards, especially along coastal areas. When Boardman needed a hand, Honeyman was happy to stump for more state parks. She also masterminded public re-

Jessie Honeyman established the Oregon Roadside Council, and worked tirelessly to keep Oregon's waysides scenic.

lations campaigns of her own, particularly her long fight for billboard regulation. Like Boardman, she loved trees and hated garishness. Late in his career Boardman would write of Honeyman, "She took great interest in the protection of our waysides. She labored on their behalf." In addition to advocacy, civic organizations often provided for small park developments, like picnic tables and water fountains—elements of parks that the conservation-minded Boardman was less likely spend time or resources on, particularly during the Great Depression. [68]

---

68 "Sam Boardman, Park Evangelist," *Capital Journal*, June 18, 1950, "Boardman Articles 1922 to Present Times." Cox, *The Park Builders*, 91; Jessie M. Honeyman, Oregon Council for the Protection of Roadside Beauty flyer, March 28, 1933, Folder 26, Box 2, Robert W. Sawyer Papers; Samuel H. Boardman to Robert W. Sawyer, September 11, 1936, Folder 10, Box 3, Robert W. Sawyer Papers; Cox, *The Park Builders*, 87.

Private citizens' help was vital in part because Oregon State Parks in the 1930s had to punch above its weight. Boardman's projects had an outsized presence in the public eye, but he estimated that in the late 1930s he had perhaps ten people working full time on parks, including himself. His narrow focus on acquisition and preservation was in part a product of the small size of his dedicated workforce. In the early years of his career, Boardman could know all of his parks and employees personally.[69]

Boardman's latter-day reputation is partly due to his mastery of the press. In addition to surrounding himself with (and sometimes creating) civic-minded conservationists, Boardman never met a newspaperman he wouldn't chat with, regularly giving interviews with the *Oregon Journal*, the *Oregonian, National Geographic* and others that wished to learn about Oregon's natural resources. The plight of Oregon's scenic spaces and Boardman's single-minded resolve to fix it was a regular newspaper feature. Sawyer was not the only Oregon newspaper editor taking a leading role in conservationist causes. When Boardman was reflecting on his career in 1950, he wrote to Marshall Newport Dana, editor of the *Oregon Journal*, that "[t]he individual from a potent standpoint is a nonentity. With the help of his brother, he builds, and you surely have been my brother." Boardman recognized that he was strong, in other words, only because of the help he received. [70]

Boardman needed every ally he could get. Particularly during the Great Depression, some members of the Highway Commission were loath to expand the park system, no matter the bargain prices or even flat-out donations. They feared the maintenance costs, and the optics of taking on such projects in such desperate times. After his retirement, Boardman described one particularly testy exchange during the acquisition of Ecola State Park in 1932, when he went before the Highway Commission in front of a crowd of 300 people:

> *Before I could explain why Ecola Park should be accepted, one of the Commission [Henry F. Spalding] jumped to his feet and proceeded to give me one of the most complete verbal tongue lashings my august person has ever been decorated with.*
> *Times were tough at this time and the Commissioner thought it sacrilege to be spending money for parks when people were tottering on the verge of starvation. His face was as red as mine was white. In some manner, I feathered my wings until the gust passed by. The Commission then voted to accept the park.*

Spalding was right that Boardman could be callous when it came to the poor—particularly those whom he deemed undeserving. Early in 1931, a day

---

69 Lawrence C. Merriam, "Oregon Parks and the Evolution of Forest Policy," March 2, 1987, pp. 1 - 3, unfiled, Oregon Parks and Recreation Collections.

70 Samuel Boardman to Marshall Dana, June 6, 1950, "Boardman Articles 1922 to Present Times."

laborer wrote to the highway department hoping to procure one of the hundreds of new highway jobs first created under Governor Norblad to combat the Great Depression. These jobs were reserved for men with families, and this laborer had none. Boardman, a hardworking, well-educated member of the middle class, expressed no sympathy. He wrote back berating the man: "The fact that you are bereft of succor is the fault of your past action. Why have you not taken a wife?" Boardman suggested instead that the unemployed man live by fishing and hunting—or just gain sustenance from the air, "peppered with the paprika of life its very self." There would be neither job nor help on offer. Boardman kept a copy of this correspondence, as was his custom when he was particularly proud of the witticisms he'd constructed. The desperate day laborer likely found Boardman's jokes about eating air less amusing. [71]

Although he had plenty of clashes with state officials over spending priorities, the losses that Boardman regretted most came at the hands of the federal government. He wrote to Robert Sawyer regarding one such failure at Quartz Mountain, where Boardman had been unable to broker a deal to protect hundreds of acres of privately-held timber along the highway.

> I am enclosing two pictures taken on the summit of Quartz Mountain on the Klamath Falls-Lakeview Highway. I took one picture, the virgin forest of 300 years to the East. I turn in my tracks and the other picture to the West, chaos, devastation. The work of a day of the woodman's axe. Once a scenic area to charm the passing traveler. What assininity [sic] to construct a road system second to none and then stand by while the very panes of the windows of our souls are shattered in a million pieces.

The Quartz Mountain issue haunted Boardman, and he placed the blame squarely on the Forest Service's inability to protect roadside timber. He viewed the involvement of the federal government on forest management as a necessary evil but scoffed at the notion that any Washington bureaucracy would know what was best for Oregon lands.

> We ask not for land or timber, though a foreign government impoverishes us, but we do ask that Government bring forth that timber which is in the background until it fronts our highways for that of private holdings. It is so little to ask for. It means so much to the future wealth of the State of Oregon. Quartz Mountain failures must not be the composite of our biographies.

---

71 Samuel H. Boardman, "Ecola (The Whale) State Park," in "Oregon State Park System: A Brief History," 206 – 210, quotation on 209; Samuel H. Boardman to Grattan L. Hoffman, Feb 2, 1931, "Boardman Articles 1922 to Present Times."

Particularly, Boardman was frustrated by what he saw as federal inflexibility. Trading federal land away from the highway for private land abutting it, he believed, would have kept the aesthetic beauty of the roadside without diminishing the timber harvest.[72]

The federal government's perceived mismanagement of land would frustrate Boardman throughout his career. Although he is remembered for the land he was able to save, Boardman was constantly attempting more ambitious acquisitions to protect himself from a Quartz Mountain legacy. Boardman's moxie garnered praise from his mentor, even when progress was slow. Judge Sawyer would comment to Boardman in 1939, "The mills grind slowly, but certainly the product as a result of your effort is very satisfactory." Boardman, however, was never satisfied. [73]

More or Less of a Hand-to-Mouth Operation:
The Civilian Conservation Corps (CCC) in Oregon Parks

The Great Depression brought cascade of calamities. Poverty, hunger, and fear stalked the lives of most Americans. For the Oregon state parks system, there were bright spots amidst this bleakness. The economic downturn of the Great Depression allowed for the cheap acquisition of lands, and some of the economic assistance that followed as part of the New Deal could flow to the state parks system. But Great Depression also threw Oregon into a period of uncertainty, increased federal oversight, and contradictory goals among politicians, conservationists, and staff over the future of the parks system. These conflicting goals would come to a head in responses to the Civilian Conservation Corps (CCC). The CCC would favor development and access to parks, rather than preservation of "untouched" landscapes. Federal involvement came with a new increase in funds to develop parks, but, as Boardman was quick to note, these funds came with new strings attached.[74]

As the Great Depression worsened in the early 1930s, the Roosevelt administration cooked up an alphabet soup of "New Deal" welfare programs meant to pull the United States out of global economic tailspin. Sam Boardman viewed the new programs with skeptical optimism. He hoped that Roosevelt could cut through the kind of smothering bureaucracy at the Forestry Department that Boardman blamed for the Quartz Mountain episode. "The red tape that they spin," he wrote to Sawyer, "may be likened unto the softest of plush. Its strands are as its forest. Numberless as to units." These hopes were swiftly

---

72 Boardman to Sawyer, June 1, 1932, Folder 10, Box 3, Robert W. Sawyer Papers; Boardman to Sawyer, June 1, 1932, Folder 10, Box 3, Robert W. Sawyer Papers; cf. Reub Long and Ron Shay, "Interview: Reub Long on the Management of Central Oregon's Rangelands," *Oregon Historical Quarterly* 88 (1987): pp. 183 – 195.

73 Sawyer to Boardman, Dec. 4, 1939, Folder 10, Box 3, Robert W. Sawyer Papers.

74 Neil M. Maher, *Nature's New Deal: The Civilian Conservation Corps and the Roots of the American Environmental Movement* (New York: Oxford University Press, 2008).

Building a footbridge in Silver Falls State Park.

The CCC in Oregon's parks reflected Boardman's disdain for development, focusing on access roads, trails, and bridges, instead of buildings. Yet, the CCC and WPA influence remains evident in the majestic architecture and stonework at a number of Oregon State Parks.

Foundational stonework for today's South Falls Lodge at Silver Falls.

The finished Lodge, 1940.

dashed. Roosevelt's conservation initiatives instead produced even more federal oversight of individual state programs. For parks, the most significant of these Depression-era initiatives was the Civilian Conservation Corps (CCC).[75]

The CCC was a voluntary work relief program aimed specifically at young men. These men were paid $30 a month, a portion of which they were required to send back to their families. For this wage, they performed manual labor throughout the country. In Oregon, where the first CCC camps were founded in 1933, work included roadside cleanup, road construction, and park landscaping. The Oregon program would have 17 camps in total, each with 200 enrollees. In addition to providing employment for young men and income for their families, Roosevelt believed that fresh air, manual labor, and camaraderie would provide moral fortitude to the generation coming of age in one of the darkest periods of American history. Like Boardman, Roosevelt firmly believed in the strength of the natural world to heal the wounds of humanity.[76] Writing about this program, Boardman said:

> *The governmental CCC movement has expanded its youth*
> *uplift throughout the terrain of the state. The birth of its*
> *inception was inspired with the lofty conception of lifting the*
> *flagstone wanderer to his place in the sun. Through the thought*
> *and its birth have come the most bewildering display of red*
> *tape administration that any government could 'best mind'*
> *into actualities.*

Boardman's frustration with federal oversight was at war with his firm belief that nature was good for the soul. He was sure that the young men of the CCC (particularly those corrupted by too much time in urban spaces) would be better for their experience, though he focused on moral uplift rather than economic survival. He was less convinced, however, that Oregon parks would survive the onslaught.[77]

Boardman wanted the labor of CCC workers, but only on his own terms. He hoped the program would focus on the construction of roads and bridges that were beyond the capacity of the cash strapped Oregon highway system. The CCC camp administrators wanted an opportunity to develop the

---

75 Boardman to Sawyer, Jan. 30 1933, Folder 10, Box 3, Robert W. Sawyer Papers.

76 Roosevelt believed the CCC could solve three issues facing the United States during the Great Depression: rampant unemployment, environmental degradation, and the moral decay of the largely urban youth population. See Maher, *Nature's New Deal*, 19 – 29. For more information on Roosevelt's views on conservation during the Great Depression, see Sarah Phillips, *This Land, This Nation: Conservation, Rural America, and the New Deal* (New York: Cambridge University Press, 2007). For a brief summary of the CCC and WPA in Oregon see William G. Robbins, *Oregon: This Storied Land* (Portland: Oregon Historical Society Press, 2005), 117 – 120.

77 Sarah Baker Munro, "The Seventy-Fifth Anniversary of the New Deal: Oregon's Legacy," *Oregon Historical Quarterly* 109 (2008): pp., 304 – 311; William G. Robbins, "Surviving the Great Depression in Oregon," *ibid*, 311 – 317; William A. Lansing, *Camps and Calluses: The Civilian Conservation Corps in Southwestern Oregon* (North Bend: Self-published, 2014); Samuel Boardman to R.H. Baldock, date unknown, "Boardman Articles 1922 to Present Times."

park themselves through buildings, trails, and concession areas. Boardman was reluctant to subject his parks to a central plan, even one in which he had authorship. The CCC administrators were unwilling to have their priorities dictated by a single obstinate state official. Mark Astrup, who worked on the CCC program in Oregon and would later become Park Superintendent from 1960 - 1962, remembered that "Mr. Boardman, of course, was interested in getting access to the parks, such as at Ecola and Saddle Mountain and such, but the CCC program was not supposed to be a road program." CCC workers would be involved in improvement projects in 45 state parks between 1933 and 1942, but the tension between CCC administrators and Boardman never fully eased.[78]

Boardman was used to having control over his parks, overseeing all construction and working with engineers he trusted and caretakers he had trained himself. The CCC camp officials were likewise accustomed to acting as foremen on their own projects. Astrup remembered,

> Boardman was always very reluctant to let anyone else do
> any planning of development in the Oregon State Parks.
> That presented a great problem because its rather difficult
> to bring 200 young boys into a camp without a program or
> any plans with which to work, so it was more or less of a
> hand-to-mouth operation.

Boardman's status as the father of state parks stood in the way of successful partnerships. Astrup's vision for parks ("accommodate visitors without despoiling the natural character of the park") was not so different from where Boardman usually ended up landing—at worst a matter of degree rather than an intractable difference. But Astrup's attempts to find a middle ground were fruitless. Years later, he recalled a specific incident in what became Jessie M. Honeyman Memorial State Park (around 1935, when it was still called Waohink Park):

> I went down, without any responsibility for having to do so,
> and spent a whole day cruising that park through that under-
> brush and salal, huckleberry and everything else. I met [Board-
> man] the following day and began to talk with him as to my
> recommendations, and he turned and walked away.

It was difficult for Boardman to make compromises when he was unwilling to even make conversation.[79]

78 Chester H. Armstrong, *History of Oregon State Parks, 1917 - 1963* (Salem: Oregon State Highway Department, 1965), 42; Mark Astrup, "Interview with Mark Henry Astrup, Third Superintendent of Oregon State Parks," Interview with Elisabeth Walton Potter, May 9, 1981, p. 7, Folder: Administrative History—Oral History—Mark H. Astrup, Superintendent 1961 – 1962, Box: Staff Biographies and Oral Histories, Oregon State Parks and Recreation Collection. Boardman did have some success getting roads to parks built with New Deal funds, particularly through the National Recovery Administration—see Samuel H. Boardman to Aubrey R. Watzek, Dec 5, 1933, Folder 29, Box 1, Robert W. Sawyer Papers.

79 Astrup, "Interview with Mark Henry Astrup," 4 – 6, 10.

Boardman tried to instill his park philosophy in the CCC Superintendents just as he did with his caretakers, demanding both a respect for his authority and a respect for the lands themselves. To one such administrator, Sam Bellah, he wrote, "Before work may start on road, trail, building, bridge, forestry, or any item contained within the application of your camp, I desire to go over said work with you in person." Although Boardman was unimpressed with the administration of CCC initiatives, he was also adamant that the workers of the CCC be treated in a way that maximized their well-being and moral instruction:

> Your first thought should be for the welfare of the boys, phys-
> ically, morally, and most of all, mentally. Most of these boys
> have been taken from a walk of life where the flagstones are
> worn smooth, the accompanying border of a picket fence. Little
> in life has been their lot, still they are the grout and mortar that
> will adheal (sic) the stones of the foundation of tomorrow…
> The intent of the CCC movement is the uplift of the American
> youth. You have a cross-section of American youth containing
> two hundred lines. How you weave these lines through the
> loom of your stewardship is your greatest duty.

He insisted that these principles be respected by all that entered his parks. Just as he warned his caretakers not to remove an errant fern, he informed federal officers that they could not improve upon nature, nor should they try:

> Don't think for a minute you can cut down and replace with
> your hands something better… whether it be a bush or tree
> in your way-side clearing, your wooded lot, your picnic area,
> LEAVE IT. Only the dead debris should be removed and
> buried. If you can't go into a forest without blazing the trees to
> find your way out, don't go in.

Boardman warned Bellah that "[w]astage through carelessness is your written order for dismissal." The purpose of this seeming threat to a man over whom Boardman had no tangible authority is unclear. Perhaps Boardman simply assumed that his own horror at excessive tree clearing would be shared by any reasonable person.[80]

Boardman saw red tape and frustration everywhere. Casting aside Sawyer's caution, he campaigned for an independent Parks Department under his sole control in the 1930s, only to be rebuffed. Power over the fate of Parks became more important to Sam Boardman than securing regular funding sources. Instead he faced a proliferation of oversight—the Oregon State Planning Board (established in 1935) and the various government organs it created produced a

---

80 Sam Boardman to Sam Bellah, November 5, 1934, "Boardman Articles 1922 to Present Times" [emphasis in the original].

number of studies and reports, solicited new experts for new kinds of advice, and (Boardman feared) added still more of the "red tape [which] fritters so much time in Governmental work." The new state-level central planning organs mirrored the proliferation of federal programs. The Civilian Conservation Corps was later widely embraced by the country, and has been lauded by historians as the birthplace of the environmental movements that would follow in the 1970s. The Works Progress Administration, another New Deal program, produced formative reports on state historic and recreational assets. But Sam Boardman was suspicious of the oversight that came with these ambitious programs, and of central planning generally. He believed that it was the individual on the ground—namely, one Samuel H. Boardman—who knew what Oregonians needed. [81]

Indeed, Boardman viewed most federal supervisors who dared to enter his parks as virtually an invasive species. When these "walking boughs of ivy enter our wilderness," he wrote, "I immediately get the itch." Those responsible for hiring CCC workers were a "mélange of governmental porch climbers [who] interwind their lean fingers into a potpourri of pork seeking job hunters." Oregon, he complained at another point, was besieged by "a passing horde of Washington tentacles." But his arsenal of metaphors could not stop the tide.[82]

Boardman, a self-taught environmentalist, was suspicious of any expertise that was not his own, and was reluctant to change his views even as understandings about ecosystems and wilderness evolved. "I am of the outdoors, the woods," he proclaimed. "[I] desire to keep them as they are." But just as he resisted the shift away from the planting of non-native trees along roadways, Boardman railed against conservationist measures not of his own making. "I have fought for weeks for the removal of shoreline logs that jeopardize the safety of boating," Boardman wrote in one of several letters to R. H. Baldock complaining about the CCC, "only to be overpowered by a wildlife technician who favored the retention of the logs for the hideout of the pollywog and fingerling." This was an inversion of sorts; Boardman was trying to alter the natural environment to allow for greater access for boaters, while the federal technician insisted on protecting natural habitat. For all his talk of honoring the natural landscape as it was, Boardman restricted that honor to particular kinds of nature. Boardman's near-infinite love for the trees, the ferns, and the birds did not extend to the humble pollywog. [83]

Probably the most conspicuous example of the Civilian Conservation Corps in Oregon State Parks was at Silver Falls. The CCC camp was established in 1935 and was first occupied by young men; in the next decade, returning

---

81   Samuel Boardman to Mark Astrup, Nov. 16, 1936, Folder: Correspondence, Box: Samuel H. Boardman Papers; Cox, *The Park Builders*, 98 – 99; Armstrong, *History of Oregon State Parks, 1917 - 1963*, p. 27; Maher, *Nature's New Deal*, esp. 225 – 226.

82   Samuel Boardman to R.H. Baldock, Dec. 2, 1936, "Boardman Articles 1922 to Present Times."; Samuel Boardman to R.H. Baldock, date unknown, *ibid.* Boardman was more forgiving when it came to long-term National Park employees, whose expertise he trusted more.

83   Samuel Boardman to R.H. Baldock, Dec 2, 1936, *ibid.*

veterans would be put to work there. In Silver Falls alone, the CCC completed 88 park projects that ranged from sewer and road work to the construction of buildings that still exemplify rustic architecture in the state. The federal government would fund 97% of the projects in Silver Falls, investing $410,000 in the betterment of this park alone—nearly as much as the entire yearly budget for Oregon State Parks in the era, and far more than Boardman could ever have hoped for from the state government in a time of economic catastrophe.[84]

The years softened but did not melt Boardman's distaste for the CCC. In his posthumously published memoir he seemed to concede that "without the aid of the CCC boys, our parks would have been years in arrears in their development." But to him the most important thing was the effect of the outdoors on the young workers:

> To me the greatest thing is not the amount of work that has been done, but the salvaging and building of the future cornerstones of the Nation.... The CCC movement has been worth every cent it has cost, even if not one lick of work had ever been struck, and may I say here that wonderful work has been done.

Despite this new enlightened outlook on the hard work of "the CCC boys," Boardman still couldn't help but make one last jab, in 1949. In a narrative report to the National Park Service, he wrote that in one park "[new] painted fog posts replaced old and decadent CCC pole constructed guard rails." Guard rails might be necessary in Sam Boardman's parks, but they certainly would not be "decadent."[85]

Compared to many other institutions during the Great Depression, the Oregon state parks system prospered in the 1930s. Boardman's aggressive (and successful) pursuit of lands—first along the valley and the coast, eventually in eastern reaches of the state—gave the Oregon parks system a large, unwieldy, and eclectic array of parks compared to years previous. Despite the hard times, the masses of tourists that Sawyer had dreamt of and Boardman dreaded finally showed up, as the new Travel Information Board claimed an increase from 300,000 to 800,000 out-of-state visitors a year between 1935 and 1941. Federal monies had paid to build conveniences that Boardman was unlikely to push for and the Highway Commission was unlikely to pay for. And then the war came.[86]

---

84 Samuel Boardman to C.H. Armstrong, Nov. 1951, 5, Folder: W.A Langille Articles, Folder 3 of 4, Box: Publications - W.A Langille Articles The Oregon Motorist, Oregon State Parks and Recreation Collection.

85 Boardman, "Ecola (The Whale) State Park," 209; Samuel H. Boardman, "Narrative Report Oregon State Parks 1948 For National Park Service," 4, Folder: Annual Report to NPS – Statistics, Acreage and Expenditures, Box: Chester H. Armstrong Papers.

86 Cox, The Park Builders, 96 – 97, 100; Ernest P. Leavitt to Henry F. Cabell, Nov. 8, 1941, Folder: Correspondence, Box: Samuel H. Boardman Papers.

"The Handicap of Our Times":
World War II and the Oregon State Parks

As Sam Boardman dealt with budget constraints, expanding federal agencies, and unending work in acquiring Oregon's treasured scenic spots, the United States was entering World War II. This conflict shaped the 1940s, and propelled a period of unprecedented economic prosperity in the years that followed the war's end. But in 1944, Boardman described the war period as "the handicap of our times." The far-reaching impact on the state park system can be easily seen in attendance and acquisition reports. After a mix of steady and rapid growth, even during the hardest years of the Great Depression, the park system slowly ground to a halt, a victim of gas rationing, closed oceanside parks, and a focus on wartime austerity.

Even before the United States formally entered the war, world events had sent attendance tumbling. In 1940, there were 2,070,238 visitors to Oregon State Parks; in 1941, that number dropped by a staggering 72% to 583,473. Beyond the business of running the state park system through challenging circumstances, the magnitude of the war was never far from Boardman's mind. Writing to his old friend and ally Jessie Honeyman, Boardman first filled her in regarding the latest in park construction and acquisitions, then turned to the war raging across much of the rest of the world. "Do you know of someone who will give me a million dollars? I could use it to such a good effect to secure living things, instead of destructive things like bombs and shells." Boardman wrote in frustration over the United States' slow response to Hitler's march through Europe. "As a Nation, we have hidden behind the horizon of a dipping ocean. The water to our eyes is as the sand to the ostrich. Wishful thinking will not stop Hitler from cleaning up Europe."[87]

After the bombing of Pearl Harbor in December 1941, Oregon's resident population (as Boardman explained to the National Conference on State Parks) "immediately turned its attention to the business of the war." Visitor counts slipped further, dropping another 31% to 402,506 by the end of 1942. Military enlistments and defense jobs disrupted family life while gasoline and tire rationing, plus speed restrictions, severely curtailed recreational travel. Oregon's parks, built as adjuncts to the highway system, were hit hard. Many towns had not yet recovered from the economic downturns of the previous decade, leaving restaurants and hotels closed even before the start of the war. [88]

On top of a general decrease in travel and leisure, parks along the coast were closed to the public and turned over to the military for defense purposes. During the war, Boardman wrote to California State Parks asking, "What is the

---

87 Samuel Boardman to Jessie M. Honeyman, April 14, 1941, Folder: Correspondence, Box: Samuel H. Boardman Papers.

88 Samuel H. Boardman, "A 1942 – 1943 Report on Oregon's State Parks to the National Conference on State Parks," Folder: Correspondence, Box: Samuel H. Boardman Papers; Eckard V. Toy Jr., "Oregon At War," *Oregon Historical Quarterly* 102 (2001): pp. 413 – 433, esp. 425 – 428.

Visits to parks nosedived as the nation turned to war. Coastal parks were closed entirely for security and national defense use.

army doing to National and State Parks in California? They are raising more or less heck with my parks, especially along the coast line." Cape Arago State Park and Yaquina Bay State Park, which were at the mouth of harbors and therefore strategically important, were requisitioned. Other points along the Oregon coast, from parks to lighthouses to giftshops, were used as lookouts and patrol stations. The majority of these were opened again early in 1945, but lookouts along the coast continued until Japan's surrender. At times, parks used by the army to house returning soldiers. In Oregon, soldiers were placed at Shore Acres State Park for recuperation. And the war tragically encroached on Oregon State Parks when a B-17 Bomber returning to its Pendleton base crashed in Cape Lookout on August 2, 1943, killing 9 American soldiers in training.[89]

Amidst the horrors of World War II, Boardman did not lose his taste for wit. In the summer of 1945, with the war having come to a close, he wrote one of his famous memos to all caretakers. Rather than reminding them to care for the parks, watch out for vandals, or appreciate the scenic values of Oregon, Boardman archly urged vigilance against Hitler's coming invasion. Conspiracy theories about the whereabouts of Hitler and other top Nazi officials were regular

89 Cox, *The Park Builders*, 101; Samuel H. Boardman, "1943-1944 Biennial Report of the State Parks Department," Folder: Correspondence, Box: Samuel H. Boardman Papers; Laura Jane Gifford, "Shared Narratives: The Story of the 1942 Attack on Fort Stevens," *Oregon Historical Quarterly* 116 (2015): pp. 376 – 383; Folder: Bomber Crash, 1943, 1 [entire], Box: Cape Lookout, Oregon State Parks and Recreation Collection; see also *Fallen Fortress at Cape Lookout* (film), Dir. Tim King, Oregon Public Broadcasting, 1993. The Look-Out on Cape Foulweather, which became a part of the Oregon State Parks system in 2013, was a giftshop/coffee shop "improbably perched" at the edge of the Oregon Coast. The Coast Guard saw the strategic potential of the panoramic views, and the giftshop was requisitioned (with full support of its owners) from 1942 – 1944. See Oregon State Historic Preservation Office and Chrissy Curran, "The Look-Out on Cape Foulweather," NRIS No. 14001159, National Register of Historic Places Registration Form, Nov 20, 2014 (listed Jan 14, 2015), esp pp. 1, 17.

reading following Hitler's suicide and Germany's surrender in 1945. Boardman's pet theory was that he had taken a submarine through the Bering Strait and would use Oregon as a landing site. It was up to the caretakers, Boardman drily suggested, to prevent invasion. "Being a porch climber by profession, you should be fully alerted against any park entry by Hitler in the parks under your supervision." He warned that although the fugitive Hitler would likely have shaved his characteristic mustache, his German accent would still give him away.[90]

As with nearly every aspect of American life, the normal day-to-day of Oregon parks was transformed during the war, but returned only gradually to an altered normalcy after it. Park acquisition had slowed but not stopped, visitation had dropped but not disappeared, and Boardman's ethos of frantic acquisition and conservation was hindered but not halted by exigencies of the war. As the United States and Oregon entered a boom in the postwar period, Oregon state parks under Boardman faced greater strains than ever before.

Betterments Are in the Blueprint Stage:
An Ethos without a Plan

Boardman and the cadre of caretakers he trained had transformed Oregon state parks from an afterthought to an institution in the span of a decade and a half, but the "Father of State Parks" was increasingly struggling to keep up with the times in the late 1940s. Boardman's growth binge had not stopped during the war, and only increased afterwards. However, the prosperity that followed the war brought an unprecedented number of visitors to state parks, and the new popularity of overnight camping exacerbated the strain on park facilities. Boardman's ethos of minimal development bent under the pressure rising attendance, and his lack of a cohesive long-term plan came into high relief. Boardman's struggle to balance the calls for rapid improvement with his fear of overdevelopment would define the last years of his career.

In 1945, there was a "immediate and marked increase [in visitation] following the abolishment of gas rationing." Oregon state parks weren't alone; tourism ramped up across the American West following the end of World War II. Wartime industry had brought hundreds of thousands of people to the coast. The growing middle class had more money and more vacation time than ever before. Roads were improving, and automobile ownership was becoming common. The two-week summer road trip quickly became, as historian Hal Rothman put it, a "badge of middle-class status." Parks that had already been crowded in the prewar era were again too small to accommodate visitors. Construction of amenities had virtually halted during the war, and partially-built projects were often in a state of disrepair. Boardman noted that "betterments are in the blueprint stage, and scheduled for the new year, provided the material necessities

---

90 Samuel Boardman to All Coastal Caretakers, Aug. 3, 1945, "Boardman Articles 1922 to Present Times."

are obtainable." By 1947, park attendance had bounced back almost entirely to the numbers in the pre-war era.

In the following years, these numbers would continue to grow, rapidly taxing the park system that Sam Boardman had cultivated. As more and more families flooded the parks, notions of recreation and scenic spaces were changing. Parkgoers increasingly wanted campgrounds, bathrooms—even running water and electricity! Boardman's final five years as Park Superintendent required him to change his own ideas of how parks should be used. However, Boardman was still required to meet at least the letter of the law, building parks adjacent to roadways and with a focus on scenic space. In a letter requesting information on his park system, Boardman acknowledged the limitations of this park mandate:

> *The State Highway Commission is the State Park Commission. A legislative act authorized the Commission to acquire 'recreational areas adjacent to, along or in close proximity to state highways, and high are so situated as to be accessible to and conveniently reached by and from state highways.'*

Because of this guideline, the "wild" spaces of Oregon—the vast forests and out-of-the-way landscapes—were usually managed by the Forestry Department, to varying degrees of success, as had been seen with Quartz Mountain. Boardman noted that every effort was being made to keep his parks as scenic as possible, and this included a prohibition on overnight camping. Still, Boardman's letter, written in 1948, conceded that the tide might be turning. His parks, which he called "sermonettes," might be required to adapt. He feared, however, that any change to his parks would come, not for the benefit of future Oregonians, but as a means of capitalizing on the land. He wrote, "I have been criticized often by those who are commercially inclined."[91]

For Boardman, this commercial inclination manifested in concessionaires and, worse yet, overnight camping. Writing to R.H. Baldock, Boardman noted that with camping "grass will turn to the dust of the earth, bush and foliage will wither and [only] stunted stumps will remain." Boardman's solution (he thought) was simple: let tourists stay in private facilities and visit his parks as a day trip. During a visit through the vast California state parks system Boardman wrote snidely to Sawyer:

> *First, I want to say that the California Parks don't hold a candle to ours. Second, I thank God that I have not destroyed the beauty of our parks thru development. They are utterly*

---

91 Samuel H. Boardman, "1945-1947 Biennial Report of the State Parks Department," Folder: Correspondence, Box: Samuel H. Boardman Papers; Boardman to Ernest Griffith, Oct. 27, 1948, *ibid*; Many preservation efforts distinguished parks completely from wilderness spaces, seeing them as fulfilling fundamentally different functions. Kevin R. Marsh, *Drawing Lines in the Forest: Creating Wilderness Areas in the Pacific Northwest* (Seattle: University of Washington Press, 2009); Boardman to Ernest Griffith, Oct. 27, 1948, Folder: Correspondence, Box: Samuel H. Boardman Papers. For information on the tourism boom of the postwar era, see Hal Rothman, *Devil's Bargains: Tourism in the Twentieth-century American West* (Kansas: University of Kansas Press, 1998), chap. 8, esp. 202 – 204.

destroying theirs, National and State, thru over development in the very heart of their scenic setting. Commercialism, get the money, seems to be their motto.

Boardman's stance on camping and his militant fight against over-developing park systems was by necessity softened during his final year as Park Superintendent in 1950. His last budget before retirement earmarked funds for the development of overnight camping in three parks: Wallowa Lake, Silver Falls, and Sunset Bay. The office of the Governor had reservations as to whether the law would allow for this type of development with highway funds. Boardman, to justify his decision, pointed to the long string of acquisitions and decisions that might have stretched the original intention of the law, but that had bettered Oregon parks. He argued that "there is need of a strong park department for the preservation and development of the present system." [92]

Boardman was grudgingly willing to allow his park lands to adapt to the changes the postwar era brought. However, because most parks had been acquired without camping in mind, the land was sometimes not up to the task. Mark Astrup was hired as Assistant Parks Superintendent in 1946 and noted these changes in park management. Astrup recalled that there was not a forward-thinking plan for development, and parks were not always large enough or well-suited for camping or other park amenities. [93]

Astrup saw this lack of access as a huge issue for maintaining public support of the park system. Boardman, Astrup said:

was preserving the natural features, and I don't think he ever appreciated the fact that he had to have public backing if it were ever to go beyond that point. And at some point, there would be antagonism aroused by people not having access to the areas.

Boardman had focused on conservation and scenery. Astrup argued that public support could be maintained only with access. If Oregon didn't adapt, it ran the risk of falling behind. In 1949, overnight camping in state parks nationwide increased 33%, as more states moved to accommodate tent and trailer camping. [94] Oregon State Parks also began to adopt new kinds of sites. Parks already run by the state were put under its purview, like Champoeg (in 1943) and Sodaville (in 1947). Other history-centered parks followed, like Collier Memorial State Park, which was acquired in 1945 and prominently featured a museum of logging equipment. Predictably, Boardman began pushing for more robust preservation

---

92 Cox, *The Park Builders*, 100; Boardman to Sawyer, March 22, 1941, Folder 10, Box 3, Robert W. Sawyer Papers; Samuel Boardman to Governor Douglas McKay, March 3, 1950, Folder: Correspondence, Box: Samuel H. Boardman Papers.

93 Astrup, "Interview with Mark Henry Astrup," 8.

94 *Ibid*; "Analysis of State Park Statistics—1949," Folder: Annual Report to NPS – Statistics, Acreage and Expenditures, Box: Chester H. Armstrong Papers.

measures only loosely connected to recreation, like the conservation of bird habitats at Cape Lookout (starting in earnest in 1941) or the creation of the Darlingtonia State Natural Site (begun in 1946). The nature of these diverse sites required more robust interpretation and education within the park system. Prior to the mid-1940s, educational signage about scenic spaces was limited to highway markers and monuments. It was in these new historic and biological spaces that signage about the area's importance and history became commonplace, particularly when the often informal network of volunteer interpreters could not keep up with demand. These interpretive efforts would continue to expand, creating a fissure in the 1960s and 1970s over whether or not a Park Ranger was, at their core, an educator or a maintenance technician.[95]

The growing pains of this era continued as Boardman's staff and their responsibilities seemed to continuously increase, especially following the war when delayed maintenance and construction projects were re-started. In 1945, there were 5 Salem office employees and 32 field employees, only 27 of which were year-round. By 1949, the State Park system was divided into 5 districts. There were 16 office staff, 43 caretakers, and 21 laborers that worked year-round. There were also 61 temporary laborers, and 30 - 60 workers for day jobs each year. Over this short period of time, the fulltime employees working on behalf of Oregon State Parks increased from 32 individuals to 80. In addition, Boardman noted, "there was an unusual amount of surface improvement and building activity carried on, and much new development was accomplished, as well as caring for the increasing and more exacting public that frequent[ed] the parks."[96]

As staff size increased, so too did the number of projects that Oregon State Parks would tackle. Boardman wrote in a report to the National Park Service, "much of the generally used state park system underwent a process of face-lifting that was pleasing to the public; but always done with due consideration for the preservation of the natural beauties of the affected areas." Astrup (whose philosophy was almost identical) remembered that Boardman had a tough time ceding control to his new staff. This included Astrup himself, at the time the Assistant Superintendent of Parks:

> I would sometimes visit a park and make recommendations for
> the caretaker to do this or that, and those recommendations
> would normally be countermanded within a day or two. It was
> not a very satisfactory arrangement, because Mr. Boardman
> would not allow anyone else to accept any responsibility.
> So you had chiefly a feeling of being a figurehead and of
> accomplishing nothing.

95   Cox, the Park Builders, 97 – 98; OPRD-Statewide Interpretive Committee, "Statewide Interpretive Services Program White Paper," July 1993, Folder: Administrative – Park Planning – Interpretation – Interpretive Planning, 1988 – 1993, Box: Planning – Interpretation and Bicentennial, Oregon Parks and Recreation Collection.

96   "Analysis of State Park Statistics—1949," Folder: Annual Report to NPS – Statistics, Acreage and Expenditures, Box: Chester H. Armstrong Papers.

Boardman was determined to impose his singular ethos on the Oregon state park system for as long as he ran it. That wouldn't be much longer. [97]

Spavined Old Maverick:
Samuel Boardman Leaves His Post

In 1950, Sam Boardman retired from the State Parks system. Between 1923, six years before he took over parks, and 1947, three years before he retired, Boardman had driven 452,097 miles in a state car, very nearly enough miles to drive to the moon and back. He was known as the "Father of Oregon Parks," not just because he was the first Superintendent, but because he had shaped the ethos and public persona of the park system so profoundly in his own image it would be hard to separate the two. As Park Superintendent, Sam Boardman was unable to stand still and unable to cede control of his parks to the federal government, or even his own staff. And now, as the country was finally finding its footing after years of depression and total war, he was being asked to take his state-mandated retirement, and distrusted the "young colts" who might be eager to put their own stamp on Oregon State Parks. Sending news of his reluctant retirement to the new chairman of the Highway Commission, Boardman wrote in his usual wry style:

> *I am enclosing correspondence in the form of a death sentence*
> *pertaining and relating to yours truly. I think Civil Service*
> *is perfectly proper and that spavined [broken-down] old*
> *mavericks should get out of the way for up and coming colt…*
> *[but] it seems so unfair to be classed by an organization*
> *that you have been a part of for 30 years, helped build that*
> *organization, to be super-DUPED when your step has lost*
> *some of its spring.*

Before he would step down, he wanted to make sure that those who would replace him knew how the lands of Oregon ought to be treated. Informed of his impending retirement in 1949, Boardman asked for another year to wrap up the loose ends of his position—and was given half that. As he wrote to a friend, "I have just received a reprieve of six months from the Retirement Board before taking the pathway to the lethal chamber." Still, Boardman was determined to use this time to gather his papers, publish his most influential letters and reminiscences, wrap up a lifetime of labor for conservation—and try to ensure his posterity. [98]

---

97 Astrup, "Interview with Mark Henry Astrup," 10. Lawrence C. Merriam, who crafted an influential 1989 history of Oregon State Parks, elsewhere said of Boardman's leadership that "as in a dictatorship, all authority and policy emanated from him, or the Highway Commission through his manipulation." Merriam, "Oregon Parks and the Evolution of Forest Policy," 10.

98 State Highway Commission to Boardman, July 24, 1947, Folder: Retirement, Box: Samuel H. Boardman Papers; Boardman to Ben Chandler, May 10, 1950, ibid; Boardman to Marshall Newport Dana, Jan. 4, 1950, Folder: Correspondence, Box: Samuel H. Boardman Papers; L.H. Warfield to Samuel Boardman, Dec. 7, 1949, ibid.

Chester Armstrong, a career engineer in the Highway Department, was chosen as Boardman's successor. Boardman hoped to shape the new superintendent as he had shaped a generation of parks personnel. In a letter to Armstrong meant for the public eye, Boardman wrote:

> *In your hands has been placed a Master's design untarnished of subject matter that the artists of the past centuries would have given their all to have canvassed... You will be the Administrator of a scenic Kingdom beyond compare. You are a trustee of an estate comparable to none in Oregon. You rule an estate for an unborn generation. The paintings have been made. From your cabinet, may you create a frame in keeping with the treasures left in your command.*

Boardman would regularly refer to his parks as places where individuals could go to be in the presence of divinity. This form of quiet awe that Boardman so favored was being rapidly eclipsed by camping and "loafing"(See Chapter 3). Boardman still fought for reverence over recreation. In his final weeks in office, Boardman worked to make sure that everyone would remember his dictum: that state parks were not for profit, or empty pleasures, but for the betterment of future generations.[99]

Boardman reminded his caretakers of their own limitations when it came to improving upon the lands that they were charged with:

> *It will soon be 20 years that I have been gathering parks and waysides for the state of Oregon. Time has about run thru my course, and another 20 years will not be for me to fulfill. Thru the years I have gathered unto the state, creations of the Great Architect. Guardedly, I have kept these creations as they were designed. When man enters the field of naturalness, the artificial enters. Remember you never can improve on the design...Your hand can conserve what I have builded [sic] thru the years... In so doing you will be director in keeping the recreational kingdom that has been a part of me thru the years.*

Boardman wanted his caretakers to act as extensions of himself, even after he had departed.[100]

This sense of ownership would shape Boardman's legacy and frustrate successive Park Superintendents. Boardman cast a very long shadow. Astrup recalled "He always regarded the areas as his, though, not particularly the public's or the Commission's—they were his, and he regarded them in that manner and

---

99 Samuel Boardman to Chester H Armstrong, Dec. 28, 1948, Folder: Correspondence, Box: Samuel H. Boardman Papers.

100 Samuel Boardman to All Caretakers, Feb, 15, 1949, Folder: Correspondence, Box: Samuel H. Boardman Papers.

was rather jealous of whatever development was accomplished." Still, when an ally on the Oregon Roadside Council suggested a Samuel Boardman Trail to honor his legacy, Boardman was quick to demur. "We are known by our deeds," he wrote, "not the perpetuation of a name plate." This may have been modesty, as Boardman did not meaningfully protest the naming of Samuel H. Boardman State Park (later Scenic Corridor) after he retired in 1950. One wonders what those donors whose names Boardman had promised to "keep green forever" through just such nameplates and namesakes would have thought.[101]

Boardman's retirement in 1950 was an event, reported in all the papers and noted by Governors past and present (including Oswald West, who sent a letter of support). One newspaper wrote that "Sam Boardman has spent the best years of his life coaxing the people of Oregon to do some of the things they ought to have had sense enough to do without being told." Boardman had focused his energies on donations, creating connections with fellow Oregonians, and becoming an amiable figurehead for the Oregon State Park system. He was described in 1946 as "a great-framed, white-haired man who occasionally gives the impression of looking like a kindly polar bear in a long overcoat." When Boardman's writings were gathered and posthumously published in the *Oregon Historical Quarterly* in 1955, a forward was written by friends at the Portland Chamber of Commerce, who, in 1954, took Chet Armstrong to task for not living up to Boardman's legacy (See Chapter 3). Boardman's accomplishments were all the more impressive, they argued, given the resources he was denied. "Lacking adequate public finance, he turned to private sources with outstanding results. Lacking an adequate work force, he turned to the men assigned to emergency relief projects. He proved with highly tangible results that resourcefulness, enthusiasm, and vision are as essential to a state parks system as money and construction." [102]

Boardman and Sawyer continued to make plans for parks, and spar over visions, even after Boardman retired. Living up to his title as the doting father of state parks, Boardman believed that the Oregon system had outgrown the cradle that the Highway Commission could provide, even if leaving meant unsteady funding. He wrote, "The parks system has come of age. It has risen to third place in state increment. The time has been reached when its importance should be recognized. Its development and enlargement should be of the first consideration." Boardman was convinced that the parks system could not survive if it was required to justify itself to the Highway Commission in charge of the

---

101 Astrup, "Interview with Mark Henry Astrup," 8; Samuel Boardman to Mrs. Daniel Heffner, Aug. 5, 1946, "Boardman Articles 1922 to Present Times."

102 Boardman Monument Dedication Pamphlet, Folder: Boardman Monument Dedication 1970, Box: Samuel H. Boardman Papers; Oregon State Parks Highway Commission State Parks Department Expenditures, June 30, 1949, Folder: Retirement, *ibid.*; "Sam Boardman, Park Evangelist," [Newspaper unknown], "Boardman Articles 1922 to Present Times."; Paul Hauser, "Sam Boardman: Collector of Oregon Beauty Spots," *Oregonian* (published as *The Sunday Oregonian*) Nov. 10, 1946, p. 64; Thornton T. Munger *et al*, "Preface: Oregon State Park System," in "Oregon State Park System: A Brief History," 179 – 181, esp. 181.

purse strings. He believed that "park men" should manage parks, not "highway men," and thus that parks needed a secure and separate funding source, one that could not be seized for road improvements at the Commission's whim. Writing privately to Robert Sawyer in 1952, after his retirement, Boardman proclaimed:

> *The time has come where there should be a Park Department*
> *separate from the State Highway Commission. There is only*
> *one other state in which the Park Department is under the*
> *Highway Commission. A Park Commission should be com-*
> *posed of members who know park values… At the time you*
> *set up the park system, you took the only method where funds*
> *could be obtained for acquisition. The park budget has now*
> *grown into about a million a year.*

Sawyer, as usual, responded pragmatically. He departed from Boardman less in his ethos than in his estimate of the economic outcomes. The growth of the parks budget in the post-war period did not mean, for Sawyer, that such growth would continue if Oregon state parks had to stand alone. He replied to Boardman:

> *I hope that someday we may have a State Park Commission,*
> *although the difficulty of financing its operations when they are*
> *set up apart from the operations of the Highway Commission*
> *may be too great. After all, the fund phase of the park activity*
> *is most important.*

Both men embraced preservation and pragmatism. Where they differed was in their perceptions of what was possible.[103]

Three years after retirement, in January 1953, Sam Boardman died in his home in Salem. The state government paused to honor his memory, and he was buried among his trees in Boardman, Oregon. In 1970, the Samuel Boardman State Scenic Corridor (the core of which was the old Samuel H. Boardman State Park) would be dedicated along the Oregon Coast, an area he had been especially desperate to save from the hands of construction and commercialization. In gathering his thoughts on the system he had created, Boardman would write, "My prayer to those who read this is - never sacrifice His works that the commercial hot dog and its odors may take over." Expressed as usual through his satirical wit, Boardman here shared what he hoped would be his legacy: let some places stand separate from modernity, so that Oregonians might rest their minds. [104]

---

103 Sawyer to Boardman, May 8, 1952, Folder 10, Box 3, Robert W. Sawyer Papers; Boardman, "Owyhee: A Recreational Area of Promise,"*ibid*; Boardman to Sawyer, Feb. 19, 1952, *ibid.*

104 Boardman, "Birth of a Park System," 182.

Wallowa Lake State Park, 1950

CHAPTER 3

All the Comforts of Home:
Parks for the People (1950-1956)

In 1957, Parks Superintendent Chester Armstrong wrote, "In the beginning, as with every infant, the State Parks Department had to learn to walk before it could run, and it had to learn in the shaky years following its birth in 1929. But like most lusty youngsters it survived childhood bumps and spills to reach a vigorous maturity in which it efficiently administers the far-flung 56,000 acres of the state parks system." When Armstrong spoke of these wobbling early years before the parks system could stand on its own feet, he was looking at the era of Sam Boardman. Boardman had approached park development as an extension of the divine, a one-man quest to save the beautiful scenes of Oregon. Armstrong considered Boardman's era to have been one of acquisition, a frenzied race to secure the landscape against encroaching forces. In contrast, Armstrong would characterize his own tenure as one of development. As he began his superintendency in 1950, the demands on park property had already changed drastically, as had the ways in which visitors wished to experience nature. Armstrong focused on building structures to maintain a growing park system, finding ways to expand recreational opportunities for Oregonians, and planning for the future of leisure and wealth that the country felt it was owed after the long hardships of the Depression and World War II.[105]

The 30 years following World War II brought not only a shift in the pragmatic development of the State Parks system but a change in the goals of the system, and the outlook of those who would run it. Boardman had looked at nature as a means of connecting to a spiritual purpose—a somewhat elitist view of nature as a pristine piece of eternal design. Armstrong and the three men who would follow him as superintendents in the 1960s and 1970s asked different questions of the landscape. The men in this period looked to a bright future, where the gems set aside at the system's birth could be widely enjoyed by "the people"—a category that gradually expanded over the decades.

After Samuel Boardman, everything seemed up in the air. In the 1950s, the "recreation" Boardman had reluctantly suffered became core to the identity of Oregon State Parks, starting with the snowballing popularity of camping. And in

105 "Parks Department Progress," *Personnel Observations* 8:3, July-August 1959, Folder: Biography, Box: Chester H. Armstrong Papers, Oregon State Parks and Recreation Collection, Oregon State Parks and Recreation, Salem, OR.

a time of unprecedented American prosperity, more people questioned the continuing marriage of convenience between parks and highways that Sawyer had counseled (see Chapter 1). In this new era of growth, some wondered, did the "vigorous maturity" of the expanding system mean that it was time to push for a new and independent department? Or was the old bargain still the best way to safeguard park goals? And in the meantime, where could they put all these people?

A General Urge to Escape:
Camping Comes to Parks and Popular Consciousness

In 1950, Chester (Chet) Armstrong took over a state park system that was bursting at the seams. Sam Boardman had been adept at acquisitions in an era of austerity. But the caution and central control he had stressed as Parks Superintendent made him reluctant to adapt the parks system to the overwhelming demands of a prosperous populace. Armstrong, Boardman's successor, had been with the Highway Department since 1914, rising steadily through engineering positions before serving under Boardman from 1948 to 1950. Boardman was less than eager to turn over the reins (see Chapter 2), and he remained a towering presence in park issues even after his death in 1953. Armstrong would have to adapt to postwar prosperity and population surges that would make Boardman's policies and procedures impossible. This period was not defined by Depression-era austerity or the magnetic and outspoken presence of a founding father, but a postwar abundance and a growing park bureaucracy designed to diffuse a central authority figure. Armstrong's tenure, from 1950 to his retirement in 1960, was defined by an unparalleled surge in attendance, from 2 million to 10 million visitors. The visitation surge was jarring enough. But these new park attendees, part of a burgeoning middle class, had new demands. The people demanded campsites. [106]

Sam Boardman, loath to admit that camping could be a necessary addition to his parks, had made only limited plans during his tenure to allow for campers. In 1948, 17,500 campers stayed at the indoor facilities at Silver Falls, the first sanctioned overnight guests to use Oregon State Park property. Boardman's reluctance to allow campers was rooted in fears of despoiling the natural environment for future Oregonians. He believed that building modern amenities for campers would surely damage the scenic views that he carefully created. In his 1948 Progress Report, Boardman grumpily admitted to the public appetite for camps, conceding that "these camps are popular and fill a desirable youth requirement that is increasing in keeping with the rapid growth of the contiguous population." When Armstrong took over, the state park system bowed to political and popular reality. In 1951, just after Boardman's retirement, the boom in overnight camping facilities began. Initially, overnight

---

106 "Biography: Armstrong," Folder: Biography, Box: Chester H Armstrong Papers; "Astrup to Succeed Armstrong to Post" *Oregon Statesmen* Dec 20, 1960, Folder: Mark Astrup Oral History File, Box: Staff Biographies and Oral Histories, Oregon State Parks and Recreation Collection.

outdoor camping was introduced to two of Oregon's parks: Wallowa Lake and Silver Falls. Silver Falls had the capacity for 40 tent camps and 10 trailer camps. At Wallowa Lake, there were 10 trailer spots and 47 tent campsites. Both were immediately popular. Many more parks followed suit as the decade continued. Unimproved camping areas might be as simple as a clearing, but the amenities enjoyed in the most developed sites of the early postwar era were quite similar to the facilities available to campers today. Campers at the new sites had access to restrooms, showers, laundry, water, electricity, stoves, and sewer outlets. [107]

In the 1951-1952 Progress Report, Armstrong pondered what might account for the surge in visitation and the new push for camps. He gave some credit to better highway systems and advertising. He noted "an increase in the number of low cost camp grounds making travel more attractive to persons in the lower income brackets." And he echoed Boardman's guess that "a general urge to escape for a time from the noise and confusion of everyday life to more pleasant and quieter surroundings" played a role. This "urge to escape" coupled with the means to do so was a nationwide trend. An increase in disposable income and vacation time in the 1940s and 50s led middle-class families into nature for vacations. In the same period, much of the public land on which people had once freely camped was being developed, logged, cordoned off, or otherwise made unavailable. More free time and less free space pushed camping to the forefront of parks.[108]

Although Boardman preferred to ignore it, the desire to camp as a means of escaping modern chaos was not new, arising alongside the parks movement. Recreational camping was mentioned at least as early as the 1860s, when upper class men and sometimes women spent weeks on outdoor camping excursions, usually hiring local scouts or bringing servants to attend to the more monotonous aspects of camp life, like cooking. The natural landscape had long been thought to heal the body and soul of those immersed in it, and the budding state and national parks systems fed the urge for untouched wilderness. Still, these trips were limited by the expense and time they took to plan, leaving them available largely to the wealthy elite.[109]

The automobile modernized the camping experience and democratized its participants. As soon as people had cars, they drove them to scenic spots for

107 "Annual Records on State Parks Land and Related Areas, 1948," Folder: Annual Report to NPS - Statistics, Acreage, and Expenditures, Box: Chester H. Armstrong Papers; "THE OREGON STATE PARKS IN 1951" *ibid.*

108 "Twentieth Biennial Report of the Oregon State Highway Commission," 16, Folder: Progress Reports, 1951 – 1952, Box: Progress Reports, 1951 – 1958, Oregon State Parks and Recreation Collection.

109 Historian Terrance Young places the beginnings of modern recreational camping with the publication of "Adventures in the Wilderness" a how-to guide on camping in the Adirondacks by William H.H Murray published in 1869 which brought national attention to the practice; Terence Young, *Heading Out: A History of American Camping* (Ithaca: Cornell University Press, 2017): 9. Camping enthusiasts sometimes trace a beginning to William Gunn's 1861 school trips to introduce his students to the love of the outdoors (and prepare them for the Civil War). Paula Gibson Krimsky, "Reading, Writing, and the Great Outdoors: Frederick Gunn's School Transforms Victorian-era Education," *Connecticut History* July 18, 2019. The differences between camping and earlier forms of recreational outdoor overnighting can be difficult to parse—see for example Francis Galton's outrageously racist *The Art of Travel; or, Shifts and Conveyances Available in Wild Countries* (London: John Murray, 1855), or Aaron V. Brown's use of the term "camping out" as a clearly well-worn idiom in an 1833 letter to James K. Polk—James Knox Polk, *Correspondence of James K. Polk*, ed. Herbert Weaver (Knoxville: University of Tennessee Press, 1969), p. 193.

rest and relaxation. Indeed, this inclination was a signature part of the parks movement in Oregon (see Chapter 1). In addition to providing access to remote wilderness (though sometimes with great difficulty), the Model T was also a fine camper, and DIY enthusiasts attached tents and cookstoves to running boards to create makeshift camp trailers. Henry Ford himself encouraged this use of his product, leading his own camping excursions with a rotating group of wealthy men he coyly dubbed "The Vagabonds." This group came to include titans of industry like Thomas Edison, Henry Ford, and Harvey Firestone; naturalist John Burroughs; and, in the summer of 1921, President Warren G. Harding. Although the name "Vagabonds" evoked a romantic fantasy of the purportedly carefree life of the wandering poor, the press releases for these camping trips showed car-camping as a luxury for men of refinement who wanted a taste of nature. The average American might not be able to afford all of the amenities of "The Vagabonds," whose inclusion of cars full of chefs and supplies in their Model T entourage harkened back to the wealthy outdoor recreationists of the previous century. But these well-publicized journeys encouraged the intrepid middle class and some working-class families to "See America First" and the auto road trip was born. Highways could provide not only scenic drives, but scenic destinations. A 1924 article in *Sunset* magazine touted this newfound vacationing option, noting that the automobile and auto camping made vacations "cheaper than staying home."[110]

Not only were these trips affordable, but camping aficionados regularly linked them to the "pioneer spirit" long romanticized in American popular culture. This notion of "pioneer spirit" was even less moored to historical reality in the 1950s than it had been in the 1920s, never mind the actual pioneer experiences of the 19th century. The new "pioneer spirit" consisted mostly of enjoying the outdoors and cooking food over fires. The celebrations of the killing of Native people and the seizing of their land that had been ubiquitous in the 19th century and into the 1920s (see Chapter 1) continued to be recreated in children's games. But killing was no longer considered by young adults to be a constituent part of the "pioneer spirit." What was now celebrated was the feeling of freedom in the out-of-doors, available by car whether the camper was playing pioneer, playing Indian, or just playing around.[111]

---

110   James B. Twitchell, *Winnebago Nation: The RV in American Culture* (New York: Columbia University Press, 2014), 71; Bill Ramsey, "The Adventures of the 'Four Vagabonds'; 1921: Camping with the President," *Model T Times* July/August 2018, pp. 24 – 27. For information on early motor camping and its impact on the popular consciousness, see Warren James Belasco, *Americans on the Road: From Autocamp to Motel, 1910 – 1945* (Cambridge: MIT Press, 1979); Emily Post, *By Motor to the Golden Gate* (New York: D. Appleton, 1916); Virginia Scharff, *Twenty Thousand Roads: Women, Movement, and the West* (Berkeley: University of California Press, 2003); Young, *Heading Out*, 95.

111   Marc James Carpenter, "Pioneer Problems: 'Wanton Murder,' Indian War Veterans, and Oregon's Violent Past," *Oregon Historical Quarterly* 121:2 (Summer 2020): 156 – 185. Playing Indian—that is, non-Native people performing caricatured "Indian" actions in approximation of "Indian" costume—had also long been one means of mystifying the experiences of the out-of-doors. This was practiced in some public and private parks, and persisted into the 1950s and beyond. Phil Deloria, *Playing Indian* (New Haven: Yale University Press, 1998), esp. chap. 4; William Harcourt, "To Camp Indian Style," *Boy's Life* June 1952, 12 – 13; Young, *Heading Out*, 103.

With the freedom of the automobile came the formation of rigid camping facilities and the prohibition of camping in certain sensitive areas. As state park systems began to be built in the early 20th century, park officials throughout the nation quickly realized that the "camp where you are" rules popular in earlier eras would no longer do. The US Forest Service began to create professionally managed campgrounds in 1918 to contain and control the crowds. The most widely used planning tool for camps, one that continues to inform many state and national parks even today, was create by botanist Emilio Pepe "Doc" Meinecke. A career government employee who consulted for several federal departments, "Doc" Meineke designed new campgrounds at Yosemite between 1926-1932, meant to keep overcrowding from damaging the popular park. Meinecke proposed that campers could be "guided by suggestion" through one-way roads and well-placed boulders or foliage that could act as a fence. The placement of picnic tables and fire pits would encourage motor campers to stay in these campsites, rather than forge their own path and risk damaging the park. One thing Meinecke refused to plan for was the travel trailer, which he called "a highly objectionable and questionable feature." But Meinecke's maxim of guidance by suggestion could be applied to trailers as well as cars, and remains a core part of camp planning.[112]

By the time Boardman was expanding Oregon State Parks in the 1930s, perceptions of camping had changed. The Great Depression turned the novel experience of auto camping into a necessity, as unemployed families packed into their cars to search for work, many driving into the American West hoping to find financial stability. Auto camps like Henry Ford's "Vagabonds" had been associated with upper- and middle-class camping vacations in the 1920s. In the 1930s, automobile camps were associated with transient labor, Hoovervilles, and houselessness. Actual vagabonds were less welcome than Ford and his chefs had been. Some free auto camps created in earlier eras were even dismantled to discourage the "unsavory" classes from congregating. When Boardman was building the state parks of the 1930s, he did not include camping amenities. He no doubt shared the popular conception of auto campers in the period—not as well-heeled outdoor adventurers, but as unwashed masses that posed a threat to his pristine parks. Boardman wanted park visitors who could afford to retire to a hotel or a private camp come nightfall (see Chapter 2). People likely camped in parks throughout the Boardman era, but without much direction, organization, or encouragement from the park designers or officials.[113]

Postwar prosperity reinvented and reinvigorated the reputation of motor camping. The expanding middle class wanted to see the country in style, and hastily constructed motorhomes, campers, and tents were replaced with a

---

112 Young, *Heading Out*, 134, 151 - 172, 229 (quote on 134); Terence Young, "'Green and Shady Camps': E.P. Meinecke and the Restoration of America's Public Campgrounds," *George Wright Forum* 31:1 (2014): 69 – 76; Linda Flint McClelland, *Building the National Parks: Historic Landscape Design and Construction* (Baltimore: John Hopkins University Press, 1998): 276 – 284.

113 Belasco, *Americans on the Road*; Roger Brandt, "Auto Courts of the Illinois Valley, a Baseline Inventory: Southwest Oregon Highway 199 and Highway 46," (Self-published, 2013).

booming industry of travel trailers and motor coaches that combined mobility with amenity. While some vacationers preferred the hardscrabble nature of the tent camp, more and more Americans saw the allure of a modern cabin on wheels to ferry them across the American landscape. It was in this era that Oregon State Parks opened to campers. They aimed to appeal not to those who wanted to experience nature without any hint of modernity, but rather the recreation crowd, weekenders from the populated Willamette Valley who valued plumbing over pristine nature.

One of the most iconic trailers of this era was the Airstream, designed by Wally Byam, born and raised in Baker City (two hours south of Boardman, Oregon). During a vacation in Oregon from California, Byam was inspired to design a hardbody trailer, purportedly to appease his wife, who was unimpressed with tent camps. Developed in the 1930s, this form of nomadic vacationing entered into the mainstream by the 1950s, even inspiring the 1953 film *The Long, Long, Trailer* starring Desi Arnaz and Lucille Ball at the height of their television fame. The Airstream may have been inspired by a trip to Oregon, but Oregon State Parks had to scramble to carve out space for trailers as camping became a quintessential middle-class summer activity in the 1950s. Streams of visitors demanded affordable, accessible facilities big enough for the bulky new vehicles, and park designers swiftly adapted. [114]

From the early development of camping facilities in Oregon State Parks, at least half of the overnight sites were designed for vehicles or camping trailers rather than tents. This type of amenity-laden camping required larger areas and more infrastructure support. It also created a clear distinction for the public and personnel between the backpackers "roughing it" in the woods and the State Park camper, snuggled in bed. This choice to appeal to the recreational camper over the backpacker defined the new conception of a typical park visitor. Boardman had envisioned his visitors in the mold of John Muir, wanderers in the woods marveling at the splendor of nature. Armstrong shaped parks for family campers in the style of Lucille Ball. They were out for a weekend to relax, not a strenuous outdoor experience.

After the success of Wallowa Lake and Silver Falls, the first two improved camps constructed on State Park property, Armstrong and his staff put their energies to the rapid expansion of camping within most state parks. In his 1952 Annual Report, Armstrong wrote

> *A new procedure was inaugurated in the Oregon State Parks*
> *in 1952 with the opening of overnight camping developments*
> *in 30 areas throughout the state. Of this number, 28 camps are*
> *of an unimproved nature ranging in size from four to fifteen*
> *campsites and provided with tables, wood stoves, water and*
> *latrine facilities.*

---

114 On *The Long, Long, Trailer* and the mini-genre of trailer pictures that followed see Twitchell, *Winnebago Nation*, 37 and 114 - 116; Bruce Hampton, "The Airstream Brand at 75: Born On the 4th of July, Wally Byam Went On to Create an American Icon," *RV Business* 57:2 (2006): p. 32+.

Wallowa Lake and Silver Falls remained the only areas that a trailer could stay in 1952 with full hookups but the next year, Emigrant Springs would join Wallowa Lake and Silver Falls with trailer camping facilities. Improving parks for the benefit of campers was no easy task. The camps in Emigrant Springs, 18 trailer sites and 32 tent camping areas, cost $35,244 to create—about 10 times the yearly salary of a ranger at the time. Advertising these new camps, the *Oregonian* noted that they had

> *All the Comforts of Home – In the improved camp sites the camper can enjoy use of a camp stove, standard camp table, rest rooms with hot and cold running water, showers, utility room for laundry and ironing, power outlets for trailer, water and waste hook ups.*

In 1953, a two-page spread in the *Sunday Oregonian* touted the ease of camping in state parks, now scattered throughout the state. "If you want the fun of camping without undergoing too much physical exertion and hardship, pack the family, food and sleeping bags in the car and drive to one of the convenient overnight campgrounds operated by the Oregon State Parks system." That year, overnight camping numbers soared while day use attendance dropped slightly. The most popular camp was Wallowa Lake, with 11,731 campers. The second full season of camping, in 1953, saw a 44% increase in use across the system, with 29 parks offering camping. Most of this new capacity was unimproved sites, as parks scrambled to build the infrastructure to accommodate demand.[115]

Armstrong and his staff had anticipated a boom in camping in 1952 and knew the parks system as it had been was ill equipped to handle the hordes. A vast new constituency would expect camping at all major parks. But that didn't mean there would be space for them. Boardman had not considered campsites in his property acquisitions, because Boardman had not wanted campers in "his" parks. Thus, while rhetorically the Oregon State Parks system was moving away from an era of acquisition, new land was needed to make space for overnight guests in existing parks, and new funds to build the amenities they desired. As Armstrong wrote in his Progress Report that year,

> *much national publicity has been given recently to public camping in federal, state, and local areas, and, while there has been public camping in some state and many federal areas for some years, the popularity of this mode of vacationing has greatly increased in the post war years, it is now possible to cover much of the country and stay in public camps allowing travellers*

---

115 "The Oregon State Parks in 1952," Folder: Reference Data - Activity and Betterment Report, 1952, Box: Chester H. Armstrong Paper.; Of course, Oregon State Parks did not, at the time, employ many professional rangers. United States Bureau of the Budget, "The Budget of the United States Government: Appendix" (Washington, D.C.: U.S. Government Printing Office, 1954), 340; "State Parks Division: Overnight Camping, October -1953," Folder: Reference Data - Overnight Camping 1953 – 1963, Box: Chester H. Armstrong Papers; "State Park Camping" *Oregonian* June 21, 1953, p. 91; "The Oregon State Parks in 1953," p. 1, Folder: Progress Reports, 1953. Box: Progress Reports, 1951 – 1958, Oregon State Parks and Recreation Collection.

freedom of attire and schedule, "home cooked meals" pleasant places to stay each night and vacations of relatively low cost.

Campers in 1953 paid 75 cents per campsite per night with a limit of one week. Sites with electricity were one dollar. At a time when the average hotel cost $5 a night and average monthly rent in Oregon was cresting $50, vacationing for a $1 a night seemed like a low-cost option. The one-week limit was probably imposed in part to keep people from simply moving to the parks full-time. Camping in

Bigger vehicles and travel trailers became firmly ensconced in the camping landscape of the postwar era.

state parks had captured the attention of vacationers, and, as a result, attendance was soaring. By 1955, Oregon ranked first in per capita attendance of all state parks in the nation.[116]

A decade later, one *Oregonian* article boasted that the era of "roughing it" in the wilderness was long over. "Today's camper in Oregon can enjoy out-door life relaxed in a lounge chair, watching his favorite TV program as his steak is being broiled over a brick fireplace next to his $5,000 camp trailer." The article noted that "[e]very park visitor likes the idea of 'roughin it' but not too rough." This vision of camping was costly to realize, and the Highway Department was frequently more focused on road building than on funding fripperies. Pressure to keep those amenities affordable for visitors meant that improvements would take longer to pay for themselves. [117]

A more bureaucratic and systematic approach to park administration led, for the first time, to attempts to determine who was actually visiting parks, and for what reason. According to surveys taken in the 1950s and 1960s, park vis-itors were largely young families or retirees, many of them coming to camp in trailers or station wagons. A 1957 survey revealed that Portland area residents made up more than half of the visitors to the parks that were surveyed, though they represented less than a third of Oregon's total population. The theory that parks were a means for citizens to escape urbanity appeared to be a reality on the ground. By 1960, there were 11 million visitors spending $170 million in Oregon and going to what was now 175 state parks. [118]

Many of the original boosters of Oregon State Parks had hoped that parks would attract out-of-state tourists to see the wonders of Oregon—and spend some money on the way. Anecdotal evidence suggested this had always been so. Wally Byam, the creator of Airstream, was hardly the only Californian touring Oregon in the 1930s. New attention to statistics showed that out-of-state visitors were a significant portion of the influx of visitors in the 1960s. A 1964 survey of visitors in 19 state parks revealed that 59% of campers were from out of state. According to the same survey, Californians made up about 15% of the total number of campers in Oregon—a significant portion that was sometimes inflated in the minds of more xenophobic Oregonians. The average camper stayed 2.5 days in the campground and enjoyed sightseeing, swimming,

---

116 "Oregon Parks Pace Use by Citizens," *Oregonian* Sept 18, 1955, p. 31.

117 "Twentieth Biennial Report of the Oregon State Highway Commission," 17, Folder: Progress Reports, 1951 – 1952, Box: Progress Reports, 1951 – 1958; "State Parks Division: Overnight Camping, October -1953," Folder: Reference Data - Overnight Camping 1953 – 1963, Box: Chester H. Armstrong Papers; U.S. Census of Housing, "Median Gross Rents By State, 1940 – 2000," **https://www2.census.gov/pro-grams-surveys/decennial/tables/time-series/coh-grossrents/grossrents-unadj.txt**; Seymour Freegood, "The Hotels: Time to Stop and Rest," *Fortune* 68 (July 1963). Whether the $1/night actually *was* a low-cost option depended in large part on the upfront costs of a camper or similar; see F. B. Green, "Recreation Vehi-cles: The Economics of Ownership," *Journal of Consumer Affairs* 12:2 (1978): pp. 364 – 372; "Pioneers Really Had To Rough It" *Oregonian* Sept 5, 1965, p. 92.

118 "The State Park Visitor in Oregon," 3 – 11, Folder: Visitor Surveys, Box: Publications- Rules, Surveys, and Reports, Oregon State Parks and Recreation Collection; "Camp Happy Urbanites," *Oregonian* Apr 17, 1957, p. 14; "State Parks, Hosts to 11 Million, Expect Event More Visitors in 1961," *Oregonian* Jan 3, 1961, p. 14.

and sunbathing. By 1969, 63% of campers came from out of state, and both day users and overnight campers listed "loafing" as one of their top activities while in state parks. That year 56% of campers surveyed were in trailer or truck campers, and the majority of them were middle-class families. As people spent more time in parks, a perceptible new appetite for programs and educational information began to grow. Campers wanted to hear from naturalists, walk guided nature trails, and read interpretive signs. [119]

The Growing Future
Planning Parks in the Age of Optimism

In the midst of this exponential growth of the 1950s, Chet Armstrong looked ahead, attempting to anticipate the needs of Oregonians in the distant future of 1975. The resulting 1956 report estimated that the population of Oregon by 1975 would swell to 2.5 million people, that visitation in state parks would be 12 million – 15 million people each year, and that the state parks budget would need to double to keep up with demand. Experts also assumed that automation and workplace efficiencies would continue to shorten the work week, which they supposed would be down to 37.1 hours by 1975, and that there would be nearly a month of vacation time for all middle-class workers by that date. As the State Parks Advisory Committee wrote, "It is anticipated that the per capita income throughout the nation will continue to rise in the years ahead and in another ten years the average family with be spending ¼ more than it does now. Leisure time is also expected to increase due to a shorter work week and additional days for vacations." The population estimate was about right—Oregon's actual population in 1975 was 2.33 million. Everything else was wildly off.[120]

Neither leisure nor prosperity increased. Bouts of inflation, depression, and eventually stagflation over the next decades meant that the budget for the park functions Armstrong was concerned about would by 1975 be lower in constant dollars than it had been in the 50s. The American full-time workweek had already stopped shrinking by 1956, and by 1975 was north of 43 hours. The expected month of vacation time had also failed to materialize for most Americans—and paid vacations would continue to shrink after the 1970s. In 1956, the report concluded that "it appears that the national trend is towards increasing recreational use in the next 20-year period, barring a nationwide catastrophe such as war, or a crippling depression, and the local trend is anticipated to be even more pronounced." The early 1970s, of course, would see both the Vietnam

---

119 In 1969, 63% of survey respondents listed an income of over $10,000 "'The State Park' Visitor in Oregon': A Report of the 1964 State Park Travel and Use Survey," Folder: Visitor Surveys, Box: Publications-Rules, Surveys, and Reports; "Here's What We're Doing," *Oregon State Park Times* 1:3, Oct-Nov, 1963, p. 4, Folder: Staff Newsletter – Park Times – 1963 to 1964, Box: Publications – Staff Newsletters, 1963 – 1994, Oregon State Parks and Recreation Collection.

120 "A 20 Year Program for Oregon State Parks" (1956), pp. 1 – 9, Folder: Administrative-Park Planning-"A 20 Year Program for Oregon State Parks," (1956), Box: Strategic Plans, 1956 – 2012, Oregon State Parks and Recreation Collection; "Report of the State Park Advisory Committee" (July 16, 1956), p. 51, Folder: State Park Advisory Committee, 1956, Box: Meetings and Events, Oregon State Parks and Recreation Collection.

Popular parks like Rooster Rock (above) and South Beach (right) both see intensive use, then as now.

War *and* a crippling depression. Armstrong assumed that there would be an ever-increasing rush of new visitors to the parks every few years, flush with wealth, freedom from long hours, and newfound mobility. [121]

While the [1956] report overestimated the future fortunes of the country, it underestimated the popularity of the parks. The visitation numbers for 1976 were 30,852,000, double the projections from 1956. Presumptions of prosperity may not have panned out, but the new focus on planning for people was prescient. But what would the people want?[122]

---

121   By 1975, Oregon Parks and Recreation had taken on many more responsibilities than had been imagined in the 1950s, so straightforward budget comparisons are difficult. Portland State University Center for Population Research and Census, "Population Estimates, Oregon Counties and Incorporated Cities" *Oregon Population Estimates and Reports* 31 (1975) ; John D. Owen, "Workweeks and Leisure: An Analysis of Trends, 1948 – 75, *Monthly Labor Review* 99:8 (1976): 3 – 8; Deborah M. Figart and Lonnie Golden, "Introduction and Overview: Understanding Working Time Around the World," *Working Time: International Trends, Theories and Policy Perspectives*, Deborah M. Figart and Lonnie Golden, Eds. (New York: Routledge, 2000). Our use of "depression" rather than "recession" here is in recognition of the long-term damage the economic downturns of the early 1970s inflicted on American workers and wages, and the particularly damaging effects on Oregon specifically (see Chapters 5 and 6). For those who measure economic health exclusively by the national Gross Domestic Product and the stock market, the economic crisis of the 1970s was only a recession.

122   Lawrence C. Merriam, *Oregon's Highway Park System, 1921 - 1989: An Administrative History, Including Historical Overview and Park Directory* (Oregon Parks and Recreation Dept, 1992), p. 43.

Amidst a rising tide of visitors, the State Parks Advisory Committee predicted a deluge of boats. Leisure time, they were assured, would turn maritime. Boat ownership had tripled since the 1940s. If that trend continued as was assumed, in 20 years the majority of American households would have boats. This was emblematic of the assumptions of perpetual prosperity common to the 1950s. While boating became an important part of Oregon Parks and Recreation, even at the peak of recreational boating in the 1960s probably only around 3 in 20 Oregon households owned boats. The crowds, however, kept growing and growing.[123]

Building on this look to the future, Mark Astrup, who took over as Superintendent in 1961 following Chet Armstrong's retirement and remained for two years, created the Oregon Outdoor Non-Urban Parks and Recreation Study. This study was designed not only to survey Oregon State Parks, but all parks in Oregon. This report would determine whether the recreational needs of Oregonians were being met and where state parks might best enable recreation. Astrup noted that the most important shift that this plan created was a movement to "people-use":

> *a pretty striking change in emphasis between the Boardman days, when we were preserving landscape qualities and scenic treasure, to the days here in the early sixties, when we were beginning to notice that people had specific needs and requirements.*

Astrup retained Armstrong's sense of urgency in this pivot to recreation. Identifying "overnight camping and [of course] boating facilities" as "areas of critical need for the future," he urged state and county governments to "give attention to getting sites now while land is available." The push for acquisition continued in the period of development. And in 1956, after decades of rumbling amidst park boosters, an old idea was finally given a hearing. Was it time, many asked, for the expanding state parks system to separate from Highways and become its own department? [124]

---

123 "Report of the State Park Advisory Committee" (July 16, 1956), p. 51, William L. O'Neill, *American High: The Years of Confidence, 1945 – 1960* (New York: Simon and Schuster, 1986); Donald Watson Christensen, "An Evaluation and Criteria for Implementation of a Recreational Motorboat Educational Licensing Practice in Oregon," PhD Diss, Oregon State University, 1978, pp. 1, 69 – 70. Boat ownership tends to be undercounted, as counts are based on registration and not all boat types need to be registered.

124 "Report of the State Park Advisory Committee" (July 16, 1956), p. 52; "A 20-Year Program for State Parks," (Apr 3, 1956), p. 2; Mark Astrup, "Interview with Mark Henry Astrup, Third Superintendent of Oregon State Parks," Interview with Elisabeth Walton Potter, May 9, 1981, pp. –14 – 15, Folder: Administrative History—Oral History—Mark H. Astrup, Superintendent 1961 – 1962, Box: Staff Biographies and Oral Histories, Oregon State Parks and Recreation Collection; "Park Usage Climb Seen" *Oregonian* Nov 5, 1961, p. 20.

Glorified Highway Waysides:
Should Parks be a Separate Agency?

Every leadership generation in Oregon State Parks faced the question of whether to remain a part of the Highway Department or strike out as an independent agency. In the 1950s, the number of park visitors was doubling every few years, and a national movement towards more robust parks and recreation programs put a spotlight on the money and resources needed to manage a growing system. As it had been from its inception, Oregon State Parks under Armstrong was still a wing of the Highway Department. But as the scope, goals, and budget of the parks programs grew, some wondered if it was time to get out from under the highway administration.

As with most issues of state, the question hinged on money. Roads had a stable income from the gas tax, plus a strong position for state funding, and a portion of those monies went to the parks. If parks were a separate agency, would funding dry up? Or were parks already losing out on their fair share of money because of the growing needs for interstates? Park administrators and advocates like Sam Boardman and Robert Sawyer had long debated this question, with Boardman arguing that "park men," not "highway men," should control park budgets (see Chapter 2). In 1955, amidst a national flowering of parks movements, the question caught the attention of the Oregon state legislature. Governor Paul Patterson convened a state advisory committee on state parks to settle the question. The committee was asked to research other state park systems, hold public meetings, and examine the inner workings of Oregon state parks as compared to other state parks. In 1956, Oregon would determine the fate of the highway parks system.[125]

According to Governor Patterson, the call for this meeting had been building for years. The Recreational and Natural Resources Committee of the Portland Chamber of Commerce seemed to lead the charge. Members had been longtime allies of Sam Boardman, and were instrumental in gathering his papers and cementing his legend after his death. Echoing Boardman's wishes, in 1954 the Portland Chamber of Commerce called into question the suitability of the Highway Department to manage parks. The main issue they identified was insufficient and unstable funding. The Chamber suggested that a fixed 3% of highway funding should be earmarked for the park system. This proposal would have increased the budget for parks from around $1 million dollars to around $1.5 million dollars. It also would have guaranteed that park funding could not be diverted to other highway projects. And the Chamber argued for a separate parks commission to administer these funds.

Armstrong reacted to this call for independence with a public response published in the *Oregonian*, saying that "the Oregon park system is well-managed and prospering under the present conditions. . . . there is no valid reason

---

125 "Report of the State Park Advisory Committee" (July 16, 1956).

for separation." Armstrong argued that the funding received by parks through highway commission allocation was adequate. Highway Commissioner Milo McIver agreed with Armstrong, stating that "there is no proof Oregon would be better off with a separate commission." He argued that the park system was in good hands and rated favorably among other state park systems. Armstrong, who had worked for the Highway Department for over 40 years, held firm to the notion that parks and highways benefited from a symbiotic relationship, in part because parks were located along highways and dependent on their maintenance. He noted that park systems in other states also fell under the umbrella of other agencies, most commonly Natural Resources—which could put park priorities in conflict with the interests of extractive industries. There was no proof, Armstrong argued, that the Highway-Park relationship in Oregon was any worse than that.[126]

Armstrong and McIver's assurances did not quell the debate. In June of 1954, another article appeared in the *Sunday Oregonian* editorial page titled "Freedom for Our Parks". Citing the continued growth of the state population and the disappearance of free public lands, this article cast doubt on the Highway Commission's ability to manage a resource so valuable to future generations. The Highway Department was:

> *a state agency that, quite properly, is chiefly concerned with the*
> *practical problems of building highways and bridges... There*
> *are well founded doubts among the lovers of the outdoors that*
> *the responsibility of acquiring new parklands for the aesthetic*
> *needs of the future should... be left in [their] hands.*

Now this was not just an issue of funding, but also one of philosophy. The editorial asked: can highway men, who are largely engineers, builders, and bureaucrats, understand the needs of nature? The stance of the Portland Chamber of Commerce and the editorial staff of the *Oregonian* was an unequivocal "no". They wrote, "members of the highway department are men of unquestioned diligence and ability, in their specialized field. But it is doubtful that they are well qualified, by temperament or training, to give the state what it should have in a parks program tailored for the future." [127]

Sam Boardman's mastery of public perceptions continued after his death. The press in 1954 seemed to be attacking the new leadership just as much as the structure of the park system. Boardman had preached the fundamental importance of acquisition, the more the better. By that metric, Chet Armstrong's modest growth seemed almost like standing still. As the same editorial put it:

> *The department still is wedded to the notion that state parks*
> *should be glorified highway waysides, and has failed to take*

---

126 "Oregon Parks Setup Backed," *Oregonian* May 13, 1954, p. 19.

127 "Freedom for Our Parks," *Oregonian* June 6, 1954, p. 42. Sentence order in the block quote adjusted for clarity.

advantage of opportunities to acquire choice sites because they have not been located adjacent to travel routes. It has also expressed the view that the limited funds set aside for park purposes should be used for maintenance alone rather than in the purchase of new areas.

They suggested a full split of the state system to a separate agency and that "such a commission could equip itself with a parks superintendent and staff trained and experienced in the specialized task of making the most of our scenic assets." The newspaper went on to boldly claim that this separate agency would fulfill the dreams of the recently deceased Sam Boardman "rightly known as the father of Oregon parks." Chet Armstrong, only 4 years into his job, seemed to be fighting a ghost. Forced by public demand to develop campsites, he was then derided for a lack of new park acquisitions. Armstrong was also called on the carpet for his background in highway engineering, rather than park administration—even though Boardman himself had taken the same path to the top.[128]

When writing a history of Oregon State Parks almost a decade later, Armstrong mentioned the controversy but deliberately noted that this discussion predated his tenure:

[P]rior to 1950, a feeling was developing among many people of the state and groups that the parks were not being properly managed by the Highway Commission. These people believed, however erroneous it may have been, that the Highway Commission had an improper conception of parks.

Armstrong made his feelings clear: "highway men" *were* "park men." The "erroneous" belief that parks should stand on their own came from the idealistic notion that funding could be easily obtained. And despite the accusations of the Portland Chamber of Commerce and the attitudes of some in the Highway Department, acquisitions had not stopped in the Armstrong era. But there were serious questions about the best way forward for a park system scrambling to keep up. Chaired by William Tugman—like Sawyer before him a newspaper editor and park advocate—the governor's commission groped for answers.[129]

One of the first tasks the committee chose was to check in with the neighbors—state park systems in California and Washington. Almost immediately, the committee discovered that the rampant growth and funding issues that were straining the Oregon system were also hitting neighboring states. In touring Washington parks, the committee noted that Washington, like Oregon, "had been forced to recognize. . . that it would be impossible to meet the demand for overnight camping facilities." The key difference between the states was not demand but supply: Washington's parks were funded directly through the legislature. While this opened up the option for more funding based on need, the

---

128 "Freedom for Our Parks" *Oregonian* June 6, 1954, p. 42.

129 Chester H. Armstrong, *Oregon State Parks: History, 1917 – 1963* (Salem: Oregon Highway Dept., 1965), p. 36.

committee found a real fear among Washington park system stakeholders that, if the political ground shifted, the parks budget might crack apart. While Oregon's park leadership constantly had to appeal to Highways for a piece of their guaranteed funding, the Washington park system depended on the public to lobby legislators for parks funding. Though at the time of their visit the parks budget in Washington surpassed that of Oregon, Tugman and his committee felt a palpable uncertainty about future funding among those they talked to on their tour. "[K]eep [the] park program out of politics," one representative "emphatically" told them, "where it is sure to be if parks must depend on the legislature for an appropriation." The Washington way was a mix of the tantalizing and the terrifying, the possibility of greater funding and independence weighed against fear of fickle funding in the future.[130]

The committee also observed the mammoth California state parks system, managed under the state Natural Resources Department. Like Oregon and Washington, California in the 1950s was struggling to keep up with the influx of campers. What set California apart was money. Amidst legislative clashes and compromises over oil extraction from public lands in the 1930s and 1940s, California state parks earmarked a percentage of all state royalties from offshore drilling along the coast. The Oregon committee visited at a particularly flush time—more than $30 million reserved for parks had finally been cleared of years of legal impediments by 1954, and the dedicated portion of future royalties had risen to 70%. This lucrative arrangement was generating $7 million dollars a year for California parks by 1956, seven times the budget for Oregon's parks. This stable funding source likely contributed to the other key difference between Oregon and California in the 1950s. California state parks already had dedicated resources for interpretation and educational programs during the summer months—programs that were extremely popular with visitors. Interpretive programs in Oregon parks, where they existed, tended to be local and/or unfunded. It would be another decade before Oregon formally allocated any state park resources toward education. The visiting committee was impressed by the scale of California's system, but couldn't think of a funding source analogous to the offshore oil that had enabled its recent capital investments. In the 1950s California parks served less as a model than a dream, a vision of what might be accomplished if Oregon state parks could somehow get their hands on millions of dollars. The committee had to head back home without a clear recipe for success from the neighbors.[131]

---

130 "Report of the State Park Advisory Committee" (July 16, 1956), pp. 19 – 22.

131 "Report of the State Park Advisory Committee" (July 16, 1956), pp.19 – 21; David Vogel, *California Greenin': How the Golden State Became an Environmental Leader* (Princeton, N.J.: Princeton University Press, 2018), Chap. 4; Melissa Tyler *et al*, "California State Parks: Preserving Our Natural and Cultural Treasures," (Exhibit, California State Archives, 2014; digital adaptation by Jessica Herrick, 2016). The Parks Advisory Committee briefly discussed the possibility of opening land to limited offshore drilling as a source of revenue in 1961. Neither the drilling nor the discussion of it moved past the exploratory phase. State Parks & Recreation Advisory Committee meeting minutes, March 3, 1961, pp. 4 – 8, Folder: State Park Advisory Committee Proceedings, 1956 - 1972, Oregon Parks and Recreation Collection; Shayla Norris-York, "Oregon Bans Offshore Drilling… Again?" *Portland Monthly* Apr 4, 2019.

The Public Would Just Raise H- - -:
Funding Fears in a Time of Plenty

The fight for parks funding in this era was frequently over priorities within the existing Highways budget. When the committee returned to Oregon and began holding hearings in 1956, austerity was not a concern. The public demanded more and better parks, and tax revenues at the time were going nowhere but up. But could a demand for costly new roads swallow up funding for parks? Some advocates for a separate park system thought so. Road building was taking center stage as an issue of national defense. The Federal-Aid Highway Act of 1956 put a nationwide focus on road improvements. The large increases in federal funding that came with this new focus might not be enough. In the grip of the Cold War, few would publicly argue against road expansions for national security. Ernest B. McNaughton, President of the pro-parks Oregon Roadside Council, voiced his support for the Highway Department's focus on interstate improvements. But he warned that given this urgent focus, "the park development and operation program has about the position of a pet dog."[132]

And many echoed Boardman's belief that highway men just didn't know parks. Thornton Munger, a retired forest scientist who was also a member of the Roadside Council, doubted that the men hired to direct the development of highways were qualified to handle the complexities of a state park system. "Businessmen chosen to direct the multi-million-dollar highway program," he proclaimed, "are not apt to find the time to develop adequately the aesthetic, sociological, and scientific factors involved in providing an adequate, well-balanced, fully functioning park system." According to Munger, the Highway Commission was simply "frying bigger fish." Munger continued by enumerating these failings, largely focusing on acquisition but mentioning also the lack of educational and cultural work done in the parks, something that a separate agency, he believed, would have the resources and legal standing to undertake. [133]

Munger was not the only conservationist skeptical that highway people would be able to handle the varied and growing needs of the park system. The Audubon Society of Oregon echoed Munger's concerns, calling for "the employment of trained personnel and emphasis on nature preservation and study in the park program." David Duniway, the Oregon State Archivist, spoke of the importance of historic sites and wished that there was a mechanism within the park structure to save historic buildings. Martha Ann Platt of the Mazamas Mountaineering Club urged the separation of parks in an effort to preserve those areas that could not be reached by auto travel. The Highway Commission,

---

132 "Minutes of the Oregon State Parks Advisory Committee Hearing on State Parks," 5, Folder: State Park Advisory Committee, 1956, Box: Meetings and Events, Oregon State Parks and Recreation Collection. The metaphor chosen implies either that McNaughton maintained the pet-keeping standards of an earlier era, or that he was more concerned about control than funding—after all, the pet dog still gets fed. On changing norms for dog care, see Katherine C. Grier, *Pets in America: A History* (Chapel Hill: University of North Carolina Press, 2006).

133 "Minutes of the Oregon State Parks Advisory Committee Hearing on State Parks," 7 – 8.

Platt argued, knew nothing of the treasures of Oregon beyond the roadsides, nor should they be expected to.[134]

Every time, the Advisory Committee brought the conversation back to money. Birds, mountains, and historic homes were worth saving, but who was going to pay for it? Reflecting on the restrictions of the current budget, Tugman noted,

> *Now one gentleman yesterday* [almost certainly Duniway] *suggested that something should be done to preserve the old buildings in Salem which were occupied by Charlie Sprague's Statesman for many years, a rather unlovely old Victorian structure, and I can assure you that if we took any considerable part of highway revenue to do that job, the public would just raise —, and I think they'd be justified.*

For Tugman, this was a numbers game. The resources were thin, and highways offered a feeling of safety for the citizens of Oregon during a period of growing atomic threats. The voting public would be appalled to see any significant amount of money diverted from that purpose to save a bird or a building. Maybe parks would be safer nestled in the Highway Department? A separate park agency might allow for a more highly trained staff to manage state parks, but that didn't mean the money would follow.[135]

Ever Be On the Watch for Sabotage:
The Parks Committee and the Spirit of Sam Boardman

As more and more Oregonians spoke to the committee, the crux of the parks issue became one of intention. Who were these parks for? Why had Oregonians donated the lands? And most strikingly, as person after person asked—what would Sam Boardman have us do? Cap Collier, a longtime park supporter and donor, wrote in opposition to a separate parks system, saying:

> *"these people gave the Highway Commission[,] for the use of the traveling public[,] these areas for Highway Parks. I am sure it would be a breach of trust now to turn these into an utterly different type of park entirely divorced from the idea for which they were created."*

Whether or not the land was donated specifically to be administered by the Highway Commission, Collier's larger point was one of legacy. Specifically, Boardman's legacy. Collier had worked closely with Robert Sawyer and Sam Boardman, and the 1950s brought swift changes to their established

---

134 "Minutes of the Oregon State Parks Advisory Committee Hearing on State Parks," 11, 30, 34.

135 "Minutes of the Oregon State Parks Advisory Committee Hearing on State Parks," 77.

authority over the park system. Camping added a stressor, and Boardman's former allies did not have the same rapport with Armstrong and his ilk, in part because Boardman had been characteristically unwilling to accept the change in leadership. The Roadside Council and the Audubon Society looked to the future, to what parks might become with specialized leadership. Men like Collier looked back at the hardscrabble glory days of the 1930s, when specialization was a hindrance, not a requirement, and "recreation" was "not our function." Although the larger question of the future of parks was important, these meetings also had to grapple with a legacy of parks as the work of a few tough men who did everything. That vision was neither accurate nor sustainable, but it was held in wildly high regard. Sam Boardman loomed large in these proceedings.[136]

Marshall Newport Dana, representing the Portland Chamber of Commerce, argued that the combination of extensive natural assets and a rapidly changing set of needs for recreation and preservation in the state of Oregon meant that there must be a separate, and permanently funded, parks agency. He used as proof a survey of recreation areas in the Pacific Northwest, noting a 300% increase in use from 1947 to 1954. To bolster his bona fides, Dana reminded the committee that he had been closely associated with parks for the last 45 years, a regular friend to Sam Boardman and the parks system. Dana argued that far from supporting things as they were now, Sam Boardman would have stood against the "crude, conservative, economical attitude that would have parks as an afterthought." He echoed Boardman's florid language when he claimed that trips to parks give those urbanites from developed states the wings to "fly into areas higher than they have ever known." In response, Tugman took a moment to stand up for the Highway Commission. "I think it's an unwarranted assumption – on the part of many people, that the State Highway Commission as such is lacking in provision or is unsympathetic toward the development of a park system or it fails to understand what parks should be." Tugman then said, perhaps exasperated with the navel-gazing idealism of the day's hearing "we haven't cut on the oil wells that they have in California." Talk all you want about what parks should be, Tugman seemed to imply. The money simply wasn't there. [137]

Arthur Kirkham, a radio journalist, in addition to recalling the holy image of Sam Boardman, brought along relics. Kirkham pulled out some of Sam Boardman's letters on the future of parks and read them verbatim. Boardman, writing in 1943, had claimed that, "The park system has been wheedled, mostly by yours truly... a poor way... If it came through the people we would have double the acreage today. It is easy to turn down the Parks Superintendent, but not so easy to turn down the people." Boardman's letter conveyed a longing for

---

136   "Minutes of the Oregon State Parks Advisory Committee Hearing on State Parks," 29; State Parks & Recreation Advisory Committee meeting minutes, March 3, 1961, p. 3, Folder: State Park Advisory Committee Proceedings, 1956 – 1972.

137   "Minutes of the Oregon State Parks Advisory Committee Hearing on State Parks," 48 – 55.

a park commission to guide his work, "a personnel schooled in park matters, an understanding heart, not a combative one." In 1950, as he was preparing to retire, Boardman had written "Ever be on the watch for sabotage of the things I have kept through the years." Kirkham continued on, quoting instances in which Boardman longed for a parks commission, a dedicated staff, and an appropriate budget that would allow for the protection of his parks. Boardman had written in 1952, in perhaps a pointed reference to his successor, "You can't have engineers interjecting emery dust on the forward bearing of park progress." [138]

In what might have been the most unguarded exchange of the hearings, Charles Keyser, a park consultant for the City of Portland, proclaimed in a letter that "a park system will not be happily contained in a drawer of a bureau of another field." "[I]f the Highway Commission continues to regard the Park Department as a stepchild with no promise of ever showing a genuine disposition to be park-minded," he spat, "perhaps a keel hauling at least would be in order sooner rather than later." At the suggestion that he and other committee members could not be "park-minded," Tugman fired back:

> It might surprise you to know that some of us were very close friends of Sam Boardman, Jessie Honeyman, Mrs. Jackson, Mrs. Rocke and the MANY Oregon people who have made notable contributions to Oregon's parks. Some of us have spearheaded campaigns for parks, playgrounds, recreational facilities in our home towns and many have a deep personal interest in Oregon history and in resource and wildlife conservation. If we are... "practical" people with some concern for costs[,] taxes[,] and such unpleasant necessities, we can bear up under that epithet, but it seems to me you are quite unfair in the implications you make.

The question, originally one of pragmatism, became over the course of these hearings a question of who could rightly guard the park system. Armstrong, present throughout, spoke up only briefly, when asked for clarifications on policy. Boardman may have been dead for three years, but his voice was heard at more length than his living successor.[139]

On March 22, 1956, the State Parks Advisory Committee was called to order to make final recommendations on whether the State Park system should be a separate agency. Tugman, perhaps still fuming from his exchange with Charles Keyser, noted that "during the hearings the various groups had been asked repeatedly for their ideas on financing these additional programs, but none had such a suggestion." The hearings and fact-finding had been wide-ranging, but in the end no one had come up with a convincing enough argument that

138 "Minutes of the Oregon State Parks Advisory Committee Hearing on State Parks," **67 – 68**.
139 "Minutes of the Oregon State Parks Advisory Committee Hearing on State Parks," 115 – 121.

By the end of 1958, the State Parks Advisory Committee was done with the question of Parks Division control and funding. Cars, highways (and their money) again reigned supreme, and Parks remained part of the Highway Commission.

funding for park priorities would expand with independence. The general consensus of those in attendance was summed up by Frank Logan of Bend, Oregon, who voiced cautious support for "the suggestion of a park advisory committee appointed under the State Highway. It would satisfy most of the people who are complaining." And at least for a while, it seemed to.[140]

Oregon State Parks would remain a part of the Highway Department, but with a new committee separate from highways providing guidance and advice. The first meeting of the State Parks Advisory Committee (appointed in 1957) was held on September 19, 1958 and seemed to solve the question of park administration. Funding would remain under the control of the Highway Commission, but those park enthusiasts who doubted the efficacy of the highway men could, it was hoped, put their trust in an independent committee appointed to oversee park issues. While the issue of a separate parks department was put to bed, the issues brought to the 1956 hearing would have implications well into the 1970s. The clamoring in 1956 for a professionalized staff and a focus on history and conservation initiatives would take root in the 1960s and 1970s—but not without some bumps along the way.[141]

---

140 "Meeting Minutes, March 22, 1956," p. 1, Folder: State Park Advisory Committee Proceedings 1956 – 1972.

141 State Parks & Recreation Advisory Committee meeting minutes, Sept 19, 1958, p. 1, Folder: State Park Advisory Committee Proceedings, 1956 – 1972; "The Oregon State Parks in 1958," p. 1, Folder: Progress Reports, 1958, Box: Progress Reports, 1951 – 1958.

1963 park managers' meeting

CHAPTER 4

There Is Money but There Are Also Strings:
Uncertainty and Excitement in the Era of Expansion, (1957 - 1970)

In 1964, Dave Talbot took over a park system that was exploding. Tourists and residents were pouring into parks faster than they could build campgrounds. Talbot was the fourth Park Superintendent in as many years. There were tensions between Highway leadership and park management, the Salem office and field staff, the new college grads and the old hands. Taking it all in, Talbot thought:

> *This machine can't possibly function.... [and yet] [i]t functions very well.... It was a total mess, in my opinion.... as I walked in the door, I very much thought about these things and realized I had a rough gem in my hands that I didn't really care so much for, all of the inner workings of the thing, but I sure did know that I ought not to screw it up.*[142]

The creation of the Parks Advisory Committee in 1956 solidified the importance of well managed state parks to Oregonians. But figuring out what "well-managed" would look like—how the "rough gem" might be cut—was still very much a work in progress. The fight for the soul of the department (see Chapter 3) wasn't over. And the issues of the 1950s, namely rapid growth and insufficient funding, continued into the next decades, despite the administration's best effort to plan for the future.

The future, it turned out, was less about boats and more about the bureaucracies, internal and external, that would shape how park people did business. Federal programs, recreation growth, and a new focus on the ranger as a trained professional were designed to answer the concerns of the public in 1956. Debates over what it meant to be a "park man" defined the hiring and firing of a growing system, which incorporated more programs for preservation

---

142 David G. Talbot, "Personal Views on the Development of Oregon State Parks," April 10, 1990 Interview with Lawrence C. Merriam and Elisabeth Walton Potter, 5 – 6, Folder: Administrative History – Oral History – David G. Talbot, Director, 1964 – 1992, Box: Staff Biographies and Oral Histories, Oregon State Parks and Recreation Collection, Oregon State Parks and Recreation, Salem, OR.

and conservation that required specialization. New layers of bureaucracy and accountability accumulated, to an extent that would have sent Sam Boardman into fits. Besides new bureaucracies creaking into place above them, park personnel had to reckon with the cultural shifts that were changing the country—and changing the parks right along with it.

Many of those who worked to expand the park system in the 1950s imagined "the people" only as the burgeoning middle class of the era. But this narrow notion of inclusivity would be challenged in the 1960s and 1970s, when new generations of park goers began to forge their own relationships to nature. Like Boardman, the superintendents that followed bristled at the supposed misuse of the landscape by the young, the poor, or the different. The places set aside during Boardman's tenure as sites for future generations to commune with the natural world were also sites of generational conflict, sexual harassment, and battles over use. In some instances, parks operated at the cutting edge. In others, parks were ill equipped to handle the changing physical and social landscape. The 1960s and early 70s saw Oregonians trying to balance both recreation and appreciation, both use and preservation, both ambitious plans and budgetary realities—balances that remain hard to define and even harder to attain. Oregon State Parks took on a familiar shape in this era, with camping facilities, recreation, coastal management, and historical interpretation becoming part of its official scope. And many of the struggles of the era—struggles against sexual harassment and racism, struggles to keep up with demand and under budget—have persisted to the present.

We Were Spending… in Big Chunks:
A Flood of Money and Bureaucracy

While rangers in the field were reckoning with an onslaught of campers in the 1950s and 1960s, Salem staff dealt with new plans and unexpected expansions. The pivot to include recreation was made official in 1959, when (at the urging of William Tugman's committee) the Oregon legislature added "Recreation" to the name of the Parks division. To Mark Astrup, who took over from Armstrong in 1961, this was part of the shift toward "people use" after the Boardman era. One of Astrup's early steps was to develop the first Oregon Outdoor Recreation Plan, completed in 1962. This plan for the first time took a comprehensive inventory of park assets and suggested paths forward based on inputs across multiple agencies. A precursor to the SCORPs (Statewide Comprehensive Outdoor Recreation Plans) of later years, the 1962 plan was a defining feature of the rest of the 1960s. Boardman's haphazard philosophy was being replaced by bureaucratic acronyms—and fact-based decision-making. Astrup came to a department where he saw "no organization," and imposed at least the bare outlines of a plan. Looking back on the 18 months he had as superintendent before he was pushed out by Governor Mark O. Hatfield, Astrup saw the

The Legislature added the word "Recreation" in 1959 to the Parks Division name, signaling a shift towards "people use."

The National Register of Historic Places is funded through the National Park Service, but administered state by state. In Oregon, that responsibility rests with Oregon State Parks and its State Historic Preservation Office.

1962 plan as one of "two outstanding things" he had accomplished. The other? The hiring of Dave Talbot, who brought political proficiency to his predecessors' penchant for planning and professionalism.[143]

Just as the increased federal push for roads guided the state of Oregon to reconsider the role of parks in the Highway Department, state and federal pushes for environmental and cultural protections would shape the continued growth in responsibilities within Oregon State Parks. Federal money for nature conservation and historical preservation transformed both from niche goals loosely linked to parkland and recreation respectively to specific agency designations in need of trained personnel. The push for conservation gave Oregon parks

---

143 Mark Astrup, "Interview with Mark Henry Astrup, Third Superintendent of Oregon State Parks," Interview with Elisabeth Walton Potter, May 9, 1981, pp. 1, 14 – 15, 19, Folder: Administrative History—Oral History—Mark H. Astrup, Superintendent 1961 – 1962, Box: Staff Biographies and Oral Histories, Oregon Parks and Recreation Collection; Outdoor Recreation Resource Review Committee, "Public Outdoor Recreation Areas: Acreage, Use, Potential," (United State Government Printing Office, 1962): pp. 97 – 101; Lawrence C. Merriam, *Oregon's Highway Park System, 1921 – 1989: An Administrative History, Including Historical Overview and Park Directory* (Oregon Parks and Recreation Dept, 1992), pp. 44 – 45, 49; Thomas R. Cox, *The Park Builders: A History of State Parks in the Pacific Northwest* (Seattle: University of Washington Press, 1988), p. 173.

a role in wetlands and waterways. Federal historic preservation initiatives added what became the State Historic Preservation Office (SHPO) to the Parks and Recreation portfolio. These programs required the rapid growth and profession-alization of a park staff that was already stretched to the breaking point. Oregon State Parks grew faster in the 1960s than any other era, but with this growth came confusion over the scope, mission, and very identity of the service.[144]

Federal initiatives may have brought national funds to Oregon problems, but they also strained state systems, sometimes without obvious benefit, and tweaked the anti-government sensibilities of some in Oregon. Talbot remem-bered that the Park Advisory Committee and Highway Department looked on the new programs of the 1960s with skepticism, because "we were starting to spend money in big chunks." Just as during Boardman's tenure, the Highway Department kept an eye on the bottom line, and new programs seemed to threat-en the budget. Most brought in new money, but not necessarily enough to cover the costs. Though the highway people were nervous, these new initiatives were exactly what park advocates had been clamoring for in 1956. As Oregon State Parks and Recreation moved into these areas officially, they had to build exper-tise in areas unfamiliar to current staff. They also had to reckon with skeptics among their supporters—people not necessarily invested in the new directions the division had been mandated to follow. [145]

We Were Amateurs:
Parks Tackle History

Historical and cultural preservation had been a part of Oregon's parks since before Oregon State Parks was created. From at least the 1900s, there had been movements to preserve Oregon's cultural assets, the long-mythologized "pioneer" era of the state (see Chapter 1). Oregon State Parks initially fell into historic preservation and education through this legacy, outsourcing expertise to "Friends" groups or other interested parties. But the local heritage organiza-tions that were tasked with historic preservation and education were too small and too sporadically funded to deal with the growing number of historic sites Oregonians wanted to protect. This issue had been brought to the attention of the Parks Advisory Committee in 1956 during public hearings, but it would take nearly a decade before the state of Oregon had a concise plan for the manage-ment of cultural resources.

In 1963, an act of the Oregon legislature gave the State Highway Com-mission the ability to acquire cultural, scientific, and historic sites with Highway Commission funds from tax revenue. No longer limited to the 1925 statute that had technically only allowed acquisitions of such lands to those adjacent to

---

144 Elisabeth Walton Potter, "The National Historic Preservation Act at Fifty," *Oregon Historical Quarterly* 117:3 (Fall 2016): pp. 378 – 401.

145 Merriam, *Oregon's Highway Park System, 1921 – 1989*, pp. 73 – 74.

More than parks and waysides: a 1963 Oregon law gave the State Highway Commission the green light to acquire cultural, scientific, and historic sites using Highway Commission funds from tax revenue. Today, there are dozens of historic sites in the system.

highways, this amendment permitted state parks to add not just scenic areas, but educational and culture assets wherever needed in Oregon. Some of these heritage sites were new; others had previously been under a patchwork of local protections. The 1963 statute placed much of the burden of preservation on the Highway Commission.[146]

State park administrators had to build capacity in a hurry. Although there had long been a push for historic preservation amongst park people, from Robert Sawyer and Jessie Honeyman to Mark Astrup, Dave Talbot, and most of the 1956 committee, there was not yet expertise in the department on preservation, history, or any of the other specialties required. We "found ourselves playing defense with people who were very knowledgeable in the business," Dave Talbot later recalled, "And we were amateurs, dealing with people who wanted us to do this or not do that."[147] In 1966, the first professionally trained State

---

146   Oregon Chapter 601: "AN ACT Relating to acquisition and administration of historic sites by the State Highway Commission; Amending ORS 366.205, 366.345, and 366.350," *Oregon Laws 1963*, pp. 1234 – 1236, found in Folder: Parks and Recreation Statutes, Box: Legislation and Statutes, Oregon Parks and Recreation Collection.

147   David G. Talbot, "Personal Views on the Development of Oregon State Parks," May 16, 1990, Interview with Lawrence C. Merriam and Elisabeth Walton Potter, p. 60, Folder: Administrative History – Oral History – David G. Talbot, Director, 1964 – 1992.

Park historian was brought on staff.[148] Elisabeth Walton [Potter] would work closely with Dave Talbot on issues of preservation and protection of historic areas for most of the next three decades. She would work not only to develop historic sites under the state parks umbrella, but also to aid local museums and work on educational and public programing initiatives.[149] In 1966, the federal government passed the Historic Preservation Act and the following year, 1967, the State Historic Preservation Office (SHPO) was created to aid in managing the federal monies devoted to historic preservation. Talbot remembered inheriting the program:

> *The Secretary of the Interior is writing the governor*
> *asking, 'Who do you want to have handle this program? There*
> *is money, but there are also strings'. So it ends up that Parks*
> *enabling statutes has the word historic in it, and there is no-*
> *body else that does other than a university, and nobody wanted*
> *to do that... so it ended up in our shop.*

This was not, in fact, a coincidence. Those who had originally pushed for Oregon state parks and scenic roadways in the 1910s and 20s had wanted to preserve history as well as nature. Under the shadow of Boardman this part of parks legacy had languished, but when new laws spotlighted history these old intentions began to be fulfilled.[150]

But in this early era of cultural preservation in the park system, places of importance to dominant White narratives of Oregon history were highlighted. Sites important to Oregon's Indigenous nations were neglected—or even damaged. A quarter century later in 1990, Dave Talbot noted, "the archeological side is still a problem. I don't know how we'll ever get it fixed." Mythic pioneer narratives had developed alongside the story of Oregon State Parks, but the stories of the people who had lived in the region before colonization were largely ignored, appropriated, missing—or outright fabricated by White rangers. Numerous parks held cultural significance for Indigenous communities, and were filled with artifacts of Indigenous culture and life. No stated policy for these areas existed. Indigenous cultural objects and even human remains were regularly relocated, or worse, collected as trinkets by park staff. As parks began to incorporate education into the park experience, programs occasionally saw volunteers and rangers in "Indian dress." Most of the time, these volunteers and rangers were not members of Indigenous communities sharing their own culture

---

148   William A. Langille filled the role of historian during Boardman's tenure, though he was professionally trained as a forester. See Box: W.A. Langille Articles—The Oregon Motorist, Oregon Parks and Recreation Collection; Astrup, "Interview with Mark Henry Astrup," pp. 18 - 19.

149   State Parks and Recreation Advisory Committee Meeting Minutes, Dec 1, 1966, p. 4, Folder: State Parks Advisory Committee Proceedings 1956 – 1972, Oregon Parks and Recreation Collection; Elisabeth Walton, "Historic Preservation Program" (1973), Folder: Administrative – Park Planning – Interpretation – Interpretive Planning, 1972 - 1987, Box: Planning – Interpretation and Bicentennial, Oregon Parks and Recreation Collection. Elisabeth Walton Potter also shaped the history of Oregon State Parks itself; many of the sources used to build this history reflect her choices about what to preserve and what to discard.

150   Talbot, "Personal Views on the Development of Oregon State Parks," May 16, 1990, p. 61.

Predictably, the places and stories that Parks deemed historically significant dismissed (or misrepresented) Indigenous history and culture.

with visitors. Rather, they were dressing up in a mishmash of "authentic... Indian outfits," meant as spectacle put on by and for White people. This was a continuation of a long tradition of redface in the Pacific Northwest, an assault on Indigenous culture that would continue with little comment into the next decades and beyond. Although the times were changing, Parks would take a while to catch up (See Chapter 7). There is no record of when White parks personnel realized they shouldn't be playing Indian.[151]

151 "DISTRICT IV" *Oregon State Park Times* 2:1, Dec.-Jan. 1964, p. 4 Folder: Staff Newsletter – Park Times – 1963 to 1964, Box: Publications – Staff Newsletters, 1963 – 1994, Oregon Parks and Recreation Collection; "Office," *Oregon State Park Times* 8:2[?], July 1969, p. 27, Folder: Staff Newsletter – Park Times – 1969, Box: Publications – Staff Newsletters, 1963 – 1994. Many of the newsletters preserved in this collection have multiple missing pages; [?] after the volume:issue numbers indicates missing pages somewhere in the document, which in turn mean that the cited page is likely to have been, rather than guaranteed to have been, in the issue indicated; "Office," *Oregon State Park Times* 8:2[?], July 1969, p. 27, Folder: Staff Newsletter – Park Times – 1969; For use of redface by White-identifying parks personnel, see "DISTRICT II," *Oregon State Park Times* 9:3, Dec 1966, p. 7, Folder: Staff Newsletter – Park Times – 1965 to 1966, Box: Publications – Staff Newsletters, 1963 – 1994; Phil Deloria, *Playing Indian* (New Haven: Yale University Press, 1998), esp. chap. 4. Native people who choose to wear traditional dress while working in parks are, of course, categorically different. In 1964, Osage teacher (and future Osage Nation leader) George Tallchief donned elements of regalia when doing interpretive work at Wallowa Lake. The newsletter writers appear to have been unaware that he was an actual Native person. "DISTRICT IV," *Oregon State Park Times* 2:6, Oct.-Nov. 1964, p. 3 Folder: Staff Newsletter – Park Times – 1963 to 1964, Box: Publications – Staff Newsletters, 1963 – 1994; "Former Osage Chief and Educator George Eves Tall Chief Walks On," *Indian Country Today* Aug 14, 2013; Vincent Schilling, "Boy Scouts 'have been one of the worst culprits' of cultural appropriation," *Indian Country Today* Sept 14, 2019.

Private Property:
State Parks Fight for Beaches, Waterways, and Trails

Amidst a growing national movement for government involvement in environmental conservation, many organs of the state and federal government took on expanded roles. Most often, Oregon State Parks and Recreation ended up with responsibility for the places where nature and recreation met. Vast new spaces and places were put under the control of the division in the 1960s and 70s. The most famous of these places was where state parks began—the long, long ribbon of public land that was the Oregon beach system. Most of the coast had been set aside as a public "highway" in 1913 at the behest of Governor Oswald West. Whether or not this was originally meant in earnest (see Chapter 1), it became clear by the 1960s that most Oregon beaches were not and had not been automobile highways—but they were still presumed to be public. Debates over public or private ownership came to focus on the "dry sand" portions of the beaches, seldom used for vehicular transportation and not explicitly covered in any Oregon law. In some communities along the shore, "private property" signs and fencing threatened beach access that had always been assumed to be guaranteed. Many still-unfenced areas of the beach still legally allowed automobile traffic, which threatened the ecosystem and endangered those Oregonians relaxing on the sand. Starting in 1947 and continuing over the next decades, the Highway Commission began restricting automobiles to fewer and fewer areas of the beach. But where should Oregon Parks and Recreation fit in? [152]

Public outcry over the beach issue spurred the Oregon legislature to act. In her 1977 history of how parks came to manage Oregon beaches, Kathryn Straton wrote that "the law was a response from a gradually developing political conscience which places value on aesthetics as well as economics, preservation as well as progress, conservation as well as development." It was also a way of catching the laws up to the customs.[153]

After a few false starts, the whole mess became a park responsibility. Legislation to turn the beaches from fictive highways to actual State Recreation Areas in 1963 failed. In 1964, the Parks Advisory Committee put their weight behind the proposal. In 1965, buoyed by new attention and support, new legislation made Oswald West's "highways" into the protected areas he'd dreamed of. Although this move clarified the legal standing of public beaches, their boundaries remained vague. There was no clear understanding on where the beach definitively started and what exactly was protected—only a general sense of public ownership. Then a cluster of cloistered cabanas forced the issue. [154]

In the summer of 1966, the Surfsand Motel in Cannon Beach fenced in the shoreline adjacent to their establishment for a series of beachfront private

---

152 Talbot, "Personal Views on the Development of Oregon State Parks," April 10, 1990, p. 4; Kathryn A. Straton, *Oregon's Beaches: A Birthright Preserved* (Salem: Oregon State Parks and Recreation Branch, 1977): p. 7.

153 Straton, *Oregon's Beaches*, 2.

154 State Parks and Recreation Advisory Committee Meeting Minutes, Dec 3, 1964, p. 3, Folder: State Parks Advisory Committee Proceedings 1956 – 1972; Straton, *Oregon's Beaches*, 19.

Playing on the beach was, and is, a "birthright preserved." The Beach Bill also directed that the ocean shore be administered as a state recreation area

cabanas, blocking public movement along the beach at high tide. Public outcry was swift, followed by private backlash among property owners who wanted to preserve exclusive beachfront for themselves. Some pushed for the abolition of public beaches altogether, arguing that their origin as "highways" had been a trick, and thus the whole enterprise was illegitimate. Parks and Highways leadership jumped into the fray, trying to find precedents for public use and work their way through the practicalities of defining a shoreline. In 1967, newly-elected Governor Tom McCall made public beaches his signature issue (with his signature flamboyance), and legislation prepared in part by parks staff was walked through the Oregon Legislature. The Beach Bill was passed in 1967, defended in court for the next few years, and affirmed and expanded in 1969. It confirmed that the vast majority of Oregon's beaches were to be publicly owned and managed. The law was now clear, but getting the public to their beaches was an ongoing issue. Oregon State Parks would continue to grapple with beach access and accessibility long after the dust from the Beach Bill fight had settled.[155]

As Oregon State Parks pushed into the ocean, it was also thrown into the rivers. A nationwide movement for preservation spurred on state campaigns for Scenic Waterways (established in 1969) and Scenic Trails (established in 1971). "All of sudden," Talbot dryly noted of the former, "I had a new baby born in the program." And dealing with waterways was fussy, as Oregon State Parks had to

---

155 Straton, *Oregon's Beaches*, 21 – 33; Talbot, "Personal Views on the Development of Oregon State Parks," May 16, 1990, pp. 66 – 72; Brent Walth, *Fire at Eden›s Gate: Tom McCall and the Oregon Story* (Portland: Oregon Historical Society Press, 1994).

Scenic Waterways (established in 1969) and Scenic Trails (established in 1971) added more complexity and administrative work to a changing State Parks Division.

zone the relevant rivers and inform property owners of certain limits to what now could or could not be done on their land. The goal of the program was to maintain a protected view from the river for those who used it recreationally. Most property owners, Talbot claimed diplomatically, had been quick to comply, as they were just as invested in the health and beauty of the rivers as the "dummies" in Salem that came in to enforce regulations. Many recreational users of the rivers, however, resented the new kinds of permitting and regulation. Especially in the early era of river management, waterways management was treacherous. Men could lose their careers if they were seen as too zealous or too lax in their regulation of rivers. Dave Talbot suggested that his role as a regulator of the riverways made him unwelcome in his hometown of Grants Pass, but that he was too soft for other members of his team, who saw any compromise with landowners as "selling the farm." Disagreements led to resignations on more than one occasion. Talbot framed these outbursts as proof of the passion that his people brought to issues of conservation, and deemed the Scenic River legislation more or less successful.[156]

The Recreational Trails bill more noticeably lacked the teeth to be enacted as effectively as its boosters had hoped. The National Trails System Act of 1968 laid out an ambitious plan for long-distance trails criss-crossing the United States—with one of the first such trails, Pacific Crest, eventually running

---

156 Talbot, "Personal Views on the Development of Oregon State Parks," May 16, 1990, pp. 78 – 84.

through California, Oregon, and Washington. Many states crafted their own legislation to build trails past those in the federal mandate. Trail enthusiasts had passed a bill giving Oregon State Parks the ability to make scenic trails, but there was no roadmap within it to successfully negotiate land use or compel land seizure. Moreover, although rural property owners were at least somewhat acclimated to the notion of shared management in waterways, land use for trails was something new and threatening. Some worried that trail creation would infringe on property rights, or that the users of the proposed trails would harm the property and persons of those who lived next to them. The result of this initiative in the 1970s was the creation of numerous *plans* to create elaborate trail systems, but very few actual miles of trails.

The Willamette Greenway, one such ambitious failure (discussed at length in Chapter 5), was later seen by many as a dismal sign of hardships to come. These federal projects gave State Parks the clout and budget of a key state agency, but with them came strings. Federal and state involvement in private properties cost the park system political capital, sometimes for only small tangible gains. Some areas were protected, but others were necessarily ignored or abandoned as outside of the scope of the federal initiative. There was also a real concern of overreaching federal oversight on state issues. Just as Sam Boardman scoffed at CCC camp bureaucrats, Oregonians of the 1960s and 1970s were hesitant to put trust in the federal government when it came to state issues and assets.[157]

These public, and occasionally explosive, fights in the legislature over conservation and cultural issues placed the Oregon State park system at the forefront of land protections. What had begun as a small organization designed to acquire roadside viewpoints was now an advocate for land usage, heritage issues, and wildlife protections. The list of programs grew, and so did the park budget. But at the same time, campers demanded parks, the highway commission demanded a balanced budget, and the new roles expected of staff demanded new skills. A bevy of new hires and a top-down pressure for professionalization pushed many of the old guard from reluctance to the edge of revolt.

The One Who Meets the Public:
Rangers Chafe at Salem Mandates

As parks grew (but not fast enough) the roles and responsibilities of rangers also adapted to the new park system (but again, not fast enough). The role of the park ranger, formally the park caretaker, was one that in the 1950s, had scarcely changed from the role that Sam Boardman had defined during the 1930s. These were men with a love of the natural world and an eye toward maintaining park properties. As the complexities of the parks grew due to camping facilities, the role of the park ranger grew in scope. But the job remained geared toward maintenance. In 1957, the rangers at last got the uniforms Boardman had

---

157 Talbot, "Personal Views on the Development of Oregon State Parks," May 16, 1990, pp. 74 – 90..

urged, which were gray with green shoulder patches—but underneath the new uniforms, it was still a blue-collar job. The cosmetic change gave them an air of authority without altering the essentials. By the 1960s, as park management gained traction as a professional field wholly separate from maintenance or engineering, the role of the park ranger was revisited.[158]

Harold Schick, who took over after Astrup was pushed out by Governor Hatfield in 1962, made professionalization a priority. Schick was the first park administrator professionally trained in park management. Boardman and Armstrong had both come up through the Highway Department. Mark Astrup, Schick's immediate predecessor, had cut his teeth on National Parks, but his training was as a landscape architect. Like Astrup, Schick saw the park system as outdated, in need of modern natural resources practices administered by trained professionals if it was to live up to its potential as what Schick called the "playground of the nation." The men handpicked by Sam Boardman and brought up on a healthy dose of folksy reverence were ill prepared to handle larger and more complex parks. Prior to state parks, Schick had worked with the Salem-Marion-Polk Regional Parks department. Though the systems were similar, he noted that the scale he was operating on with state parks dwarfed his previous experiences. And the pushback on professionalization was categorically more fearsome. Schick lasted two years. [159]

Professionalization in the 1960s meant a movement away from maintenance and caretaker responsibilities and towards more polished, public-facing roles of visitor service and education. Under Boardman, the interpretive roles of a caretaker were present, but more nebulous. Boardman had no formal parks training, and neither did his staff. He may have dreamed of parks specialists with a wide suite of interpretive skills (see Chapter 2), but the primary role of caretakers had been protection and maintenance. Now, as more and more people flooded parks, caretakers were also tasked with the role of wildlife specialist, teacher, and Oregon spokesperson, a role some did not relish. At the same time, work once handled on the park level, like park planning and engineering, was now handled by the trained experts in the Salem office. The men that spent their careers in parks were suddenly answering to recent college graduates who had never dug a ditch.

Schick's educational background and desire for systems and order marked him as an outsider. And his shift in management style had reverberating consequences. The staff was becoming divided by education level, age, and priorities. Those who had worked within the Park system since its inception resented

---

158   Merriam, *Oregon's Highway Park System, 1921 – 1989*, p. 44.

159   "Parks Chief Sure System Will Grow," 1962, Folder: Administrative History – Biography – Harold Schick, Superintendent 1962 – 1964, Box: Staff Biographies and Oral Histories, Oregon State Parks and Recreation Collection; Tom Wright, "State Parks Chief Switched to New Post in Surprise Move," *The Statesman [Journal]* March 23, 1962; "Schick Is Chosen as Parks Director," *Heppner Gazette-Times* May 24, 1962, p. 2:2; Elisabeth Walton Potter to Jo Ann [Cline] Schick, Feb 28, 2000, Folder: Administrative History – Biography – Harold Schick, Superintendent 1962 – 1964, Box: Staff Biographies and Oral Histories, Oregon State Parks and Recreation Collection.

changes in style and leadership, and the new folks coming in looked at the older staff with derision. The old guard, Talbot speculated, looked at the new college-educated young leadership with one thought: "those 'idiots' from Salem are going to screw everything up."[160]

Schick, the head "idiot from Salem," attempted to differentiate the park system proper, and its staff, from the maintenance crews of the highway department. Educational requirements and title changes (from Foreman to Park Manager) were only the most visible of these shifts. Schick also hoped that the work and the mindset of park employees would move with the times. He worked to place more interpretive signage, and to push the workers into embracing their role as educators. But he quickly found that although he could compel the men running parks to put up the signs, he couldn't ensure that those signs would be maintained. Downed and neglected interpretive signs might not teach visitors any lessons, but they sent a clear one to the folks up in Salem. [161]

Undaunted, Schick worked to create information booths, slide programs, and nature trails, the success of which he touted in a 1964 staff newsletter. But however much Schick might frame these changes as victories, many on his staff remained rigidly opposed to the new order. Schick noted in a newspaper article, when comparing this job to his previous positions, that "it is also harder to keep contact with the man with the shovel, the one who meets the public." This disconnect was certainly felt in both directions. The rangers and caretakers that cut their teeth in the Boardman and Armstrong eras did not appreciate or comply with the changes in procedure. Despite the friction, Schick saw the importance of a well-trained staff. "It is real [sic] important to have high quality personnel in such places as registration booths at parks and camping places. This is the first public contact some tourists have in Oregon and they ask such varied questions." But these mandates fell on deaf ears. After fighting the tide for two years, Schick left Oregon for a position in Philadelphia. Schick's successor Dave Talbot said his predecessor's changes "raised holy heck, but… laid the foundation for a professional organization."[162] The ground had been broken, but Talbot would still have difficulties fostering the growth of professionalism in the organization.[163]

Dave Talbot replaced Harold Schick at the end of 1964 and remained at the head of Oregon State Parks until 1992. Like Schick, Talbot had been professionally trained. Unlike Schick, he had worked regularly with both Oregon parks and the Highway Department as a recreation director prior to his new appointment. Officially, the Highway Department was looking for someone within their organization with five years of park administration experience and

---

160   Talbot, "Personal Views on the Development of Oregon State Parks," April 10, 1990, p. 7.

161   Talbot, "Personal Views on the Development of Oregon State Parks," April 10, 1990, pp. 7-8.

162   Merriam, *Oregon's Highway Park System, 1921 – 1989*, p. 71.

163   "WHAT WE'RE DOING," *Oregon State Park Times* 2:5 [?], Aug – Sept 1964, p. 3, Folder: Staff Newsletter – Park Times – 1963 to 1964; "Parks Chief Sure System Will Grow." On Schick's preference for college-trained staff, see Don Cochran, interview with Margie Walz, Oct 16, 2008, found in "Three Rivers District Oral History Project" (Plymouth, MN: Three Rivers District Administrative Center, 2008 [ongoing?]); "One of Current Staff to fill Parks Post," *Capital Journal* Nov. 27, 1964, p. 11.

a college degree. Unofficially, after Schick's tenure, there seems to have been a desire for someone who already knew the region and the workers. All three of the finalists were familiar names to the Highway Department. Talbot, ambitious, politically savvy, and young for the position at 31, got the job.[164]

Talbot's initial reaction to the Park staff was similar to Schick's. "When I looked at the kind of people, the structure, communications and lines of responsibility and all that, it was a total mess," he later reflected. Talbot was a young professional trained in the latest in parks policies, ready to make a splash in the world of state parks. He saw a lot wrong with the system as it was. But he also recognized that, however "wrong" it was, the parks system was working—"the output of the product was terrific." Talbot, like Schick, saw a lack of education, a lack of training, and holes in programming and interpretation. But he also noted a widespread devotion to the park system. So, Talbot decided that any changes would need to be slow. He remembered thinking "I ought not try to change the institutional personality overnight. The group would have to do it themselves."

Talbot knew he needed to find footing with the park staff, but he also had to convince the Highway Department that he could be trusted not to "go crazy and start spending a lot of money." Talbot, at least as much as Boardman, would have to fight for every penny from the Highway Fund. He noted that, for those that held the purse strings, "the money goes for roads, and the money goes for asphalt on new roads." Moving into the 1970s, Talbot would have to convince not only a reluctant staff but a skeptical series of bosses that the new complexities of the park system were necessary. And he would have to do so while also taking up the same battle for expansion that had been raging since the 1950s.[165]

Smile – Company's Coming:
The Public Demands Growth

In the 1960s, just as Armstrong's report had predicted, the tourist industry in Oregon boomed, and the strain on the campsites and parks boomed right along with it. In 1964, more than 210,000 people were turned away because the "full" sign was up at many campgrounds. Frustrated campers, taxed resources, and exhausted park personnel defined this era of rapid growth. In his first year as superintendent, Dave Talbot urged his staff to (cheerfully) brace for another summer season:

> *The theme of Oregon's 1965 tourist promotion is 'Smile*
> *— company's coming!' While this is but a slogan and*
> *primarily intended for chambers of commerce, service*
> *station operators, and restaurant waitresses, I cannot think*

---

164 Floyd McKay, "State Park Chief Search Narrows To 3 Assistants," *Statesmen Journal* Nov 26, 1964; State Parks and Recreation Advisory Committee Meeting Minutes, Dec 3, 1964, p. 4, Folder: State Parks Advisory Committee Proceedings 1956 – 1972.

165 Talbot, "Personal Views on the Development of Oregon State Parks," April 10, 1990, pp. 5, 11.

*of a more appropriate thought to convey to you as we enter
our heavy-use summer season... The very people whom
you seek to serve will be the greatest sources of frustration
and disappointment in the months ahead, but their pleasure
and appreciation are your constant reward.*

The concern among park employees, aside from their own frayed nerves, was how many visitors would even fit into the current system. By 1965, 17 million visitors were coming through state parks. Glenn Jackson of the Highway Commission cautioned that "20 million visitors was 'about the limit' – then the federal government must take over the cost of providing the public facilities." Park staff felt the strain on resources, lamenting in staff newsletters the entitlement of some peak season campers. One woman was told that the campground was full at Cape Lookout, so she left her trailer parked in the roadway, blocking traffic, and started knocking on trailer doors until she found someone who was about to leave. Her success was met with irritation among park rangers. In 1967, a ranger complained:

*The more they get, the more they want, tourists are getting
harder to please. One woman called Betty [Davis] asking the
name of a park in Central Oregon which had hot and cold
showers, a play area for the children, and a boat dock, and
where her family could water ski and camp near the water....
Another insisted on being told what spray was used in Central
Oregon parks to keep the rattlesnakes out.*

Tales of the latest unusual demands tourists had made of the "Betty Davis Telephone Service" became a regular feature of staff newsletters. [166]

More than the demands for amenities, campers called Davis demanding more access. In 1969, the *Oregonian* reported that five out of every six campers were turned away each summer weekend at more popular parks. The Oregon State Parks system was reaching a breaking point and the public was noticing. As Talbot later remembered,

*in the late '60s and early '70s we were turning people away
in droves... I can't recall where or when, but I remember
Glenn Jackson just made a decision... 'I think it's time to
build some more campsites,' and in the conversation some-
body said. 'How many?' And he said 'Well, How about a
thousand?' And we did.*

---

166 "Oregon Park System Known as Best in Nation, Campsites have Modern Luxuries" *Oregonian*, Sept. 5, 1965, 92; "Superintendent's Note," *Oregon State Park Times* 3:1, May 1965, p. 1, Folder: Staff Newsletter – Park Times – 1965 to 1966, Box: Publications – Staff Newsletters, 1963 – 1994; "Private Park Concept Watched as Solution to Camping Crush" *Oregonian*, July 24, 1966, 25; "Cape Lookout," *Oregon State Park Times* 4:2, Aug 1966, p. 4, Folder: Staff Newsletter – Park Times - 1965 to 1966, Box: Publications – Staff Newsletters, 1963 – 1994; "NEWS FROM THE FIELD," *Oregon State Park Times* 5:2, Aug 1967, p. 1, Folder: Staff Newsletter – Park Times – 1967 to 1968, Box: Publications – Staff Newsletters, 1963 – 1994; "DISTRICT I," *Oregon State Park Times* 4:2, Aug 1966, p. 2, Folder: Staff Newsletter – Park Times - 1965 to 1966, Box: Publications – Staff Newsletters, 1963 – 1994.

Jackson's 1,000 sites were the last major campgrounds built until the 1990s, but didn't even meet the ever-increasing demands of the 1970s. Faced with over-flowing campgrounds and wanting to avoid the aggravation of turning people away, staff spearheaded a reservation system to avoid the gridlock of the first-come first-served system that had previously dominated campsites. This measure helped, but the park system in the 1960s and 70s simply could not accommo-date the growing number of campers. This issue would only be compounded as funding began to dry up in the new decade.[167]

The call to "Smile" was a small part of a broader push toward more visi-tor-oriented work. After Schick's tenure, Talbot might initially have seemed like a welcome respite to staff who thought that they could return to the "good old days" when parks were about maintenance rather than education. But Talbot would orchestrate a fair bit of change, albeit slowly. Oregon State Parks and Recreation would now demand new skills and new standards. Talbot saw the toll professionalization took on the old guard, those men who could accom-plish anything, who loved parks, but who lacked the education and long-range planning that would define the upper management of the 1970s and 1980s. He admired the old-timers in park positions as "self-made people for the most part who had risen in life through sheer determination, guts and native intelligence." But he also noted that they were, at their heart, "highway guys." Talbot echoed the fears of the Portland Chamber of Commerce a decade prior. Could men trained in highway maintenance be park men? As much as Talbot admired the work ethic of the staff he inherited, he also viewed them with skepticism. His solution was to infuse into the old staff more college-educated park specialists to slowly change the park system from the inside. But in moving toward a more educated staff, Talbot mourned the loss of the chummy, almost familial atmo-sphere woven through the old department, a "love affair with one another, the social group." [168]

This love affair can be seen clearly in the staff newsletters, started in 1963 during Harold Schick's tenure. Used as a means of tracking projects throughout the state, early newsletters also included news on families, banter between park managers, kudos from park visitors and Salem staff, and a fraternal tone among those who fit in with the "ranger" ethic. These newsletters were also a means of creating clear distinctions between the park staff and secretaries, rural and urban, young and old. Perhaps written in good fun, this "love affair" shared among those dedicated to parks was an exclusive club, not just based on educa-tion or outlook, as Talbot intimated, but on a wider notion of belonging that the rangers rigidly cultivated.

---

167 "Oregon '69: The Future of Oregon" *Oregonian* Feb. 2, 1969, p. 53; Talbot, "Personal Views on the Development of Oregon State Parks," April 10, 1990, p. 22.

168 Talbot, "Personal Views on the Development of Oregon State Parks," April 10, 1990, pp. 10, 28.

The Girl with the Pretty Eyes:
Women Forge a Path into Parks Careers

This fraternity of rangers, so admired by Dave Talbot, was built and maintained as a boy's club. Women, long a part of the state parks system, both in the Salem office and the field, were mentioned in newsletters and correspondence as beautiful anomalies and were largely tasked with interpretation, a job that male rangers were loath to participate in. In 1965, there was one female employee working at Cove Palisades, and her presence was so notable that she was one of five news items mentioned by that park. "Only one feminine employe[e] will be at the Cove this year. She will handle the information and slide program." In 1966, female park staff, listed simply as "the girls," were charged with developing more interpretive programming at the Cove. The work of women as park advocates and park employees dated to the program's beginnings. Nonetheless, a hard line was drawn professionally between the work of women and that of men, especially in the field. They could run a slide show, or hand out brochures, but the "real" park work was for the men. [169]

The bemusement of male park employees at the presence of women in any labor capacity was unfortunately not new. Sam Boardman, writing to R.H. Baldock in 1939, noted in great detail the physical features of a woman hired by the highway department to mow grass along North Santiam Highway. He wrote,

> *No, I didn't stop, but confessing to you – it was the first time that I actually enjoyed the "Curves" between Mill City and Detroit... If this woman mower is a new innovation in the highway department, I should like to make a suggestion on behalf of the traveling public. Pick them skinny and wrinkled. Perch the statue of liberty, and you will have everyone in the ditch.*

Though not as explicit, this "boys' club" mentality continues to the present day (see Chapter 7). Boardman was perfectly willing to have women on staff as his secretaries and eager to honor the work of women as lobbyists for the parks' interests. But he was also flabbergasted by women in caretaker or maintenance roles, and did not have any women working for him in that capacity during his tenure.[170]

Women were a more common fixture in office and park settings in the postwar era, and yet the distinction between men and women in the workplace was palpable. In an August 1966 newsletter, three new staff were announced in the Salem Headquarters: Jim Ramsden, Elisabeth Walton, and Laura Barrows. Laura Barrows was described as "the very attractive brunette opening the mail." Elisabeth Walton, in addition to her impressive credentials as an expert in historic

---

169 "Cove Palisades State Park," *Oregon State Park Times* 3:1, May 1965, p. 4 Folder: Staff Newsletter – Park Times – 1965 to 1966, Box: Publications – Staff Newsletters, 1963 – 1994; "DISTRICT III," *Oregon State Park Times* 4:2, Aug 1966, p. 7, Folder: Staff Newsletter – Park Times - 1965 to 1966, Box: Publications – Staff Newsletters, 1963 – 1994.

170 Sam Boardman to R.H. Baldock, July 17, 1939. Folder: Correspondence, Box: Samuel H. Boardman Papers, Oregon Parks and Recreation Collection.

preservation with an advanced degree, was referred to as the "stately blond historian." Jim Ramsden's hair color and level of attractiveness was not listed. Laura Barrow would later be replaced by a woman with an "attractive Southern accent," joining a receptionist with "merry blue eyes." In 1968, it was determined that husbands and wives could not work in the same Division, and many Salem staff (the women) were moved to new divisions or found other employ. The newsletter noted "We hate to lose two girls, who are not only congenial and attractive, but are excellent secretaries as well." These women, even when—in the case of Elisabeth Walton—they were heads of complex federal programs, were consistently diminished in newsletters—described first, and sometimes exclusively, by their physical attributes and marital status. [171]

Although women made up a majority of jobs in reception and assistant capacities in Salem, they were still an anomaly in the field. The presence of young women in the information booth, or even on the sidewalk, was enough to throw male staff into fits, if one is to believe the staff newsletters of this period.

> *We have wondered why there are so many men in the reregister line. Could it be the four young pretty new Park Aides in mini-skirts? If so, thing will soon be back to normal. It seems that a note was posted in the booth, stating that uniforms should not be mini. We're not mentioning any names, but the party who posted it says that he doesn't mind the view, but it is causing too big a traffic jam.*

Girl watching was a regular feature in the staff newsletters, as male staff and volunteers ogled visitors in bikinis, female staff, and even inmates at local penitentiaries.

> *If there are any requests for binoculars or complaints about a sharp drop in work (male, of course) at the District II office, it may have something to do with those huge windows in the new East Salem Highway Building. There is an excellent view of the Women's Correctional Institution where the girls are planting flowers and working on the lawn.*

Just as Sam Boardman had been unable to contain himself at the sight of a woman mowing grass, 30 years later the idea of a woman bending over to plant

---

171 "OFFICE," *Oregon State Park Times* 4:2, Aug. 1966, p. 22, Folder: Staff Newsletter – Park Times - 1965 to 1966, Box: Publications – Staff Newsletters, 1963 – 1994. Amidst decades of newsletters wherein women's physical features were noted constantly, we were able to find only one reference to the attractiveness of a male employee, in 1967—and even this spoke only of a "smile" that "melts... feminine" campers. See "DISTRICT IV," *Oregon State Park Times* 5:2, Aug. 1967, p. 11, Folder: Staff Newsletter – Park Times - 1967 to 1968, Box: Publications – Staff Newsletters, 1963 – 1994; "Meanwhile, Back at the Office," *Oregon State Park Times* 4:3, Dec. 1966, p. 16, Folder: Staff Newsletter – Park Times - 1965 to 1966, Box: Publications – Staff Newsletters, 1963 – 1994; "Meanwhile Back at the Office," *Oregon State Park Times* 6:2 [?], Aug. 1968, p. 20, Folder: Staff Newsletter – Park Times - 1967 to 1968; Nor was the focus on physical appearance a function of youth. The redoubtable Betty Davis was congratulated at one point as having gotten "her trim figure back" after several children and was teased for "NOT modeling" a new bikini for staff. "DISTRICT II," *Oregon State Park Times* 6:2 [?], Aug. 1968, p. 10, Folder: Staff Newsletter – Park Times - 1967 to 1968.

More often than not, women rangers spent their time in informational booths. Collier Memorial State Park, c. 1965

flowers ranked as important news for the park system. The tenor of the times was such that the editors of the staff newsletters, typically women themselves, thought it was humorous and appropriate to publish stories of co-workers ogling women or jokes (?) about a male ranger giving a female receptionist a spanking at an after-hours event.[172]

Despite the challenges, some women chose to continue with parks, working towards promotions out of the informational booth where they were regularly placed. In 1967, Vivian Hudson was transferred to head up Chandler Wayside after working at Tumalo. The newsletter noted a young boy, on sight of Vivian in uniform, exclaimed "Gee, a woman Forest Ranger." A slide operator (essentially an early interpretive ranger) at Cape Lookout returned for the summer season and, as noted in the newsletter, "[staff] wonder if she knows that the first year she worked here she was tabbed "the girl with the pretty eyes.""
These women, excelling in their positions, fought stereotyping, sexism, and the potential (and assumption) of a career cut short due to marriage or raising a family. Park staff seemed more comfortable with traditional roles for women,

---

172 "DISTRICT II," *Oregon State Park Times* 8:1 [?], Apr. 1970, p. 7, Folder: Staff Newsletter – Park Times – 1970 to 1971, Box: Publications – Staff Newsletters, 1963 – 1994; "DICTRICT I," *Oregon State Park Times* 5:2, Aug. 1967, p. 4, Folder: Staff Newsletter – Park Times, 1967 to 1968; "DISTRICT IV," *Oregon State Park Times* 8:2 [?], July 1969, p. 18, Folder: Staff Newsletter – Park Times - 1969, Box: Publications – Staff Newsletters, 1963 – 1994; "DISTRICT I," *Oregon State Park Times* 5:1 [?], May 1967, p. 5, Folder: Staff Newsletter – Park Times - 1967 to 1968; "DISTRICT 1,", *Oregon State Park Times* 5:2, Aug. 1967, p. 2, Folder: Staff Newsletter – Park Times - 1967 to 1968.

and, in 1967, gave out "Doll Awards" which were "presented to all the wives of the Park Managers because they are always so nice in taking messages and running errands."[173]

The distinction between the men and women of the park system was apparent in the highest offices. The Park Advisory Committee, which guided the planning and purchase of park lands since 1956, existed for 20 years before the first woman was appointed, Lucille (Lu) Beck. Dave Talbot remembered that Beck's presence caused great concern, largely due to the Advisory Committee Tours, a yearly event of touring parks in specific regions that had been punctuated by "raucous, joke-telling, good 'ol boy outrageous drinking bouts, among other things" (see Chapter 5). Talbot noted that the tone of these trips was required to shift, now that a lady was present. His concerns were perhaps misplaced. Remembering her first trip with the boys, he noted that "Lu could handle it." And, Talbot noted with amusement and perhaps chagrin, "horrible racist, sexist stories" and "old jokes" continued to be an informal part of Parks Advisory Committee meetings well into the 1980s. In parks as in broader American society, sexist jokes were normal and harmful.[174]

Reflecting on his tenure, Dave Talbot was quick to say that affirmative action, specifically the hiring and promotion of women, had long been an important issue for him—but his actions told a different story. He prioritized perceived pragmatism over more proactive steps to address the rampant culture of sexism in the park system. He approached his role in affirmative action as largely passive. If women met the qualifications for management positions, he would happily hire them. But women rarely gained the experience in maintenance and construction that were essential for those positions, as they were more often than not relegated to the information booth. Many managers, Talbot thought, would be unwilling to put in the time to train women workers on tractors or construction work. Many men would be unwilling to take on roles that were associated with women's work. And neither Talbot nor his managers were willing to create or enforce a policy that would ensure women had access to the training and experience they would need to advance. Fretting that promoting unprepared women would have "doomed them to failure," Talbot did not seem to comprehend that he had a duty to prepare them for success.[175]

The boys' club mentality of the rangers during this era relied on strict exclusions. Whether it was the professional, the college man, the woman, there

---

173 "DISTRICT IV," *Oregon State Park Times* 5:2, Aug. 1967, p. 12, Folder: Staff Newsletter – Park Times - 1967 to 1968; "CAPE LOOKOUT," *Oregon State Park Times* 6:2 [?], Aug. 1968, p. 7, Folder: Staff Newsletter – Park Times - 1967 to 1968; "DISTRICT I," *Oregon State Park Times* 5:3, Dec. 1967, p. 2, Folder: Staff Newsletter – Park Times - 1967 to 1968.

174 David G. Talbot, "Personal Views on the Development of Oregon State Parks," June 6, 1990, Interview with Lawrence C. Merriam and Elisabeth Walton Potter, pp. 123 - 124, Folder: Administrative History – Oral History – David G. Talbot, Director, 1964 – 1992, Oregon State Parks and Recreation Collection; University of Oregon, *Oregana*, ed. Sue French (Eugene: University of Oregon Student Publications Board, 1956), p. 262; Julie A. Woodzicka and Thomas E. Ford, "A Framework for Thinking About the (not-so-funny) Effect of Sexist Humor," *Europe's Journal of Psychology* 6:3 (2010): pp. 174 – 195.

175 Talbot, "Personal Views on the Development of Oregon State Parks," June 6, 1990, 118.

was little room or tolerance for difference in the ranks. The "shared love affair" rangers treasured included a troubling commitment to stasis and sexism. But the staff newsletters also suggest a camaraderie that united parks in different parts of the state. These men held big retirement parties, met for summertime campouts, and saw themselves as stewards of an important job. Under Dave Talbot as under superintendents before him, the parks leaned on this scrappy group to function, however resistant they were to change. So, while the campsites grew and the sites were maintained, state parks started to fall out of sync with the rapidly changing world around them. For the rangers of the 1960s and 70s, the most frightening change came wearing paisley—or nothing.

It's Hippie Time Again:
Parks grapple with the counterculture

One thing that it seemed the entire parks department was willing to agree on in the 1960s: hippies were ruining the state. Hippies, seemingly defined by most park personnel as any person with long hair, were deemed a menace to the park system and were regularly mocked in newsletters and monitored by staff. A distrust of spirited youth was a longstanding tradition in parks. In the 1930s, Sam Boardman had focused his attentions on the young vandals desecrating his trees. By the mid 1960s, there was an all-out culture war on the beaches, in the forest, on the plains and the hills: the buzz-cut ranger vs. the long-haired youth. Alongside miniskirts and campers behaving poorly, the antics of hippies were regular newsletter fodder. Largely jovial, the newsletters and later actions by park staff and the state government suggest an undercurrent of fear. A 1968 newsletter joked "Have you heard about the park manager who bought a pair of hair clippers? That is just in case the hippies come back this summer. He thought he should be prepared. Don't you think a bath would be more apropos?" Pointedly, stories like these in the newsletter sat alongside mentions of those serving in Vietnam, either park staff or family members. The same 1968 newsletter noted that a long-time seasonal employee at Champoeg had just been made a lieutenant in the U.S. Army, noting

Officially sanctioned "uniform" at Rooster Rock, 1971.

"[w]hen he worked at the park, he had to call the park manager 'sir' and now I guess we will have to call *him* 'sir.'" Park newsletters attempted to skirt controversy, but these two versions of American youth, one an unwashed parkgoer, the other a soldier, hinted at the political unrest of the era. When the park system of the 1970s was planned in 1956, staff had expected leisure time and family boat trips, not nude sunbathing and motorcycle races. The hippies were not the people parks had been built for.[176]

The complaints among the staff followed clichéd generational lines. They also revealed incessant voyeurism. One 1971 newsletter noted, "With the new camp and all, it has been pretty dull for Dennis – there haven't been any hippies to watch skinny-dipping." This was not a one-off; the newsletters often made light of opportunities rangers took to ogle naked hippies, sometimes without their knowledge. "Four hippies camped one night under Merlie's watchful eye," the news section of a 1970 newsletter read. "The next morning he observed them taking a shower under a stand pipe. With the aid of binoculars, he was able to determine the bare fact – two of them were girls." Such showers notwithstanding, stereotypes about the unwashed nature of the youth were particularly fascinating to the highway men. "It's hippie time again – different hippies, but the same problems with them – at least we think they are different ones, although the crew has agreed that they all look and smell pretty much alike. That makes it hard to tell for sure." In addition to hygiene complaints, there was bemused bafflement at political actions. One newsletter noted,

> We hope that Bill Wright appreciates the extra attention he received at the park – a sprig of wild flowers and a peace note – left on his flashy red convertible. But you weren't the only, Bill. Jerry Lucas' pickup and a State Police truck received the same treatment.

These cultural differences manifested in more than tasteless jokes about bathing or creepy instances of spying. Park personnel, especially those in management, feared that the presence of the hippie youth would destroy a park system that was meant for families. Parks along the coast, always the most crowded in the summer months, became a tipping point over the hippie issue.[177]

In 1970, rumors spread that Oswald West State Park, located south of Cannon Beach, was a hotbed of illegal activity among hippies due in large part to its proximity to Portland. This rumor was enough to attract the attentions of

---

176 "DISTRICT I," *Oregon State Park Times* 6:2 [?], Aug. 1968, pp. 3 and 7, Folder: Staff Newsletter – Park Times, 1967 to 1968 [emphasis in the original]; see also "CONGRATULATIONS," *Oregon State Park Times* 4:2, Aug. 1966, p. 1, Folder: Staff Newsletter – Park Times - 1965 to 1966.

177 "CHAMPOEG STATE PARK," *Oregon State Park Times* 9:2 [?], Aug. 1971, p. 7, Folder: Staff Newsletter – Park Times – 1970 to 1971, Box: Publications – Staff Newsletters, 1963 – 1994; "FAREWELL BEND STATE PARK," *Oregon State Park Times* 8:1 [?], Apr 1970, p. 19, Folder: Staff Newsletter – Park Times – 1970 to 1971, Box: Publications – Staff Newsletters, 1963 – 1994. Apparently the editors of the *Oregon State Park Times* used Volume 8 for the years 1969 and 1970 alike; "FAREWELL BEND STATE PARK," *Oregon State Park Times* 8:1 [?], Apr 1970, p. 14, Folder: Staff Newsletter – Park Times – 1970 to 1971; "THE COVE PALISADES STATE PARK," *Oregon State Park Times* 8:2 [?], July 1969, p. 18, Folder: Staff Newsletter – Park Times – 1969.

the *Oregonian*, who sent reporter Steve Erickson out to investigate. According to the resulting article, "straight" campers were forced out of the area "in fear or disgust." The problem was so rampant that it was suggested the park should close. A lifeguard interviewed said, "I guess the state could close the park to campers, but that would ruin it for the decent people, too." The line was clearly drawn: there were hippies, and then there were decent people.

Though the ranger on duty was unwilling to comment on the issue, he did point the intrepid reporter to the hotbed of hippie activity. Following a secluded trail, Erikson approached a hastily constructed shrine, built to honor "all religions — except Satanism" according to its creator, Ishmial Aliva. When told that the park rangers had labeled him a hippie, Aliva replied "they're up-tight and paranoid about our long hair. They think we're some religious sect. They're very sad and have narrow little hearts." Aliva proceeded to explain the shrine and his own spiritual journey, stopping only to marvel at his pet cat stalking and nearly eating a chipmunk. When Erickson asked the ranger on duty if this hippie camp posed an issue, specifically with garbage, the ranger simply replied, "their garbage is no worse than anyone else's."[178]

This somewhat innocent exchange between a reporter and an eclectic park user was enough to stoke the already-existing fear of the Salem parks administration, even if the staff in the field didn't see much of an issue. Reports of hippies taking over Oregon State Parks, specifically Oswald West, trickled into Dave Talbot's office. In June of that year, regional supervisor Cliff Lenz wrote to Dave Talbot asking that the camp be closed, "because of the undesirables that have been using the area for the past 3 or 4 years." The exasperated supervisor noted that camps at Oswald West were "used mostly for wine or narcotic parties" and would surely impact the reputation of the whole system. To prove his point, Lenz attached local police reports to his letter to Talbot. These reports noted illegal camping, narcotics, and occasionally, fights.[179]

Lloyd Shaw, second-in-command at Highways, asked for a "hippie check" in August, which he received from Dale Hoeye, Park Manager at Oswald West State Park. Hoeye reported back with the written equivalent to a shrug. His men checked in on the family campers, and no one was reporting any issues with the "so-called long hair set." He noted one noise complaint, but he also acknowledged that noise happened at all campgrounds from time to time. At the end of his letter, he called out the lifeguard at Cannon Beach, quoted in the recent newspaper article, as "giving us a black eye." The problem that Lenz had complained of, Hoeye seemed to say, was a tempest in a teapot.[180]

---

178   Steve Erickson "'Let that Chipmunk Go': Aliva's Cliff Shrine Belies Hippie Appearance"

179   C[liff] H. Lenz to David Talbot, June 8, 1970, Folder: Oswald West State Park – Issue – Hippies, Box: Oswald West State Park, Oregon State Parks and Recreation Collection, Oregon State Parks and Recreation, Salem, OR; Walter C. Woolfolk and Claire McMillan, "Beach Patrol S[h]ore Sands Beach," March 21, 1970, *ibid.*

180   Dale Hoeye to Lloyd Shaw, August 12, 1970. Folder: Oswald West State Park – Issue – Hippies. Hoeye's son was likely a Marine in Vietnam, but this doesn't seem to have led him into the reflexive anti-hippie stance often assumed for people of his status and time. Hoeye's son is mentioned in "HONEYMAN STATE PARK," *Oregon State Park Times* 4:3 [?], Dec 1966, p. 10, Folder: Staff Newsletter – Park Times – 1965 to 1966

Talbot found evidence that supported both Lenz and Hoeye. In July 1970, undercover police officers infiltrated hippie enclaves set up in coastal parks. They swept up one drug dealer and a handful of users, but found nothing of note in terms of violence or property damage. What Lenz had reported as a fight was, perhaps, the conclusion of a sting operation.[181] In the end, Talbot chose not to close the campground in 1970, noting that the nearby towns preferred hippie containment. "If we run them out of Os West," the locals purportedly said, "they'll just go somewhere else, and as it is now, we know where they are."[182]

Warren Gaskill, Talbot's second-in-command, kept a close eye on the situation during the 1971 season. He encouraged a focus on "the actual problem." Was the issue "Drugs, Hippies, Not enough camping space? 'Good' people not using the area?" Regional supervisor Val Jones reassured Gaskill that "a good percent of park users [were still] older family people." The problem was that "the park has been a stopping-off spot for traveling hippies and young people who want to do as they please without interference from anyone." This created a frustrating situation for park staff, but Jones noted that it was getting better and that strict enforcement of the rules seemed to discourage the rampant drug use and partying of earlier years. G.R Leavitt, the Field Operations Supervisor, agreed with Jones, writing "I believe, by everyone's determination, we have nearly won the battle with the hippies."[183] Park personnel, from rangers all the way to the top, defined the success of their parks by the "right" kind of visitors. The problem at Os West was not just the presence of "long haired brethren" but the potential absence of "straight" ["normal"] campers—the "Good" people. But Oswald West State Park was not the only, or the most conspicuous display of these anxieties. A month after a reporter for the *Oregonian* hiked to a hippie shrine in 1970, Oregonians all got a close look at the spectacle of the counterculture.[184]

Inferior Wine and Hot Weather:
Vortex I

In 1970, on a cool day in late August, tens of thousands of people streamed into a state-sponsored rock concert at Milo McIver State Park. The event, Vortex I, might have been remembered one of the largest rock concerts of the era—if anyone had been keeping track of how many people were in the cars backed up for miles or in the crowds arriving on foot, day after day, as the temperatures rose. But with free entry, free food, and a free pass from the governor when it came to nudity and drug use, the records kept by the organizers remained hazy. And as long as it was peaceful, state officials didn't want to know anything about it. Except for Talbot.

---

181   Holly V. Holcomb to Dave Talbot, Sept 29, 1970, Folder: Oswald West State Park – Issue – Hippies.

182   Dave Talbot, "Os West State Park Recommended Closure," *ibid*.

183   G.R Leavitt to Warren Gaskill, Oct 15, 1971. Folder: Oswald West State Park – Issue – Hippies; Val Jones to Warren Gaskill, Oct 8, 1971. Folder: Oswald West State Park – Issue – Hippies.

184   Ibid.

Milo McIver State Park became a mini-Woodstock for a couple of days in 1970.

Vortex I was meant as an idiosyncratic answer to a summer of violence. The cultural divide over the war in Vietnam had reached a point of crisis, and protestors in the streets were answered with batons and bullets from law enforcement. Portland was scheduled to host a parade of the American Legion, with a potential speech by President Richard Nixon. Amid a swirl of rumors and planned protests there were isolated threats of riots, violence against police, and other mayhem among possible protesters (amplified by FBI speculation). And there were threats from members of the American Legion that they would respond to disruption with overwhelming force. This was enough to scare the city and Governor Tom McCall into something drastic. In stilted meetings with local peace groups, McCall hammered out the free rock concert as counter-programming, hoping it would lure would-be rioters out of Portland and thus prevent political violence. It seemed to work. The free music festival was well attended, and the originally planned protest against the Vietnam War melted away. The American Legion marched and met Vice President Spiro Agnew unimpeded. Lambasted by many during the preparation phase as a surrender, the success of Vortex I became a triumph for McCall, who presented himself as a man who could maintain peace without jackboots and was swept into reelection.[185]

185 Matt Love, *The Far Out Story of Vortex I* (Nestucca Spit Press, 2004). The legacy of Vortex I is contested, with some authors proposing that it was a political touchstone, and many attendees arguing that it "wasn't about politics… it was about listening to music for free." Isabel Gautschi, "The price of admission was love," *Estacada News* Aug 13, 2014. At the time, the American Legion gleefully used the inconstancy of the "ordinary hippies who like their pot and rock" to critique the anti-war movement as a whole. "The American Legion's 52nd National Convention," *American Legion Magazine* 89:5, Nov. 1970, pp. 23 – 25. In later decades, some participants celebrated the festival as a beautiful dream, others came to believe they had "inadvertently participated in a sellout." Love, *The Far Out Story of Vortex I*, 225.

For Oregon State Parks and Recreation, however, Vortex I seemed like a nightmare in the making. Dave Talbot and other park administrators went on high alert, treating the concert as a potential invasion. Talbot noted during preparations for the event that "Intelligence reports show that hard-core &#%!@*#!@* want to have a confrontation with the American Legion. There will be intelligence people in the park while this is going on, but no uniformed police." Talbot was tasked with keeping the peace in the park, a job he was loathe to take on, as altercations between park officials and the hippie groups of the 1960s and 1970s were regular fodder in park communications. But this was a political situation out of his control. Talbot noted that the "governor would just as soon sacrifice a park as downtown Portland."[186]

To prepare for the festival, Dave Talbot reached out to Bill Crouch, head of parks in Nashville, Tennessee, who dealt with rock festivals on park property. When Talbot asked if there was any semblance of self-control within hippie enclaves, Crouch recommended that Talbot "keep an eye on their leader." As was common among many at the time, Crouch differentiated a leftist leadership he was frightened of from the everyday hippie. "So many of those kids are good kids that are out for the thing they enjoy," he warned, but the national news would be looking for the violent exceptions. "The news media will be your biggest problem."[187]

But there were no reports of violence. Local media watched with fascination as the largely peaceful crowds filled the park. The *Oregonian* noted "the total amount of clothing being worn in the park would have failed to fill the back of a pick-up truck. Clothing has become more an oddity than nudity." Another newspaper attempted to estimate the amount of sewage that would need to be hauled out in "honey trucks" due to the hippie invasion. The *Oregon Journal* placed the number at 250,000 pounds. Dave Talbot admitted that the toilet needs at the concert were really anyone's guess, but noted the literal tons of food flowing into the kitchens—that would have to end up somewhere after it had flowed through the participants. Still, after reporting on the mud baths and long hair of the "youths" in the park, the *Oregonian* conceded that the park itself was being respected by all the concert goers they spoke with, only one of whom had even heard of the American Legion protest that was supposedly going to destroy Portland that week. Many were just there for the music, a mix of a few niche national acts like the blues legend Charles Musselwhite and an array of local groups such as Jacob's Ladder and the Portland Zoo Electric Band. Thousands

---

186 David G. Talbot and Bill Crouch, transcribed telephone conversation, [undated], Folder: Milo McIver State Park - Vortex I Rock Festival, Box: Historic State Park Documents: Milo McIver State Park to Minam State Recreation Area, Oregon Parks and Recreation Collection. The underscores used to indicate swearing in the original text have been changed to more varied punctuation for clarity. For more information on the government planning for Vortex I see Brent Walth, *Fire at Eden's Gate: Tom McCall and the Oregon Story* (Portland: Oregon Historical Society Press, 1995).

187 David G. Talbot and Bill Crouch, transcribed telephone conversation, [undated], Folder: Milo McIver State Park - Vortex I Rock Festival; Timothy Tyler, "The Cooling of America: Out of Tune and Lost in the Counterculture, *Time* Feb 22, 1971; Charles DeBenedetti, *An American Ordeal: The Antiwar Movement of the Vietnam Era* (Syracuse, N.Y.: Syracuse University Press, 1990): 216.

gathered around a log stage built with donated equipment. Thousands more camped down by the river.[188]

And Talbot kept eyes on it all, as the parks collection of aerial photographs taken at regular intervals throughout the festival demonstrate. Reporting on the event after the fact, Talbot was pleased to say that drug dealing, vandalism, and other non-violent crime had been kept to a minimum, largely due to "Vortex-appointed 'Monitors'" whose "policing was very effective." He estimated the crowd at 30,000 - 40,000 each day and informed the Parks Advisory Committee that "the majority of the first-aid and hospital cases were reportedly the result of foot cuts, burns, inferior wine and hot weather" rather than drugs or violence. Vortex I organizers made good on at least part of the promise of what they had titled a "biodegradable festival of life." There had been tens of thousands of those who Talbot labeled "'people'" (in scare quotes) rather than the "visitors" label he typically applied to those who came to parks. But despite the unwelcome crowds, there was "no deliberate vandalism," no extraordinary staff hours needed for clean-up, and no unusual damage reported that year. The hippies hadn't hurt anything. "Apparently," Lloyd Shaw wrote that October, "some reports of the activities of the hairy brethren were exaggerated or completely false."[189]

Two decades later Talbot had come around on the concert, if not the concertgoers. He praised McCall for having avoided a "horrible confrontation of these hippies and young people coming from all over America to raise hell." But at the time, Talbot claimed, the whole of state government had sought deliberate ignorance regarding Vortex I. Whether it was about attendance, cost, or another subject,

> *nobody wanted to know anything. But more than that they didn't want to know anything. It was total silence. I'd say "well do you want to…?" "nope, get out of here" they got it behind them, and it was such a distasteful thing to the general public that they just heaved a sigh of relief when it was over, and to this day nobody wants to talk about it.*

Despite the fears of invasion and the enormity of the event, Vortex I quickly became a punchline for park staff too. "We're in pretty fair shape after

---

188   Leonard Bacon, "6,000 Flock to Park as Vortex Starts to Spin," *Oregonian* Aug 28, 1970; David G. Talbot, "Summary: Vortex I, McIver State Park," [undated], Folder: Milo McIver State Park - Vortex I Rock Festival; Isabel Gautschi, "The price of admission was love," *Estacada News* Aug 13, 2014; Eric Cain, "Vortex I," Oregon Experience S4 E403 (original broadcast: Oct 28, 2010). Oswald West State Park – Issue – Hippies. The fact that the Vortex I festival had occurred without issue between the time of Hoeye's letter and Shaw's response may have shaped the latter.

189   Vortex I Aerial Photographs. Milo McIver State Park Photographs. Oregon State Parks and Recreation Collection, Oregon State Parks and Recreation, Salem, OR; James Long, "15,000 Expected at Vortex," *Oregon Journal* Aug 27, 1970; David G. Talbot, "Summary: Vortex I, McIver State Park"; "McIVER STATE PARK," Oregon State Park Times 9[?], May 1971, p. 4, Folder: Staff Newsletter – Park Times – 1970 to 1971; Matt Love, The Far Out Story of Vortex I (Nestucca Spit Press, 2004); Lloyd Shaw to Dale Hoeye, Oct. 5, 1970. Folder: Oswald West State Park – Issue – Hippies. The fact that the Vortex I festival had occurred without issue between the time of Hoeye's letter and Shaw's response may have shaped the latter.

Vortex I," staff from McIver Park wrote in 1971. "The deer and gophers are back, but we haven't caught any of them using pot as yet." Then they moved on to irrigation, and the new overnight campground that would soon finally be ready. After all, the hippies had only descended for a week. Fitting in the crowds of campers was still the pressing problem.[190]

The Oregon State Park system entered the 1970s with decades of expansion under its belt. For all the talk of having moved from an era of expansion to an era of development, expansion *and* development had been near-constant in the 1950s and 60s. As usual, the mission grew faster than the money. Although park budgets and projects had expanded, although the new Advisory Committee offered new legitimacy and expertise, coming up with the money for parkwide overhauls and even basic maintenance was growing difficult. Although park staff rose to the challenge in creating new campgrounds, they failed in areas of interpretation, cultural resource management, and allowing changing demographics within their ranks. Sexism went virtually unchecked, and racism virtually unnoted. And still, more and more people were coming into the parks. But in the 1970s and 80s, economic catastrophes and political convulsions would force Oregon State Parks into hard decisions amidst hard times.

---

190   Talbot, "Personal Views on the Development of Oregon State Parks," May 16, 1990, pp. 51-52; "McIVER STATE PARK," *Oregon State Park Times* 9[?], May 1971, p. 4, Folder: Staff Newsletter – Park Times – 1970 to 1971.

Cape Lookout, 1973

CHAPTER 5

We Learned How to Live with Less:
Running on Fumes, (1970 - 1990)

In 1990, nearly thirty years into his career as the head of Oregon State Parks and Recreation, Dave Talbot sat down for a series of interviews for a new history of the Oregon parks system. The questions posed largely dealt with ideas, mission, and accomplishments. What was he most proud of? What was the ethos of state parks? He was tasked with looking back, but he couldn't help but return numerous times to the one thing that would define the future of the park system: money. "The whole funding issue is yet to be resolved," he proclaimed more than once, and he worried that parks would "have to live with a hand-to-mouth existence." This issue was never far from his mind. Finding enough money to pay for parks while still "do[ing] the thing that's right" would always be a constant concern.[191]

Through the 1970s and 80s, shifts in funding required shifts in philosophy. From the beginning of Oregon State Parks in the 1920s, the gas tax had been the largest single source of revenue in park budgets. During the international oil crises of the 1970s, this revenue was removed— "temporarily" in 1977, then permanently by constitutional amendment in 1980. But the oil crises were only the beginning of two decades defined by recession. By the 1980s, Oregon State Parks and Recreation was reliant on the General Fund and the whims of the legislature. Left with no other options, Oregon State Parks in the 1970s and 80s had to borrow against the future. Fewer parks were established than ever before, and critical maintenance was delayed in the hope of better times to come.

The budget crunch collided with an expansion of responsibility. Federal and state initiatives of the 1960s and early 1970s expanded the role of state parks along the coast and in communities across the state. Conservation and

---

191   David G. Talbot, "Personal Views on the Development of Oregon State Parks," April 10, 1990, Interview with Lawrence C. Merriam and Elisabeth Walton Potter, p. 25, Folder: Administrative History – Oral History – David G. Talbot, Director, 1964 – 1992, Box: Staff Biographies and Oral Histories, Oregon State Parks and Recreation Collection, Oregon State Parks and Recreation, Salem, OR; David G. Talbot, "Personal Views on the Development of Oregon State Parks," June 6, 1990, Interview with Lawrence C. Merriam and Elisabeth Walton Potter, 109, *ibid*.

historical preservation—aspects of Parks that had been underemphasized for decades—were now mandated. These new programs and priorities had to grow even as budgets shrank. New programs also served to highlight the fissures among the staff. As Oregon State Parks expanded, relations between employees and management became less fraternal and more professional. Discrimination and sexual harassment, which had been a part of Oregon State Parks from the beginning, became more visible and less acceptable—though these issues by no means disappeared (see Chapter 7). As Talbot and the rest of Parks leadership attempted to meet the needs of Oregonians and the demands of the legislature, they looked to layoffs, unpaid volunteer labor, and restructurings that left field staff shaken.

The 1950s and 60s had been an era of possibility and growth, both in the size and scope of the parks system. Throughout the 1970s and 80s park staff and management found ways to do more with less. Constant crises wore on morale and sanded down ambition. Land was given up, maintenance deferred, plans put on hold. And yet the parks soldiered on, by the end of 1980s serving more visitors than ever before despite the losses of money and employees. But park staff could barely hold it together. These decades came to define the tenure of Dave Talbot. He had started in 1964, a young man ready to bring Oregon State Parks in step with the nation. But when he sat down in 1990 to remember his time with parks, all questions led back to one. How could parks survive without a source of stable funding?

We Were Hunkered Down in Full-Scale War:
Budget Fights Amidst Prosperity

Even before the budget crunches of the 1970s, there was tension over how much highway money to dedicate to parks. Dave Talbot later remembered the period immediately following his appointment in 1964 as the low point of relations between Parks and Highways, despite or perhaps because the deprivation of later decades had not yet set in:

> *[E]lements of the Highway Department who were always afraid the park people were going to go crazy and start spending a lot of money and doing a lot of crazy things. I think this was a control issue. It was clear to me that the money was certainly there. Large quantities of money to further park objectives, if I could get a hold of it.*[192]

For state parks supporters, this had been a worry since the 1920s. Being nestled into the budget for highways allowed parks to get much of their funding without a bruising appropriations process, but parks boosters from Robert

---

192 David G. Talbot, "Personal Views on the Development of Oregon State Parks," April 10, 1990, p. 9.

Sawyer onwards had feared the possibility of Parks ceasing to be a priority. The ambitious and expanding agenda of Oregon State Parks in late 1960s had to be enacted under the supervision of highway administrators who considered it their duty to limit highway spending to road construction and maintenance, rather than parks or heritage programs. Oregon in the 1960s made some substantial investments in state parks and infrastructure. Talbot remembered this period of success as a "full-scale war"[193]:

> *We were hunkered down in full-scale war mode. I spent all day and all night for I don't know how many years in that ugly situation of working in a place where you knew you really weren't welcome, and people in important places would get you if they could.*[194]

Dave Talbot noted in a 1968 staff newsletter that funding issues were at the forefront of his mind. Acquisition programs continued in 1968, but construction projects were completely shut down and staff salaries were kept abysmally low. Talbot hoped that the end of the year would bring an end to these shortages.[195]

In the late 1960s, possibly in response to this battle for funding, there was a push within the Highway Department to make state parks a subordinate arm of Highway Maintenance. Park supporters used to worry that parks had the position of a pet dog under the Highway Department. This move would have turned the parks division into a hungry stray. Dave Talbot, only a few years into his leadership, threatened to quit—already, as he put it, "burning my bridges behind me by having confrontations with the [managers] of the world." State Parks had friends in high places, and State Highway Commission Chair Glenn Jackson and Chair of Parks Advisory Committee Loren "Stub" Stewart intervened. The move to put parks further down the pecking order was quickly quashed.[196]

Tensions eased following the reorganization of Highways into the Department of Transportation in 1969, but the feeling of being under siege still fueled the drive for independence. The generally bountiful budgets of the era and high-profile support for expansion suggested that boom times might continue with an independent park system. By the end of his career, Talbot had come to view these early clashes with Highways leadership as useful training for brutal choices on politics and staffing to come. "I learned how to fight inside like you wouldn't believe," he later reflected. "I know how to do terrible things."[197]

---

193 Lawrence C. Merriam, Jr., *Oregon's Highway Park System, 1921 – 1989: An Administrative History* (Salem: Oregon Parks and Recreation Department, 1992), 50 – 51.

194 David G. Talbot, "Personal Views on the Development of Oregon State Parks," April 10, 1990, p. 17.

195 David G. Talbot, "The Superintendent Says," *Oregon State Park Times* 6:3 (Nov. 1980), p. 1.

196 David G. Talbot, "Personal Views on the Development of Oregon State Parks," April 10, 1990, pp. 15 – 16.

197 David G. Talbot, "Personal Views on the Development of Oregon State Parks," April 10, 1990, p. 21.

Tak[ing] a bloody beating:
The Willamette Greenway

The Highway Department's desire to relegate parks to a subset of maintenance was one sign that the growth and prosperity of the 1960s and 70s would not spell success for parks. The other was the disastrous Willamette Greenway project. Large-scale projects such as Scenic Waterways and Ocean Shores were able to make real progress in the move for scenic spaces for all Oregonians. Despite grumblings of government overreach, these successes solidified the position of State Parks as an agency to be reckoned with. In contrast, the rise and fall of the Willamette Greenway Project marked an epochal shift in Oregon parks. One of the most ambitious of the mammoth plans taken on in the 1960s, the Willamette Greenway was at its inception the largest project Oregon State Parks had attempted. In 1965, with calls for Willamette River protections from many directions and the just-passed federal Land and Water Conservation Act poised to pour funds into Oregon, the time seemed ripe to try something ambitious.

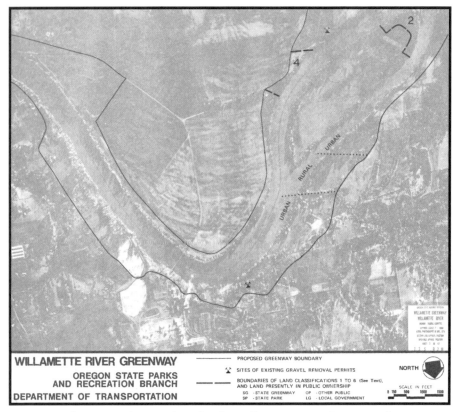

An excerpt from one of many plans for the Willamette River Greenway drawn up in the 1970s. Plans were no doubt prepared with great (but unfounded) hope.

In 1967, with both Governor Tom McCall and his erstwhile opponent Bob Straub supporting intervention along the river, what became the Willamette Greenway Project began to take shape. It was initially conceived of as a continuous greenway and park system stretching along the banks of the Willamette from Eugene to Portland, as a sort of riverine analog to the free travel available along Oregon beaches. In 1967, a committee convened by McCall released a plan full of ambition but light on specifics, promising "the preservation and enhancement of the river's natural environment while at the same time developing the widest possible recreational opportunities." It called for camping spots, recreation areas, boat launches, scenic conservation easements, large tracts for recreational centers, a vast network of trails—and no concrete plans regarding how any of it would be paid for. Supporters, the Highway Department, and the parks would have to find a way.[198]

The project needed millions and got thousands. Estimates of the costs for the full plan ranged from $10 million dollars on up; after a heated campaign the Oregon legislature was coaxed into ponying up $800,000. In 1969, Highway Commission Chair Glenn Jackson got some headway with a plan to convince local areas to put up matching funds for a single Greenway park in each relevant county. But the biggest break would come in 1970 at the federal level, when Talbot had to respond to a schmoozing emergency. As he later recalled:

> *I was on Sauvie's Island one day when a State policeman pulled me over, and I couldn't imagine what I had done wrong...*
> *as it turned out, [State Legislator] L. B. Day had secured $5,000,000 from the Secretary of the Interior. I was to get myself to Washington, D.C. as fast as I could to help get all the paper work and news releases and everything fixed. So, I just dropped everything [and] jumped on an airplane.*

Within a day, five million dollars in matching federal funds for Greenway projects was in the bag. Suddenly there was "a lot of pressure down the pipe[,] with all this money to move it." Although some legislative reluctance remained, there was enough commitment in the governor's office and the Highway Commission to set aside some funds for the project even without additional monies being allocated. As a sort of triage, the focus came to be on preserving the river banks themselves, a natural corridor that might or might not be useful for recreation at a future date. Some tracts were easy to acquire; other property owners refused.[199] In 1972, the Willamette Greenway Project ran headlong into a backlash from many rural constituencies. The key point of contention was eminent domain.

---

198   Thomas R. Cox, *The Park Builders: A History of State Parks in the Pacific Northwest* (Seattle: University of Washington Press, 1988), pp. 137 – 152, esp. 151 – 152.

199   Cox, *The Park Builders*, 152 – 158; David G. Talbot, "Personal Views on the Development of Oregon State Parks," May 16, 1990, Interview with Lawrence C. Merriam and Elisabeth Walton Potter, 49 – 53, Folder: Administrative History – Oral History – David G. Talbot, Director, 1964 – 1992, Box: Staff Biographies and Oral Histories 49 – 53;

It was impossible to realize the original vision of the project—a riverfront recreation area that stretched from Portland to Eugene—without forcing at least some property owners to sell at market value. The legal right of Parks and Recreation to do so was well established. The original laws on state parks in 1921 and 1925 had endowed them with the power of eminent domain where necessary. But this was little known and less accepted by the 1970s. Many Oregonians still supported the original vision of the Greenway, not least governor-elect Bob Straub, one of the foremost champions of the idea from its inception. But even the mere threat of involuntary seizure of riverfront property was a bridge too far for a critical mass of citizens and their legislators.[200]

Oregon State Parks and Recreation faced a new statewide organized opposition, the Willamette River Frontage Owners Association, created in 1972 to beat back the Willamette Greenway. Responding to the "army of Highway right-of-way agents" sent to acquire riverfront land, this group pushed the legislature to cut off funding for acquisition in 1972, then pushed through legislation that sharply curtailed the possibilities of eminent domain for the Willamette Greenway. "[W]e were really in a hole over the condemnation thing," Talbot later recalled, "even though we hadn't condemned anything." He had hoped to ease off and soothe the tensions of the moment, but Governor Bob Straub insisted on moving forward with the project he'd campaigned on. As Talbot floridly recalled it, the governor told him to "get on your horse and get your spear and get going, you wimpy bureaucrat." But Talbot was unable override the storm of opposition that was brewing.[201]

Opponents passed the 1973 Willamette River Greenway Act which (together with its 1975 successor) effectively torpedoed the original vision of the park. It banned the use of condemnation along the riverfront to seize farmlands for park purposes, redefined conservation to include current farming practices, and shifted substantial decision-making power from the Department of Transportation to local governments. Legislative attempts to resurrect the original conception of the Willamette River Greenway as a park were unsuccessful, despite having the support of Governor Bob Straub. Indeed, the legislature came perilously close to stripping eminent domain from the State Parks' toolbox altogether. The original Greenway project "was effectively shut down" in the late 1970s. Efforts for conservation continued, but vision of a continuous park along the river faded. The Willamette Greenway Park remained an unrealized dream. The "low key program" that bore the name going into the 1980s turned into an umbrella term for the uneven development of a checkerboard of parkland near the river. An attempt at the end of the decade to pursue the more ambitious version under a different name—"possibly just drop[ping] the 'green'"—came

---

200   Sam A. Kozer, compiler, *State of Oregon Constitutional Amendments...Together with the General Laws...* (Salem: State Printing Department, 1921), Chapter 343 [S.B. 365], 654.

201   Talbot, "Personal Views on the Development of Oregon State Parks," May 16, 1990, p. 52; Cox, *The Park Builders*, 158 – 159.

to nothing, and a 1988 call to "implement [the Willamette Greenway] with high priority" fared little better. The Willamette Greenway never lost its name, and the dream has never died (see Chapter 7).[202]

Talbot saw the defeat of the Willamette Greenway Park as the end of era, the point at which Parks and Recreation "moved from a land purchase program to a land-use planning program." After "tak[ing] a bloody beating" on the Greenway, Talbot and the Parks Commission became more cautious in their approach to acquisition, and in their approach to politically sensitive issues. The budget crises to come would turn this caution from strategic wisdom to economic necessity.[203]

People with a Common Interest:
The Parks Party Bus?!

Fights over the Willamette Greenway highlighted both the threat of rural backlash against parks, and also the need for coalition building. Managing a sprawling parks portfolio meant serving several sometimes contrary constituencies. New monies from federal programs also meant new forms of federal oversight. State parks had to navigate and complement moves for local parks on the one hand and National Parks or Natural Areas on the other. And most critically, Oregon State Parks and Recreation had to find ways to serve the whole population of Oregon amidst a deepening divide between urban and rural residents—a divide that came to threaten the bedrock the department was built upon.

Building relationships with rural residents had long been a critical part of building the park system. Parks served many functions, but their role in bringing urban dwellers "back to nature" had been at the forefront of many parks movements from the beginning (see Chapter 1). This framing ran the risk of alienating rural residents, who might feel excluded from park planning or even coerced into giving up rights or property for the enjoyment of others. From the beginning of Oregon State Parks, the help of influential power-brokers able to build support for parks in rural regions had been critical. Sam Boardman had Bob Sawyer. Dave Talbot had Stub Stewart.

---

202 Talbot remained convinced that a gentler approach might have succeeded; he blamed the failure in part on Highway men used to wielding eminent domain as a matter of routine. Talbot, "Personal Views on the Development of Oregon State Parks," May 16, 1990, pp. 49 – 53, quotations on 52 and 50; Webb Sterling Bauer, "A Case Analysis of Oregon's Willamette River Greenway Program," PhD Diss., Oregon State University, 1980, 102 – 152; David Talbot Memo to File, "Meeting with Governor Atiyeh," Jan 22, 1979, p. 2, Advisory Committee Minutes & Actions 1971 – 1981, Oregon State Parks and Recreation Collection; State Parks and Recreation Advisory Committee meeting minutes, Nov. 14, 1980, p. 9, Folder: Advisory Committee Minutes & Actions 1971 – 1981, Oregon State Parks and Recreation Collection; 2010 Citizen Advisory Committee, "Oregon State Parks 2010 Plan" (Salem: Oregon Parks and Recreation Division, Department of Transportation, 1988): 8 and 37 - 39, Box: Strategic Plans 1956 – 2012, Oregon State Parks and Recreation Collection.

203 Talbot, "Personal Views on the Development of Oregon State Parks," May 16, 1990, p. 53; Bauer, "A Case Analysis of Oregon's Willamette River Greenway Program," 180 – 181.

Loren "Stub" Stewart was an upstart lumber baron and a canny conservationist. He made a fortune building a midsized lumber empire in Oregon in the 1950s and 60s, where his company found special success by finding new uses for "waste" products, and by diversifying into areas like recreation and construction. Among many educational and conservationist causes, he spent over 40 years volunteering his time, services, and money for Oregon State Parks. For most of those years he was on the State Parks Advisory Committee, wielding power and influence both subtle and overt to shape the course of state parks.[204]

Along with his hard-nosed approach to organization, many Park personnel remembered Stewart's Advisory Committee annual trips as especially significant. Likely starting in 1962 and (at least initially) funded by Stewart himself, the State Parks Advisory Committee would pile into a bus and visit a series of parks or potential parks in Oregon (and occasionally visiting parks in neighboring states). They would bring along a smorgasbord of park personnel and visiting officials, and would meet with local community leaders and would-be donors at each stop.

These annual tours were an educational opportunity and an outreach program, a way to connect those making decisions about state and national parks with local conditions and constituencies. As Talbot later recalled, the idea was:

> *to be out and around talking to people about State Parks, how*
> *we could better coordinate with the counties, how we could*
> *help in a variety of ways. You have these people with a common*
> *interest in the bus talking (thirty-five to thirty-seven people from*
> *a wide variety of interests and agencies). Just being on the bus*
> *together for two, three or four days, especially for the new peo-*
> *ple, they could make contacts so fast that paid off for so long.* [205]

In addition to networking between state and national advisors and personnel, the trips also served to cultivate and demonstrate dedication to the areas of Oregon they were visiting:

> *Go to Eastern Oregon, go to Southern Oregon, go to these peo-*
> *ple and say 'We are here to help. What do you think?' They liked*
> *it a lot. They deserved that a lot, and they don't get very much*
> *of it by organized government. And here you are bringing in the*
> *National Park Service from Seattle and the head of this and the*
> *head of that and the guy from Washington, D.C., and local peo-*
> *ple feel better about their relations with government as a result.*

This was a lesson that stuck with Talbot in the hard times to come, and this (he thought) was the core purpose of the tours. For many, the early trips were

---

204 "Bohemia, Inc. History," *International Directory of Company Histories* 13, Tina Grant, Ed. (St. James Press, 1996); "Loran L. Stewart" Biography, World Forestry Center Leadership Hall Exhibit (Portland, OR: 2003).

205 Talbot, "Personal Views on the Development of Oregon State Parks," June 13, 1990, p. 130.

remembered most vividly as a sort of roving party—"raucous, joke-telling, good 'ol boy, outrageous drinking bouts, among other things. Just crazy stuff." Eventually "Stub and his cronies had to clean up their act" in later decades—out of chivalry when Lucille "Lu" Beck became the first woman on the committee in the 1970s (see Chapter 4), and out of necessity as norms changed in the 1980s. But the underlying function of the tours as a means of connection remained. The parties had a purpose. The warm relations built on these tours became especially vital as government ambition for state parks began to cool.[206]

Fear of the "White Elephant": Planning Parks in a More Modest Era

This coalition building became more important as the decades wore on and the role of State Parks as a highway agency grew more tenuous. In 1973, the Oregon Legislature created a distinct Parks and Recreation Branch within the Department of Transportation. Still subject to the Highway Division, Parks and Recreation nonetheless had their status as a separate entity confirmed and clarified at this juncture. But 1973 also marked the onset of a difficult period. Throughout Talbot's long career with Oregon State Parks (1964 – 1992), almost every move towards independence was coincident with calamity. Even as the new Parks and Recreation Branch gained more independence and responsibility, funding was in decline and popular support was wavering.[207]

One thing has always been true of Oregon State Parks: there is never enough money in the budget to do all that has been asked of the department. Park staff and the Advisory Committee spent most of their time together on budget concerns, even in the comparatively flush 1960s. During his time on the committee, Alfred "Cap" Collier was perhaps the most likely person to grill staff on the fundamentals. Like many others on the Committee, he combined business success (like Stub Stewart, in the lumber industry) with a commitment to state parks (including Collier Memorial State Park, much of which was donated to memorialize his family). In meetings, he combined folksy stories with practical questions. In conversations about new parks, he could be relied upon to bring up the necessity of adequate toilets. Collier was willing to get into the muck of the details.[208]

In 1972, Collier expressed his fear of spending state money on a "white elephant," a park that did not fit the goals or needs of the system and would create continuing expenses if accepted. Looking back on decades of acquisition, staff and committee members in times of economic stress saw several white

---

206 When he was told to "take care" of a journalist in 1962, Dave Talbot took him to a tavern and taught him a gambling game to keep him out of trouble. If that was the "tame" activity, one can imagine what else the tour might have gotten up to. Talbot, "Personal Views on the Development of Oregon State Parks," June 13, 1990, pp. 132 – 135, quotes on 132 and 135.

207 Dave Talbot to Parks Staff, Feb 21, 1973, Folder: State Parks Departmental Bill, Steps towards Independence, 1985 – 1990, Box: Legislation and Statutes, Oregon Parks and Recreation Collections.

208 State Parks and Recreation Advisory Committee conference call minutes, April 6, 1972, Folder: Advisory Committee Minutes & Actions 1971 – 1981.

elephants on the horizon. The move from "land purchase" to "land-use planning" that Talbot voiced regarding the 1970s was far from absolute—park acquisition continued in the decade, and even trickled on amidst the economic shocks of the 1980s. But fear of "white elephants" began to play a larger role in acquisition decisions. The reflexive protective purchasing of the Boardman era had been superseded by more deliberate strategic decision-making.[209]

In a special meeting called on December 19, 1972, "Stub" Stewart, the Advisory Committee, and Oregon State Parks leadership hammered out a set of park priorities. The first order of business was to speak to the balancing act that had been bubbling since Boardman: "Should emphasis be on recreation or preservation?"

> *Even though 87% of the total Parks System acreage is currently undeveloped [they answered], it is not our intention to duplicate the preservation job now being done by other agencies, especially the federal agencies. Emphasis should be placed on recreation development, but at the same time protecting what natural resources we have under our jurisdiction.*[210]

Preservation would persist, but moving forward the "Recreation" portion of the mission would gain increasing prominence. This was a culmination of a decades-long push in the direction of land use rather than land protection (see Chapter 3). The Committee also urged a continued focus on "land ac[qui]sition, especially when unique land areas become available." Particularly, they urged that "[l]ands acquired should have some attraction and be located where demand is greatest." The attraction could be a natural feature, a historic space, or something purpose-built for recreation (motorbike raceways were the example given). "Commercialism" would "not be encouraged," but neither should the Boardman-esque "present policy of discouraging almost all commercial services" be continued. Fear of "white elephants" notwithstanding, the Committee and staff planned for steady growth with a more careful eye to the needs and desires of visitors. What they didn't anticipate was the quarter-century of economic shocks that would slowly push the park system to the brink of oblivion.[211]

Worries of "white elephants" in 1972 must have seemed extremely prescient when the "black swan" oil embargo of 1973 sent the United States economy into a tailspin. Oil prices jumped 350%, helping to precipitate a series of economic crises that consumed the rest of the 1970s. Because of their reliance on gas taxes, Highways and State Parks in Oregon were hit especially hard. One of the arguments for placing and keeping Oregon State Parks under the

209 State Parks and Recreation Advisory Committee conference call minutes, Aug 7, 1972, Folder: Advisory Committee Minutes & Actions 1971 – 1981.

210 State Parks and Recreation Advisory Committee meeting minutes, Dec 19, 1972, p. 1, Folder: Advisory Committee Minutes & Actions 1971 – 1981, *ibid.*

211 State Parks and Recreation Advisory Committee meeting minutes, Dec 19, 1972, pp. 1 – 3, Folder: Advisory Committee Minutes & Actions 1971 – 1981.

Preservation and recreation: The inherent tension between recreation and preservation has existed since day one at Parks. Leaders from Boardman forward have grappled with the mission.

jurisdiction of the Highway Department had been the perceived stability of the gas tax. Parks seemed prized by the public but vulnerable to cutbacks in times of economic stress. The assumption had been that gas revenues would be comparatively more reliable, as they had been during the Great Depression. But with gas prices at the center of the current crisis, gas taxes faced new scrutiny and protest. The main source of funding for Oregon State Parks and Recreation seemed like it might sputter out, just as the visitor boom that had propelled the breakneck pace of the 1960s flattened and fell. As lines for gasoline grew, state park use dropped by a third, and was still significantly below previous years by 1974. Although there remained "sufficient funds for the basic program," the acquisition goals that had been the agreed-upon focus began to idle. Visitor numbers would recover and reach all-time highs by the late 1970s. The budget would not.[212]

---

212 On the energy crisis that began in the 1970s, see Meg Jacobs, *Panic at the Pump: The Energy Crisis and the Transformation of American Politics in the 1970s* (New York: Hill and Wang, 2016); State Parks and Recreation Advisory Committee meeting minutes, Dec. 15, 1977, p. 1, Folder: Advisory Committee Minutes & Actions 1971 – 1981; State Parks and Recreation Advisory Committee meeting minutes, April 12, 1974, p. 1. The term "black swan" has come to refer to a catastrophic unanticipated event. Kenneth A. Posner, *Stalking the Black Swan: Research and Decision Making in a World of Extreme Volatility* (New York: Columbia University Press, 2010).

The whole system was running on fumes. Rural counties hit especially hard by Department of Transportation cuts to the highway budget pushed for a removal of parks from the highway fund, and/or an effective "moratorium on immediate and future plans for state park acquisition and development until the State's financial picture is improved." By 1976, the proposed budget for Oregon State Parks and Recreation was roughly half of what it had been a decade earlier (when adjusted for inflation). Without at least a few cents increase in the gas tax, ODOT Director Bob Burco warned, "layoffs will continue and programs will suffer." Voters, still feeling the sting of stagflation, soundly rejected every proposed gas tax increase. The layoffs continued. The programs suffered. And before the end of the 1970s state parks would be out of gas entirely, as first politicians and then voters prevented parks from getting any of the gas tax funds.[213]

Amidst hard budget decisions, "Cap" Collier's fear of "white elephants" combined with a narrower sense of what state parks should strive for amidst the tapestry of park and nature organizations and governmental bodies in Oregon. He saw more "natural" spaces in the template of Boardman as the right niche for Oregon State Parks. "What we want mainly," he proclaimed in 1977, "is a place for people to wind-down." If a particular acquisition seemed like "more of a wind-up park," Collier thought it was best left to the counties or the country, rather than the state. Made at one of "Cap's" last meetings, Collier's call for state parks only as places of refuge seemed from an earlier era. He was listened to, in this case, because the "wind-up parks" he rejected were often more expensive to staff and run.[214]

Increasingly, Oregon State Parks began moving land to county control, at least where the counties could reasonably pursue parks and recreation goals on their own. As late as 1971, this had seemed unlikely. When one such potential transfer was raised, "Cap" Collier had wondered if it would "establish a precedent," and was assured it would not. Yet by 1972, transfers of parks were often considered and occasionally enacted. This could be a way of attempting more harmony with local governments, which might want to shape parkland on their own. Particularly, as Talbot later pointed out, the move toward county control helped to fund locally desired "small, relatively appealing, no sex appeal kind of projects" that lacked the "pizzazz" of big, splashy parks. And it seemed like a way to get more parks for less money.[215]

---

213 State Parks and Recreation Advisory Committee meeting minutes, Nov 18, 1976, p. 3, Folder: Advisory Committee Minutes & Actions 1971 – 1981. The estimate of "roughly half" includes adjustment for inflation; if not so adjusted, the budget was around two-thirds. Exact budget calculations vary depending on the nature of the records used and what is and is not included. State Parks and Recreation Advisory Committee meeting minutes, Nov 18, 1976, p. 9, Folder: Advisory Committee Minutes & Actions 1971 – 1981; State Parks and Recreation Advisory Committee meeting minutes, Aug 10, 1979, p. 2, *ibid*. "Stagflation" is the term of art used to describe a state of high inflation, high unemployment, and stagnant demand—a particularly nasty kind of economic crisis.

214 State Parks and Recreation Advisory Committee conference call: Scoggins Reservoir, July 13, 1977, p. 3, Folder: Advisory Committee Minutes & Actions 1971 – 1981.

215 Talbot, "Personal Views on the Development of Oregon State Parks," Apr 10, 1990, p. 37; State Parks and Recreation Advisory Committee conference call, Oct 7, 1971, p. 2, Folder: Advisory Committee Minutes & Actions 1971 – 1981; State Parks and Recreation Advisory Committee meeting minutes, May 22, 1981, p. 4, Folder: Advisory Committee Minutes & Actions 1981 – 1989, Oregon State Parks and Recreation Collection.

Whether to move to local control was a complex question, one that was often scuttled by feasibility issues or the wishes of original donors. But at a time when Oregon Parks and Recreation could not afford to develop the land under their purview, local control and local dollars could make the difference between success and condemnation. By the mid-1980s, "Stub" Stewart and the rest of the Parks Advisory Committee praised efforts for "Parks to dispose of surplus lands" that did not fit into goals of a streamlined system. By 1989, in one of their last meetings, a majority of the Parks Advisory Committee pushed against efforts from the legislature to put an old-growth forest under state park control. The era of automatic acquisition was dead. Boardman's long shadow had been eclipsed.[216]

We Fell into Hard Times:
Gas Runs Out of the Park Budget

Park staff hoped in vain that the budget shortfalls and austerity measures of the mid-1970s would not continue into the new decade. In 1979, the legislature made Oregon State Parks and Recreation a coequal branch of the Department of Transportation. This marked a shift to equal footing between Parks and Highways. But as was the case with every move toward independence in the era, the change was coupled with calamity. The move to equality was enabled in part by the loss of gas tax revenue. With the state budget feeling the squeeze of a tough economy in 1977, the state park system was "temporarily" deprived of its share of the gas tax. This money didn't come back. After three years of temporary measures, the deprivation was made permanent. In May of 1980, by state constitutional amendment approved by over two-thirds of Oregon voters, Oregon Parks and Recreation was severed from this portion of highway funds. Attempts to get these moneys back in 1983, 1987, and especially 1992 did not come near success.[217]

Revenue from other sources, particularly visitor fees, provided for many of the day-to-day costs of running parks, but they were not sufficient to meet demands for expansion, or even maintenance. The loss of gas tax income was a wrench. But it was not a surprise. Dave Talbot remembered being attacked many times over the years for not, as he put it, "throw[ing] myself on the spear as many thought I should." But he thought this loss of funding was inevitable. And he was not alone. New Governor Victor Atiyeh and old Highway Commissioner Glenn Jackson echoed feelings across park leadership when they concluded in 1979 that "the constitutional amendment seemed to be inevitable

---

216   State Parks and Recreation Advisory Committee meeting minutes, Dec. 2, 1986, p. 2, Folder: Advisory Committee Minutes & Actions 1981 – 1989; State Parks and Recreation Advisory Committee meeting minutes, April 28, 1989, p. 2, *ibid.*

217   David G. Talbot, "Personal Views on the Development of Oregon State Parks," April 10, 1990, p. 18; State Parks and Recreation Advisory Committee meeting minutes, April 1, 1983, p. 6, Folder: Advisory Committee Minutes & Actions 1981 – 1989; City Club of Portland, "Constitutional Amendment Limits Uses of Gasoline and Highway User Taxes (State Measure No. 1)," (Portland: City Club of Portland, 1980); *FYI* 153 (July 26?, 1996).

and we shouldn't fight it." Voters feeling an economic pinch and the first tail-winds of 1980s anti-tax movement (see Chapter 6) seemed determined. The official position of state parks became that they would "[s]tand back and let the chips fall where they may." As they maneuvered through a fundamental funding shift, Dave Talbot and other park personnel tried to reframe the continuing financial fallout as an opportunity. To Talbot, this loss signaled a need to move from specialized funding to the General Fund. "To risk the loss of money to strike out for independence was worth it," he proclaimed. But what many would later see as foolhardy bravado was, arguably, making the best of it. The money was already gone.[218]

Despite shifts in the parties, platforms, philosophies in the governor's office through the 1970s and 80s, Oregon's state parks remained a popular cause. But there was a tangible shift in the sense of the possible, particularly when it came to budget. The 1980s saw significantly more collaboration with local groups and local governments—both in terms of decision-making and in terms of where the money for parks would come from. When it came to funding major acquisitions, Talbot wrote in the margins of one report, "the Gov. choked." As Oregon's economy limped through the 1980s, state parks remained popular, but getting enough money to run them seemed nearly impossible.[219]

It was initially unclear how devastating the loss of the gas tax would be. Budgets and staff would have to be cut, but in its first year thrown into the state budget process Parks seemed to be "fairly successful." But then the 1980 crash hit and the economy tanked, again. As inflation, unemployment, and the worst recession since the 1930s gripped the nation, Oregon State Parks were at the mercy of a General Fund reeling from losses and dealing with crises. "We knew it would be tough financially, but we had no idea how bad it would be," Talbot confessed to park staff a few years later. "The transition… could not have come at a worse time." As Talbot remembered in 1990, "It took us a decade coming out of that vote in '80, and the terrible recession, and the game plan falling apart, the General Fund not being there, we then fell into hard times and learned how to live with less." This lesson was forced on parks time after time after time.[220]

Budget shortfalls came hard and fast. Almost every year Oregon state parks had to make up for another deficit by firing staff, abandoning projects,

---

218 David Talbot Memo to File, "Meeting with Governor Atiyeh," Jan 22, 1979, pp. ii and 13, Folder: Advisory Committee Minutes & Actions 1971 – 1981; Talbot, "Personal Views on the Development of Oregon State Parks," April 10, 1990, p. 19.

219 Talbot had been referring specifically to Gov. Vic Atiyeh, but his assertion was soon applied generally across state government. David Talbot Memo to File, "Meeting with Governor Atiyeh," Jan 22, 1979, p. 1, Folder: Advisory Committee Minutes & Actions 1971 – 1981.

220 State Parks and Recreation Advisory Committee meeting minutes, Aug 10, 1979, p. 2, Folder: Advisory Committee Minutes & Actions 1971 – 1981; David G. Talbot, "From the Administrator's Desk," *Oregon State Park Times* [issue unknown] (Dec 1984), Folder: Staff Newsletter—Park Times—1984 to 1990, Box: Publications – Staff Newsletters, 1963 – 1994, Oregon Parks and Recreation Collection; Talbot, "Personal Views on the Development of Oregon State Parks," April 10, 1990, p. 23.

Strict divorce from Highway Division seen

Measure 1 poses dilemma for parks funding

By SUE HILL
Oregon Statesman Reporter

Use is down, fees are fewer, state legislators are critical, and now a two-month-old interoffice memo has surfaced to add to the woes besetting the once-respondent state park system.

The memo, from the attorney general's office to the state Highway Division, says the severance of parks from the state highway fund — an issue up for a statewide vote this May — would be a greater financial setback to the Parks Division than originally thought.

The opinion, written by Jack Sollis, an assistant attorney general assigned to the Transportation Department, says that if Measure 1 passes in May, the fiscal divorce between parks and highway will be "strict."

"IT IS NOT LEGALLY possible to stretch the meaning of the words ..." Sollis wrote to state Highway Engineer H.S. Coulter last November." ... the new language ... is probably the most restrictive of any constitutional dedication language relating to highway funds than will be found in the United States."

Sollis sp practice of leasing eq have to be in resp

Highway Division, Sollis also outlines other mutual aid areas that parks will no longer be able to enjoy

THAT MEANS, IF VOTERS pass Measure 1, the Parks Division may have to go to the legislative Emergency Board seeking additional money to reimburse the highway fund for capital equipment, rentals in joint offices and other administrative services

Parks officials said Friday they are not sure of the budgetary implications of Sollis' opinion. However, an Oregon Statesman reporter learned of one $400,000 estimate that one would officially confirm.

Measure 1 seeks to limit use of the tax and motor vehicle taxes making up the Highway Fund exclusively to highway and maintenance

Up until last year, parks and state drew partial funding from the Highway But the 1979 Legislature tossed ther used the $60 million savings to f highways.

MEASURE 1 WOULD SIMPL budgetary separation into the tion so that future legislatures

The Secretary of State's office is required to attach an estimated fiscal impact to all ballot measure The fiscal impact on Measure 1 — officially zero since the budgets are al ──ted   Norma Paulus said last ──t certain all   ──tion

public to turn to smaller cars and make fewer trips As a result, the once booming gas tax now cannot keep pace with inflation.

GAS SHORTAGES ALSO HURT the parks' budget. Parks officials said Friday that park use in 1979 was down 17 percent, leaving a $400,000 hole in its revenues in the first 6 months of the 1979-81 budget.

──es recur this spring and sum- ──ing, the Parks Divi- ──oney from

Times may turn tough for state parks system

By CHARLES E. BEGGS
Associated Press Writer

Oregon's state park system, after years of feasting on highway funds, is adjusting to what may be a permanently leaner diet.

Concerned that parks now have to compete with such programs as welfare and education for General Fund tax dollars, officials are considering options including a statewide property tax ··

staple on the menu.

"We're going to see a dir ── on," says Dav ──

DOT officials report no danger to parks if Measure 1 approved

The Department of Transportation convinced Secretary of State Norma Paulus this week that the state Parks Division will suffer no hidden financial peril if voters approve Measure 1 at the polls in May.

Measure 1 would permanently restrict use of state gas and motor vehicle taxes to highway construction, repair and maintenance. Until last year, part of the highway fund was used to finance operation of parks and state police.

The 1979 Legislature jumped the gun and removed parks and state police from the highway fund in order to release $60 million extra to repair potholes.

The secretary of state is required to attach a fiscal im- ──wide ballot measure. Origi-

1 passes When the November memo came to light several weeks ago, it gave rise to fears that parks would have to buy thousands of dollars of equipment that wasn't budgeted.

Parks has been leasing about $200,000 worth of equipment a year through the highway fund

The Department of Transportation, parent of the parks division and guardian of the highway fund, reviewed the whole issue and decided this week that there is no fiscal impact

Department officials now point out that rental rates charged to parks include a depreciation charge to finance new equipment. Accumulated depreciation should provide enough equity to allow purchase or replacement of ──ment the department argued this week when ──

Money crunch may close some state parks

PORTLAND (AP) — A money crunch may prompt the Oregon State Parks and Recreation Division to close or lease remote parks,

parks superintendent David Talbot said Friday.

The loss of gasoline tax funds has crippled the division's ability to purchase or maintain parks in areas remote from urban centers, he said. He said the division must "concentrate bucks where the people are going to be."

Ballot Measure 1, passed by Oregon voters in the May primary, limits gas tax and license fees to highway maintenance. The measure forces the parks division

into competition for funds with other state government programs, Talbot said.

Recreational vehicle taxes are retained for parks but Talbot said high gas prices in future years could annihilate that source. He said recreational vehicle taxes provide about .34 percent of the division's money.

If the parks division does find itself crimped for money, maintenance of Oregon's parks system could suffer, Talbot said.

"We would rather start closing parks than cut back on the quality of service people are used to," he said.

The number of out-of-staters in Oregon parks is declining while more Ore-

gonians are using them, Talbot said. Last year 35 million persons cruised through the state's parks, he noted.

The parks division may have to charge visitors if money gets tighter, Talbot said, but he isn't in favor of that approach.

"We will have to get the money from the guy that goes to the beach and to the river, but we would rather go fight for general fund money than try to collect it at the gate of every small park in the state," he said.

Bill to aid U.S. fishermen progresses

WASHINGTON (UPI) — A bill that could end foreign fishing in American

zone he introduced last fall at the request of Oregon fishermen.

The 1980 constitutional amendment removing Parks from the gas tax coffers was a watershed moment for Parks, leading to decades of financial struggle.

or deferring maintenance. Almost every year, these hard decisions were by a command to brace for more cuts. "[S]ome cuts are drastic," as Warren Gaskill, Talbot's second-in-command, warned the Advisory Committee in 1981. "[B]ut we are looking at a $1 million dollar problem." In the worst predictions, the gap yawned to 30-plus million dollars. The popularity of parks (and the political wiles of their supporters) kept the worst of these disasters at bay. There was little doubt in the 1980s that the "real gems in the parks system would be preserved at all costs." But park staff had to reckon with near-constant uncertainty about their projects and their job prospects.[221]

The most at-risk programs were centered on interpretation. Due to continuous budget shortfalls, "the history stuff in parks…languished." The more ambitious plans of Elisabeth Walton had to be put on indefinite hold. "We have done bits and dabs," Dave Talbot said of the history programs of the period, "but there is so much to be done." As with all funding issues, "history stuff" was a question of priorities. In a later interview Talbot mourned that colleges were turning out too many "people who want to get into 'interpretation,'" a "certain kind of people," instead of "the kinds of people that we need." Talbot did not clarify what "kinds of people" they needed, but interpretation people weren't it. But Talbot also said that one of the "most satisfying parts of my career has been the rounding out of a good basic park system with historic properties that are really valuable and important." To Talbot, interpretation in these properties (and parks generally) mattered. But it was a benefit rather than a necessity. Attempts in 1981 to make History its own department was beaten back—but then, there was little money to devote to *anything*. The State Historic Preservation Office still received federal funds, but those areas of history not under their purview, like museums and interpretation, withered. In the triage of the 1980s a lot of things that mattered went unsupported.[222]

Nickel and Dime Fees to the Public:
The Cents of Desperation

With the gap in the budget looming larger, park personnel had to take a hard look at services previously provided for free. Sometimes this was a matter for the legislature, as in 1982, when parks were finally given a sufficient share of boat taxes to pay for the boat services they provided. Other perks previously

---

221 State Parks and Recreation Advisory Committee meeting minutes, Feb 19, 1981, p. 5 - 6, Folder: Advisory Committee Minutes & Actions 1981 – 1989 State Parks and Recreation Advisory Committee meeting minutes, May 22, 1981, pp. 4 – 5, *ibid*; State Parks and Recreation Advisory Committee meeting minutes, June 16, 1982, p. 2, *ibid*.

222 David G. Talbot, "Personal Views on the Development of Oregon State Parks," April 8, 1990, Interview with Lawrence C. Merriam and Elisabeth Walton Potter, 64, Folder: Administrative History – Oral History – David G. Talbot, Director, 1964 – 1992, Oregon State Parks and Recreation Collection; Talbot, "Personal Views on the Development of Oregon State Parks," June 6, 1990, pp. 115 – 116; Talbot, "Personal Views on the Development of Oregon State Parks," June 13, 1990, p. 136; State Parks and Recreation Advisory Committee meeting minutes, Feb 19, 1981 , p. 2, Folder: Advisory Committee Minutes & Actions 1981 – 1989; State Parks and Recreation Advisory Committee meeting minutes, Feb 25, 1982, p. 2, *ibid*; State Parks and Recreation Advisory Committee meeting minutes, June 16, 1982, p. 6, *ibid*.

given for free to visitors had to become fee-based to survive. The "days of free firewood [were] gone forever" by 1980, and fees for camp reservations were reinstated the following year. Many new small fees and taxes were suggested to try and make up the constant shortfalls in park budgets. Big-ticket items, like a one cent tax on cigarettes, were longer-term goals (in part because cigarette taxes had to increase by five-cent increments, since vending machines [!] didn't take pennies). In the meantime, rental fees had to be hiked up, vehicle fees were rolled out in selected parks, and RV licensure costs were increased. There were worries about these efforts to patch the budget. Would visitors read these fees as an attempt to "nickel and dime them," and get angry? But with holes in the budget looming large and "Highway funds…no longer available as the 'balancer' for [the] budget," many at Oregon State Parks and Recreation felt they needed every

"Two dollars!!? Do you think I'm *made* of money?!!

Campsite surcharges for out-of-state visitors had little impact on Parks revenue, but generated ill will in the tourism industry for the 10 years it existed.

dollar they could get. By end of 1981, "nickel and dimes fees to the public" were a regular agenda item for the Parks Advisory Committee.[223]

The crisis also meant a slow acceptance of unpopular measures. In 1977, the Oregon legislature had added a $2.00 surcharge for campers from out of state. This was a popular measure among many Oregon voters. Indeed, amidst the "Unsolicited Comments" in the 1975 visitor survey "[m]any comments were received from Oregonians suggesting that nonresidents should be charged higher fees." Parks personnel, on the other hand, protested this shift, correctly predicting that it would generate significant ill-will and insignificant revenue. Despite the protests of personnel in 1977 and a unanimous call from the Parks Advisory Committee to repeal the surcharge in 1978, the special fee for out-of-state visitors remained.[224] And by 1981, the Parks Advisory Committee and Dave Talbot had quietly dropped their previous protest against the surcharge. Every dollar counted. And then these surcharge dollars, too, disappeared in 1987.[225]

Some attempts at usage fees, however, proved immediately impossible. One such proposal was the charge of an extra $1 fee for those who brought dogs to the parks, the logic perhaps being that dogs inflicted more wear and tear and required more kinds of clean-up and maintenance. The blowback at the very idea was immediate and enormous. Unable to fully express just how badly the notion had fared with the press and the public, Talbot had staff and the Parks Advisory Committee watch a "Dog Fee Tape" to see visceral reactions to even the suggestion of a fee to take pets to parks. Hearing the "howl of protest [that] was raised by the canine community... the idea was quickly dropped."[226]

Replacing gas tax dollars with money from the General Fund had been unavoidable. When Talbot tried to spin this into a positive, he relied on popularity. The immediate solution for budget shortfalls, he suggested early in 1982, should be: "More General Fund [money]. People love parks—we need and deserve it—give us more money."

---

223 State Parks and Recreation Advisory Committee meeting minutes, Dec 3, 1982, p. 1, Folder: Advisory Committee Minutes & Actions 1981 – 1989; State Parks and Recreation Advisory Committee meeting minutes, June 16, 1982, p. 2, *ibid*; State Parks and Recreation Advisory Committee meeting minutes, Oct 15, 1980, Folder: Advisory Committee Minutes & Actions 1971 – 1981; State Parks and Recreation Advisory Committee meeting minutes, Nov 14, 1980, p. 7, 8, 4, *ibid*; State Parks and Recreation Advisory Committee meeting minutes, Dec. 3 – 4, 1981, p. 7, Folder: Advisory Committee Minutes & Actions 1981 – 1989; State Parks and Recreation Advisory Committee meeting minutes, Dec. 3 – 4, *ibid*.

224 Parks and Recreation Branch, Department of Transportation, "Oregon Parks Visitor Survey, 1975," (Spring 1976), 16; State Parks and Recreation Advisory Committee meeting minutes, Nov 1, 1978, p. 4, Folder: Advisory Committee Minutes & Actions 1971 – 1981.

225 Arguably, the disappearance of the surcharge in 1987 was a net positive, signaling a shift toward bringing in more tourist dollars overall. However, many Californian would-be visitors remembered the surcharge even a decade later, and some assumed it was still in force. State Parks and Recreation Advisory Committee meeting minutes, Feb 19, 1981, p. 3, Folder: Advisory Committee Minutes & Actions 1981 – 1989; State Parks and Recreation Advisory Committee meeting minutes, May 22, 1981, p. 7, *ibid*; State Parks and Recreation Advisory Committee meeting minutes, Dec. 4, 1987, p. 10, *ibid*;; "Californians See OPRD Road Show," *FYI* 225 (Jan 16, 1998).

226 State Parks and Recreation Advisory Committee meeting minutes, Dec 9, 1983, p. 2, Folder: Advisory Committee Minutes & Actions 1981 – 1989; State Parks and Recreation Advisory Committee meeting minutes, April 17, 1984, p. 7, *ibid*.

Love of parks could be used to pry vital dollars out of a Governor or a committee at the last minute, but the positive associations Oregonians had with state parks did not lead to a demand for more taxes to fund them. In the political economic climate of the 1980s, such a move would have been unlikely. Park revenues improved over the summer of 1982 (with "the return of the nonresidents") but did not fully rebound. Unable to thrive on a shrinking budget, Oregon State Parks in the 1980s pursued new donors, new rank-and-file supporters, and a new unpaid labor force.[227]

The Long-Term Salvation of Oregon State Parks:
Volunteer Programs and Citizen's Groups

From 1980 on, Oregon State Parks and Recreation came to rely on unpaid labor, particularly from expanding and empowered groups of volunteers. Of course, the system had leaned on volunteers nearly from its inception, from the park improvements Jessie Honeyman had organized to the interpretation offered by citizens' groups at Champoeg. But now the park system could not function without them. At the beginning of the hard times in 1970s there had still been "sufficient funds for basic operation." In the grim 1980s, that was no longer the case. Volunteers and donations made up the difference. New park host programs had volunteers doing work previously accomplished by paid personnel. Growing "Friends of" groups enabled significant improvement, fundraising, and advocacy. As park budgets were cut to the bone, donations of time and money became the lifeblood of the system.

Donors had always been key. Most of the state park system had been built from donated land, and now more and more of the funding had to come directly from the citizenry. Just as Boardman, Sawyer, and Honeyman had done in the 1930s, Talbot, Stewart, and much of the rest of the Parks Advisory Committee found a lot of their work for parks was fundraising. Cultivating donors large and small was a critical part of getting big projects off the ground. For what became the Deschutes River State Recreation Area, much of the funding was raised by thousands of people giving through organized groups like the Oregon Wildlife Heritage Foundation. But Talbot also borrowed a helicopter through "Stub" Stewart to court a big donor who, just as Boardman had, "liked green stuff" in her wilderness rather than "the brown country"—and so needed to be flown to the green center of a proposed acquisition. "Stub," of course, was a major donor in his own right, and a soft touch. Talbot remembered that when he was closing in on the last of the funding for the Deschutes River project, "[Stub] said, 'I think

---

227   State Parks and Recreation Advisory Committee meeting minutes, Feb 25, 1982, p. 2, Folder: Advisory Committee Minutes & Actions 1981 – 1989; State Parks and Recreation Advisory Committee meeting minutes, June 16, 1982, p. 2, *ibid*; John L. Mikesell, "The Path of the Tax Revolt: Statewide Expenditure and Tax Control Referenda since Proposition 13," *State and Local Government Review* 18:1 (1986): 5 – 12; Clarence Y. H. Lo, *Small Property versus Big Government: The Social Origins of the Property Tax Revolt* (Berkeley: University of California Press, 2018).

I can get you [an additional] $50,000. But you've got to pay me back.'" Talbot never did. Stub kept giving anyway.[228]

"Friends of" groups rose to new importance in the 1980s. Citizens groups for parks predated the state system, of course, from Champoeg on (see Chapter 1). But now "Friends of" groups would work hand-in-glove with state parks people. "Lu" Beck came to the Parks Advisory Committee in 1976 after co-founding the first of this new kind of group, the "Friends of Tryon Creek," in 1970. The group coordinated place-based volunteer labor, advocacy, and education—and built a base of donors small and large.[229] In the 1980s, with Lu's encouragement and eager acceptance by a cash-strapped state park service in need of allies, "Friends of" groups expanded. The Tryon Creek model, Talbot expounded in 1990, was

> *the forerunner of what I think might be the long-term*
> *salvation of Oregon State Parks. That is the development of*
> *citizens groups [such as]; Friends of Tryon Creek, Friends*
> *of Silver Falls, a Friends of whoever movement that will*
> *take another decade…. At the end of that decade we will*
> *have twenty or thirty of those things with membership of*
> *thousands with a constituent body who really cares, who will*
> *go to "war" for Oregon State Parks.*[230]

It was increasingly clear in the 1980s that Oregon State Parks needed all the Friends they could get. Drawn by love of a specific park, these groups might become advocates for park affairs generally. In 1985, the state legislature made these already-growing relationships official, clearing the way for enduring partnerships between Oregon Parks and non-profits. In 1990, asked about how parks had changed since the 1960s, Talbot reflected:

> *the business of doing things by yourself is long gone… has been*
> *gone for a decade. Very few things will ever occur anymore*
> *where you don't have a whole host of people being a party*
> *to it. The simplistic, one agency things aren't going to happen*
> *anymore in Oregon very much unless the financial situation*
> *changes a lot. And it's probably for the good."* [231]

"Friends of" groups, Talbot hoped, could act as foot-soldiers for parks in the budget battles to come. This new army of supporters would perhaps be a more organized and comprehensive evolution of what had come before.

228 Talbot, "Personal Views on the Development of Oregon State Parks," June 13, 1990, pp. 145 – 146..

229 Anon, "Founding Story of Tryon Creek,"
https://tryonfriends.org/stories-of-tryon-creek/2020/3/founding-story

230 Talbot, "Personal Views on the Development of Oregon State Parks," June 13, 1990, pp. 134 – 135.

231 David G. Talbot, "Personal Views on the Development of Oregon State Parks," June 13, 1990, p. 156.

But the park host program: that was brand-new. In the summer of 1979, Talbot's second-in-command Warren Gaskill oversaw the beginning of a volunteer host program at a few coastal parks, patterned after U.S. Forest Service campground volunteer programs. These new hosts would do a mix of guidance and maintenance tasks, in exchange for a free campsite and the pleasure of their work. Talbot reported in fall of 1979 that the new host program:

> *has worked very successfully in most cases. The public and our own employees appreciate the assistance provided by the hosts and the hosts "love their work."* [232]

The park host program was rolled out officially in 1980, with immediate popularity. In addition to the badly needed free labor, it served to drum up excitement for the park system: park hosts, largely retirees, acted as ambassadors for the beauties of parks. Indeed, it proved so popular that by 1981:

> *a problem [had] arisen in that competition for the Host position was keen in certain parks. An Oregon couple complained that they were not selected for the park of their choice—a California couple was selected instead. They felt that Oregonians should have preference for Park Host positions over out-of-staters.*

The Committee tended to agree, and backed down only after park personnel pointed out that "many of the apparent out-of-staters were actually Oregonians who wintered elsewhere but 'came home' for the summers." Oregonians' tendency to blame Californians notwithstanding, it was clear that the host program had generated plenty of interest.[233]

But what could hosts or volunteers reasonably be expected to do? What about the hard and grubby work of maintenance and cleaning? As host and volunteer programs were being rolled out across the state in 1982, Talbot praised the more long-standing Friends groups but worried that "generally we could expect a long-term loss of quality in many volunteer operations dealing with maintenance." Committee member Lynn Newbry warned that "volunteer workers get pretty tired of cleaning restrooms—after about a day," and fellow member Darald Walker worried that "poor maintenance would reflect on State Parks."

But worries couldn't stop the change. Volunteers were already essential, and Parks leadership were eager to expand their use into struggling parks where staff had already been laid off. They judged volunteers "well worth it" for the work they did in hosting and trail maintenance, whatever small prob-

---

232   State Parks and Recreation Advisory Committee meeting minutes, Oct 15, 1979, p. 9, Folder: Advisory Committee Minutes & Actions 1971 – 1981.

233   State Parks and Recreation Advisory Committee meeting minutes, Dec 3 – 4, 1981, p. 3, Folder: Advisory Committee Minutes & Actions 1981 – 1989.

lems might crop up. The "'hard times,'" Talbot reported in 1983, "forced us into many volunteer programs." Some of these volunteer programs involved specific and temporary efforts, like the "Company's Coming" beach clean-up campaigns begun in 1986. But it was the longer-term host programs that raised thorny questions about labor.[234]

Were the park hosts workers, even though they received no salary? Early in 1984, the state of Oregon said yes. After one park host succumbed to an illness on the job, his widow filed and won a Workers' Compensation claim. Although Oregon State Parks and Recreation did not contest this ruling, the precedent made staff and the Parks Advisory Committee nervous. There were serious considerations of scrapping the whole host program over liability concerns. Park staff suggested mandatory health screening for park hosts, but such screenings would have stood on tenuous legal ground even before the passage of the 1990 Americans with Disabilities Act. More serious consideration was given to pursuing the exemption of park hosts from Workers Compensation laws. There was precedent for this, both in the national Domestic Volunteer Service and in state-level volunteers at ski areas or sporting events. But in the end, the employees and advisors at Oregon State Parks and Recreation accepted the hosts as essential *and* unpaid workers, covered as such.[235]

And it was clear by the end of 1984 that the expansion of the volunteer program was a runaway success from a management perspective. As park administrator Steve Johansen tabulated the hours put in and the tasks done, he estimated that volunteers had done work "equating to nearly 31 full-time positions." But, as he proclaimed,

> *[t]he real value of the program, beyond the money saved, is the positive response of the public to the volunteers, such as the park hosts, and the enjoyment the volunteer themselves receive from performing this service.*

Leadership across parks agreed, proclaiming that despite "great initial reluctance" the program quickly drew "universal rave reviews." The rise of volunteers had enabled parks to do more with less, and had helped to build out a constituency to fight for park programs. Many of the initial worries about the program faded. The worries about workers' comp faded as problems remained minimal. Visitor satisfaction with cleanliness remained high even after volun-

---

234   State Parks and Recreation Advisory Committee meeting minutes, Feb 25, 1982, p. 2, Folder: Advisory Committee Minutes & Actions 1981 – 1989; State Parks and Recreation Advisory Committee meeting minutes, Dec 3, 1982, pp. 2 and 6, *ibid*; State Parks and Recreation Advisory Committee meeting minutes, June 16, 1982, pp. 3 – 5, *ibid*; State Parks and Recreation Advisory Committee meeting minutes, Dec. 9, 1983, p. 6,*ibid*; State Parks and Recreation Advisory Committee meeting minutes, Dec. 2, 1986, p. 2, *ibid*.

235   State Parks and Recreation Advisory Committee meeting minutes, April 17, 1984, p. 3, Folder: Advisory Committee Minutes & Actions 1981 – 1989; Legislative Council Committee, *ORS 656.027* (2019), **https://www.oregonlegislature.gov/bills_laws/ors/ors656.html**; U.S. Government Printing "Compilation of the Domestic Volunteer Service Act of 1973 As Amended Through December 31, 1987," Serial 100-F (Washington, D.C.: U.S. Government Printing Office, 1988).

Volunteers, and especially campground hosts, have become indispensable to park operations.

teers took over many of the on-the-ground responsibilities for park cleaning and maintenance. From interpretation to guidance to restroom maintenance, the volunteer program was flush with success without costing much money—only a little training, a free campsite, and (as the official 2013 park host guide put it) "recognition[, which] is indeed a volunteer's pay."[236]

But free labor often means fewer jobs. Some, perhaps much, of the 31-full-time-positions-worth of work done by volunteers in 1984 would never have been done without them. With budgets tight, volunteers filled in the gaps. The more than 30 Parks jobs that were eliminated between 1980 and 1984 would never return. The success of volunteer programs and other means of bringing "free" labor to the parks (see Chapter 6) may well have whittled down how many paid positions there could be. Even as visitor numbers rebounded and reached new heights by 1988, staffing did not fully recover, much less expand

---

236 State Parks and Recreation Advisory Committee meeting minutes, Dec 11, 1984, p. 7, Advisory Committee Minutes & Actions 1981 – 1989, Oregon State Parks and Recreation Collection; Parks and Recreation Division, Department of Transportation, "Oregon State Parks Visitor Survey, 1984," (Winter, 1984),p. 17; "Volunteers and Constituency," 1, Folder: The Governor's Conference on State Parks, 1985, Box: Meetings and Events, Oregon State Parks and Recreation Collection; Oregon Parks and Recreation Department, "Oregon State Parks Host Program," p. 7 (Jan 2013), **https://stateparks.oregon.gov/ckfiles/files/2013_parkhostprgmbasics.pdf**.

to keep up with unprecedented demand. Volunteer hours did increase, with the hosts alone now doing work equivalent to roughly 50 full-time positions, and numerous other volunteers providing free labor for trailblazing, interpretive work, and numerous other tasks. The parks could not go on without them.[237]

The move to volunteers let state parks keep running after funding had fallen. And despite the stutters of the early 1980s and the anti-government tenor of the times, parks remained popular. Unbowed by the "bloody beating" of twelve years of increasing austerity, in 1984 park boosters and personnel began gathering allies for a new campaign. Talbot dreamed of volunteer groups with a membership of thousands ready to "go to war" for the park system. The budget battles to come would be more grueling than he had dreamed.

Up Until Now, Everything Has Been Okay:
Burnt Toast and Town Halls

As the national economic crises began to ease in 1984, Oregon Parks and Recreation pushed for an end to the austerity. Parks budgets had been slashed time and time again since the late 1960s, and had almost been bled dry by the early 1980s. Like Boardman before him, Talbot knew that public relations were a key to park success. Boardman, who had spent his tender years wandering the great outdoors, played the part of a lone philosopher, sending wisdom and wisecracks into the newspapers. Talbot, a track-and-field champion in his youth, launched a sort of democratic decathlon to win over the public. Staff, donors, the Committee, the community, and Talbot himself would each have roles to play. The sparse Parks successes of recent years had typically come from one of two paths. Sometimes a specific project was pushed past the finish line because it had enough champions. Other times, a particular park issue became an emergency, and that urgency moved the needle at the last second. Now the task was to frame the many issues plaguing Oregon State Parks as a single grand project and a singular emergency—and to bring enough champions on board to solve it all.[238]

One element of the strategy was what became known as the "Burnt Toast Tour." For six months between 1984 and 1985, Dave Talbot embarked on a media marathon. He visited at least 22 Oregon communities, convened 13 open "Town Hall" meetings, and did enough interviews to flood the airwaves and

---

237 2010 Citizen Advisory Committee, "Oregon State Parks 2010 Plan" (Salem: Oregon Parks and Recreation Division, Department of Transportation, 1988): 20 and 48, Box: Strategic Plans 1956 – 2012, Oregon State Parks and Recreation Collection; Carol Jusenius Romero, "The Economics of Volunteerism: A Review," in *America's Aging: Productive Roles in an Older Society* (Washington, D.C.: National Academy Press, 1986): pp. 23 – 50; Dylan Lewis, "Unpaid Protectors: Volunteerism and the Diminishing Role of Federal Responsibility in the National Park Service," in *Protected Areas in a Changing World: Proceedings of the 2013 George Wright Society Conference on Parks, Protected Areas, and Cultural sites*, Samantha Weber, ed. (Hancock, MI: George Wright Society, 2014): pp. 95 – 100. The implications of a cause and effect between the volunteers taking over duties that had previously been done by paid employees and the continued reduction in paid positions that had previously included those duties are put forward by the authors alone (based on conjecture, implication, and evidence from sources primary and secondary), and do not necessarily reflect the views of OPRD, the Oregon Public Employees Union, or any other body.

238 University of Oregon, *Oregana,* ed. Sue French (Eugene: University of Oregon Student Publications Board, 1956), pp. 307, 310.

op-ed pages with parks business. Field and headquarters personnel worked behind the scenes to make sure the tour would be well-attended and well-covered: distributing surveys and fliers, prodding reporters, and calling up anyone who had expressed an interest in attending. When one early meeting attendant was asked how he'd heard of the event, he said:

> *Well, I read it in our local newspaper, heard it on the radio, received a personal letter from your administrator, and had two telephone calls yesterday from local field people wanting to make sure I know about the meeting tonight and that I was planning to attend.*[239]

Through the dogged work of parks personnel, the "Burnt Toast Tour" drew 745 people from 82 different Oregon communities to the "Town Halls," with thousands more hearing about the events from newspapers, radio, or television. The "Burnt Toast" moniker came from the anecdote with which Talbot started most of the meetings:

> *There once was a five year old boy who had never uttered a word....*

> *At the breakfast table one morning, like a bolt from the blue, the lad spoke his first words ever: "This toast is burned."*

> *His mother, recovering from a near faint, let out a scream of joy, hugged her son and asked why he had never spoken before.*

> *"Up until now, everything has been OK," he said.*[240]

In other words, Parks was speaking out because there was a crisis. The budget crisis that had been building for the better part of a decade would finally get attention.

The "Burnt Toast Tour" was billed as a community problem-solving event, where Talbot would outline the problem parks had and solicit solutions from the public. "We'll provide the questions," a flyer for the Newport Town Hall read, "you bring the answers." And parks staff did collect plenty of answers, from surveys handed at the townhall and distributed across the state. Talbot was in part applying lessons he'd learned on "Stub" Stewart's party bus back in the 1960s. Coming face-to-face with people in their own communities mattered. "DAVE TALBOT, state parks administrator[,] will be there to listen to you and answer your questions," the flyer concluded. Having the head of Oregon Parks and Recreation explain the problem personally, it was hoped, would help to build a constituency.[241]

---

239 "The Future of Oregon State Parks... The Town Hall Tour" (1985), p. 7, Folder: Governor's Conference on State Parks, 1985, Box: Meetings and Events, Oregon State Parks and Recreation Collection.

240 "The Future of Oregon State Parks... The Town Hall Tour" (1985), p. 1.

241 "The Future of Oregon State Parks... The Town Hall Tour" (1985), attachment 1.

In fact, the meetings were less about getting answers than educating about the problem and figuring out which answers would be acceptable. Using flipcharts on a display easel to work through the studies that parks had already done, sometime standing on tables in his shirtsleeves to be seen, Talbot made the case that the park system in Oregon was critically underfunded, and needed both more General Fund money for the present and some special source of funding (to replace the gas tax) for the future. He went through alternatives for funding, then opened the floor for questions and comments. As staff later reported:

> *Participants suggested dozens of ways to raise money, took*
> *exception (usually in a good natured way) to some existing policies*
> *and procedures, debated without resolving some continuing*
> *problem areas, and pledged time after time to do whatever is*
> *necessary to maintain and improve Oregon State Parks.*[242]

Few new ideas came to light in these "Town Halls." But they were highly effective in raising awareness, within and beyond the meetings, that Oregon Parks and Recreation had a budget problem that was not of their own making. The attendees were not average Oregonians—they were those people who chose to spend a night out of their week listening and talking about Oregon State Parks problems and solutions. Although Talbot and others would sometimes use the survey responses from these meetings as a proxy for the wishes of Oregonians generally, this was more a matter of bad statistics and/or good PR than fact.[243]

A majority of those surveyed would have agreed with Boardman about everything but camping. Large majorities favored stronger preservation efforts, above any other question of priorities. Nature was the most important thing, but about two-thirds of those surveyed also wanted more interpretation and history. A bare majority of 51% were in favor of selling books on Oregon history in parks, but every other possible commercial activity drew more negative than positive responses. Respondents were particularly disdainful of "Gift shops" (78% opposed), "Fast food service" (82% opposed), and "Full service restaurants" (84% opposed). Boardman's line against hot dog water, it seemed, would hold.[244]

Although an earnest desire to protect the natural world motivated town hall attendees, in appeals to the legislature and the governor parks people leaned on the bottom line: State parks bring in more money than they cost. Since the time of Robert Sawyer, a central argument for the expansion of Oregon State Parks has been the tourist and visitor dollars they bring to the surrounding areas. From 1959 on, report after report has backed up this argument with facts. Armstrong and Astrup's Progress Reports had pointed to profits. Visitor surveys included calculations of how much the draw of park had spurred tourist

---

242 "The Future of Oregon State Parks... The Town Hall Tour" (1985), p. 9,

243 "The Future of Oregon State Parks... The Town Hall Tour" (1985), pp. 7 – 8.

244 "The Future of Oregon State Parks... The Town Hall Tour" (1985), attachment 3, Folder: Governor's Conference on State Parks, 1985, Box: Meetings and Events, Oregon State Parks and Recreation Collection.

State Parks Director Dave Talbot, making the case to the public in 1985.

spending locally. Research in the 1980s corroborated all that had come before. The fact that money spent on state parks bring a net profit to the state as a whole has seldom been sufficient to prevent budget cuts. But it was enough, in the business-minded 1980s, to bring Governor Victor Atiyeh on side. The promise of tourist dollars and the momentum of "Burnt Toast" were enough to convince Atiyeh to call for a "Governor's Conference on State Parks," bringing together stakeholders, by the end of 1985.[245]

When the time arrived, Recreation Director Kathryn Straton kicked things off. She had been recommending something like the town halls since at least 1980, and had years of experience shaping the message of Oregon state parks for the public. Like Talbot, she focused her comments on the problem of money. Parks were popular, but popularity wasn't enough to pay the bills. Where could the money come from?[246]

This time, checking in on the neighbors suggested a clearer solution. When the Parks Advisory Committee had consulted with neighboring states in the 1950s (see Chapter 3), they had found no obvious model to replicate in Oregon. Now,

---

245 Advanced Studies Unit, "The Economic Value of State Parks in Oregon, 1959," (Salem: Oregon State Parks & Recreation Division, Oregon State Highway Dept, 1959); Chester H. Armstrong and Mark H. Astrup, "1960 Progress Report," (Salem: Oregon State Parks & Recreation Division, Oregon State Highway Dept, 1961): 20, Box: Progress Reports 1959 – 2003, Oregon State Parks and Recreation Collection; "The State Park Visitor in Oregon: A Report on 1964 State Park Travel and Use Survey," esp. 8 – 11, Folder: Publications – Administrative—Visitor Surveys, Box: Publications—Rules, Surveys, and Reports, Oregon Parks and Recreation Collection.

246 Kathryn Straton to All Participants in the Montgomery Report Meetings, Feb 17, 1981, Folder: Outdoor Recreation Planning 1980s, Box: Meetings and Events, Oregon State Parks and Recreation Collection.

as Kathryn Straton argued before the 1985 Governor's Committee, the model was clear: "more *general* funds ought to support the system," because "*general* Oregon citizens as well as the specific park users benefitted from it" [emphasis in the original]. Oregon State Parks at the time received a low 19% of their budget from the General Fund, whereas Idaho received 39%, Washington 65%, and California (peak oil production notwithstanding) 60%.[247] Straton's focus on the "general Oregon citizens" was not (just) a fun play on words. It reflected the many duties of Oregon State Parks and Recreation beyond the "recreation" for which admission could be charged, particularly preservation. "We protect a lot of land purely for scenic, historical[,] or natural resource purposes," Straton explained. "[B]ut there is no way to recover those costs through user fees." Some things could not be nickel and dimed.[248]

Oregon State Parks faced two related problems from budget shortfalls: there was not enough money to perform existing duties, and practically none to continue acquisitions to meet the evolving needs of Oregonians. Nickel and dime charges could fill in small gaps, but something bigger was needed. Parks leadership came to the 1985 Governor's conference with two potential strategies. Should parks get more money from the General Fund, to raise Oregon to parity with neighboring states? Or should there be a push for some special funding source, like the oil money that had funded California parks in an earlier era?

Both! A culmination of the plan to reframe the story of Oregon State Parks came in 1987, when a Citizen Committee spent the better part of the year crafting a blueprint for parks for the next two decades. The Oregon State Parks 2010 Plan, which was published in 1988, gave an ambitious overview of the problems and solutions facing the division. Money remained central, with an array of budget fixes large and small suggested. But the 2010 Plan also generated the best data the division had ever gotten on usage, and brought together the disparate dreams that had been collected over the years.

A Vision without a Task Is a Dream:
The Citizen Committee Gets Down in the Weeds

The Oregon State Parks 2010 Plan tried to build support and appeal through data and specifics. Parks, after all, were already popular in theory. The work was in showing what had to be done, how much it would cost, and why it mattered. After gathering all the necessary expenses together under one mantle, the writers of the report could then speak to budget solutions. If the myriad issues were framed this way *and* solved, the division could move past scattershot nickels and dimes to a more stable source of funding.

One central building block of the plan was an enormous set of surveys. A survey of visitors to parks in July and August of 1988 netted 18,000 completed

247 Kathryn Straton, "Amended Speech Draft," Nov. 27, 1985, pp. 1 – 2, Folder: Governor's Conference on State Parks, 1985, Box: Meetings and Events, Oregon State Parks and Recreation Collection.

248 *Ibid*, 2.

questionnaires. There was also a phone-and-mail survey in 1986 and 1987, which got detailed opinions on recreation from a little more than 2,000 Oregonians. Both surveys were rigorous compared to what had come before, with very high response rates for the targeted populations.[249]

They found a population with a wide mix of interests, but more room for rest and reverence than had been recorded in the ad hoc surveys of the 1960s and 70s. "Loafing" had topped the activity list back in 1963, and its less judgmental equivalent "Relaxing" still topped the list in 1988—tied with "Viewing scenery" at 81% of all visitors. "Solitude" was enjoyed by 69%, whereas "Getting together with friends" came in for 56%. Boardman's dream of quiet contemplation still held sway for many.

Visitor surveys had been standard since Armstrong, but the State Parks 2010 Citizen Committee was unprecedented in the scope and range of its inquiry. In an "eleven-month, whirlwind schedule" of meeting, tours, and hearings, they took in the thoughts of hundreds of Oregonians, read the survey responses of hundreds more, and spoke to staff and volunteers at every level. They inspected not only current parks and future sites, but campsites, restrooms, sewer treatment facilities, and structures half-consumed by dry rot after almost two decades of deferred maintenance. It was the most comprehensive investigation of Oregon State Parks and Recreation yet attempted.[250]

That time on the ground showed. The top priority, the Citizen Committee insisted, had to be "[t]he rehabilitation or replacement of existing park facilities." In the 1980s, when any park expenditure needed a champion, the unglamorous work of upkeep had been deferred again and again. Previous top-down charges had often begun and ended with a single "grand scheme" (as Talbot put it). This time, the Citizen Committee had spent time in the proverbial trenches, and they knew "maintenance and rehabilitation of the system [had] been compromised." Big dreams needed to be built on a stable foundation—with working bathrooms and rot-free walls.[251]

Most of the recommendations boiled down to "more, please." More parks, more trails, more history. More, in other words, of what park personnel had already identified as necessary but impossible with the budget as it was, in meeting after meeting, report after report, standing in front of the governor or standing on top of tables. Carefully phrased over several pages, the main finding of the Citizen Committee had already been summed up by Talbot almost a decade before: "People love parks—we need and deserve it—give us more money."[252]

---

249 The visitor survey had a return rate of about 60%, the phone-and-mail survey of a little over 70%. The response rates in previous surveys seem to have been much lower and/or unrecorded. 2010 Citizen Advisory Committee, "Oregon State Parks 2010 Plan" (Salem: Oregon Parks and Recreation Division, Department of Transportation, 1988): 12 – 13, Box: Strategic Plans 1956 – 2012, Oregon State Parks and Recreation Collection.

250 2010 Citizen Advisory Committee, "Oregon State Parks 2010 Plan," 5.

251 Talbot, "Personal Views on the Development of Oregon State Parks," May 16, 1990, p. 87; 2010 Citizen Advisory Committee, "Oregon State Parks 2010 Plan," 7 and 18.

252 State Parks and Recreation Advisory Committee meeting minutes, Feb 25, 1982, p. 2, Folder: Advisory Committee Minutes & Actions 1981 – 1989.

A newer element the Citizen Committee added was marketing. There had been parks advertising for decades, from simple billboards, to governor sloganeering, to 30 second TV spots featuring mostly silence and trees (perhaps even Boardman might have approved). But the Citizen Committee recommended Oregon Parks and Recreation market not only its parks but itself. "[E]ducate Oregonians about their park system," the Citizen Committee instructed. "Emphasize the value of the park system as a market for attracting tourists... [and] as a crucial part of the state's livability." A major way to "enhance revenues to help the park system perform its mission" was to educate Oregonians about what that mission was and how much it helped the state. [253] The plan reached a crescendo that balanced hope with crisis:

> As State Parks approaches its 60th* birthday with a history of great success and public support, we can't help but reflect on the fact that the system has been dormant for more than a decade—no new parks, no new campgrounds, no new programs. The legacy of Oregon State Parks is clearly in jeopardy....
>
> [T]he time has come for a major, new parks program... State Parks has the people, the resources, the skills and the vision to begin to meet the challenges of the future. What is needed is the support and financial backing from Oregonians to make the 2010 proposals a reality.[254]

This was the core intervention of the 2010 plan. Rather than a "grand scheme" around a single big idea, like a coastline or a river, the plan was more a grand bundle, a thousand and one things that could be done to bring Oregon parks closer to their potential. All that was needed was funding—"$3.40 each year" for each Oregonian.

Could they replace the nickel-and-dime with the big ticket? The 2010 plan was meant as blueprint for the future, but it was also hoped that bringing all of the major needs under one roof would allow for a clearer path towards paying for them. If parks supporters could get the right raise support for the right targeted tax, or get the right levy passed, the years of triage could finally end. The focus on specifics and process, it was believed, would help make the case.

The 2010 Plan was distilled into a glossy brochure that meshed inspirational quotes with specific actions. The cover page read, "A vision without a task is a dream," a quote sometimes ascribed to Jessie Honeyman back in the 1930s.

---

253 2010 Citizen Advisory Committee, "Oregon State Parks 2010 Plan," 10.,

254 The notion that there were *no* new parks or programs was an exaggeration, one that echoed what Talbot had been saying for years at this point. Although there had been a few additions to parks in the 1980s, the rhetorical weight of "no" outweighed the more accurate blandness of "few." 2010 Citizen Advisory Committee, "Oregon State Parks 2010 Plan," 10. *The 60th birthday celebration posited Sam Boardman's ascension to superintendency in 1929 as a sort of Year Zero, with all state parks activity before that consigned to an earlier era of darkness. See especially Elisabeth Walton Potter to Craig Tutor, cc Jim Lockwood and James Hamrick [email], Dec 1 1999, Folder: Tracing the Origins of OPRD, Box: Park History, Oregon Parks and Recreation Collection.

The rest distilled the wonky specifics of the full plan to a collection of major points, beautiful pictures, a long Boardman quotation (of course), and maxims of varying quality—leading up to "a vision with a task is victory." The only missing ingredient was money.[255]

In 1989, as this new fight for park funding began in earnest, the possibility of new independent department came unexpectedly to the fore. When the 2010 Plan began to seem difficult to pursue under the mantle of ODOT, independence came through in a matter of months with little debate (see Chapter 6). At long last in 1990, there would be an independent Oregon Parks and Recreation Department. Every previous move toward autonomy had been met with incidental disaster. The creation of a distinct Parks division in 1973 had coincided with the slide into years of austerity. Becoming a co-equal branch of the Department of Transportation in 1979 had also marked the end of the gas tax moneys and the beginning of even harder times. But maybe this time would be different. Writing to staff about impending independence in 1990, Director Dave Talbot praised them for their efforts during the "turbulence and change" of the prior decades, and expressed his hope that the inauguration of the new Oregon Parks and Recreation Department would mark the end of the hard times.

But there was much, much more turbulence and change ahead.

"Independence" meant turbulence and change, but it also meant cake.

255 "Oregon State Parks 2010 Plan" brochure (1989?), Box: Strategic Plans, Oregon State Parks and Recreation Collection; Lynn Newbry to "Friends of Oregon State Parks," Jan 19, 1989 [public letter], Folder: Agency Publications, Box: Strategic Plans, Oregon State Parks and Recreation Collection.

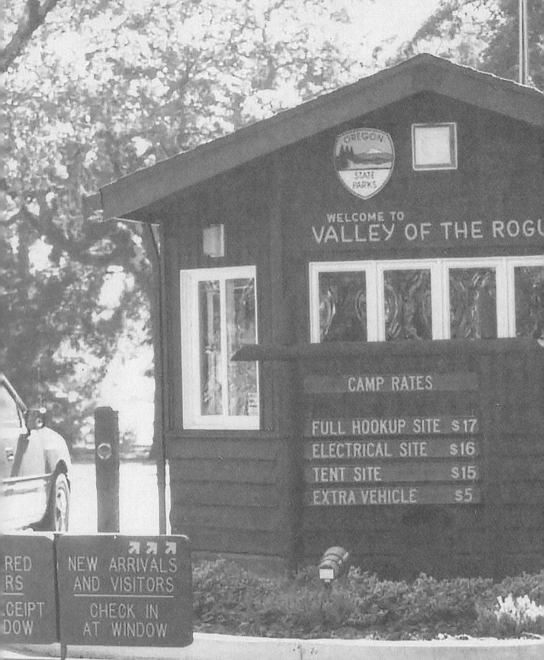

Valley of the Rogue, 1990's

CHAPTER 6

Rising to the Challenge:
Desperate Measures and the Search for Stable Funding

On the morning of August 2, 1989, the new and independent Oregon Parks and Recreation Department was born. A picnic bench was brought from Champoeg to Salem for the signing of the bill that made it so, and a crowd of 500 feasted on a purportedly 250-pound cake shaped like the state of Oregon—"hyped as Oregon's largest birthday cake." Similar festivities at a smaller scale were arranged at parks across the state. Celebrating the 60-year anniversary of Sam Boardman's appointment as Parks Engineer as well as impending independence, many hoped more distance from the Department of Transportation would help turn the corner after two decades under siege. The new Oregon Parks and Recreation Department (OPRD) officially became an independent state agency on Jan 1, 1990. But the search for stable funding that had consumed the 1980s would continue.[256]

Public opinion shaped Oregon parks in the 1990s even more than it had in previous decades. Building public engagement and support had always been a priority. But in this new decade, public ballot measures shaped how the parks would be run, how they would be funded, and at times even threatened their ability to operate. The decade opened with catastrophic losses, with funding for government slashed in 1990 and move to fund parks through new gas taxes decisively rejected in 1992. Unprecedented layoffs, innovations in funding, new volunteer initiatives, and more troubling labor practices followed. But the period closed with measured success. In 1998, Oregonians definitively demonstrated their support for parks by mandating for them a dedicated portion of lottery funding. In the 1990s, then, parks turned around an almost three-decade drought and found funding through popular demand. But the search for stability, in funding as in so many other park matters, was still ceaseless.[257]

---

256 Via: Oregon Department Transportation 14:9 (Sept, 1989), p. 4; Via: Oregon Department Transportation 14:8 (August 1989), p. 1; Monte Turner to Parks 60th Anniversary Committee, "Proposals from Brainstorming Sessions Celebration of Parks 60th Anniversary" [e-mail], June 1, 1989, Folder: Folder: Tracing the Origins of OPRD 60th Anniversary Observed 1989, Box: Park Histories, Oregon Parks and Recreation Collection, Oregon Parks and Recreation Department, Salem, OR. Accounts of the weight of the cake vary wildly, in part because the plans for its size kept getting bigger and bigger. Neil Goldschmidt, the governor of Oregon from 1987 – 1991, later confessed to having committed third degree rape over a period of years. Because of this history, and relatively peripheral position Goldschmidt has in the narrative of this book, we have chosen not to name him in the text. See Nigel Jaquiss, "The 30-Year Secret: A Crime, a Cover-Up, and the Way It Shaped Oregon," Willamette Week May 12, 2004.

257 William M. Lunch, "Budgeting by Initiative: An Oxymoron," Willamette Law Review 34:663 (1998): pp. 663-674.

It's Not a Divorce:
Parks and Highways Split Up

In truth, Parks and Highways had only stayed together so long because of the money. When the relationship began in the 1910s and 20s, parks had been seen as an outgrowth of movement for beautiful roadways (see Chapter 1). But almost from the beginning, the main reason to keep the two together was funding. Sharing a department could mean sharing costs, with engineers, scientists, and lumbermen able to work for parks and highways alike. And it could mean keeping parks away from the worst of the budget cuts. Highways got a lion's share of the gas tax, and the scraps left for state parks had still been enough to fund basic operations even in the leanest of times. This sense of security had sunk Boardman's dream of his own department, hovered over the committee decisions to keep parks with highways in the 1950s, and blunted Talbot's early efforts at independence (see Chapters 2, 3, and 5). But, as Kathryn Straton proclaimed in 1985, the "Highways/Parks relationship ended in 1980 when Oregonians voted to restrict gas taxes to highway purposes only."

With the main reason to stay together gone, all that was needed was a push. Asked if an independent department would help bring park goals to fruition, Talbot said yes. In 1989, with relatively little debate or resistance, independence was achieved. Boardman's appointment in 1929 was elevated to the "official" start of the department, in part to make the year 1989 an important anniversary, news media was contacted to make new independence part of the story of a (hopefully) rising parks department, and it was off to the races. With fanfare and cake, the new Oregon Parks and Recreation Department was celebrated in the capital, in newspapers, and in parks across the state.[258]

"It's not a divorce," Talbot proclaimed to park and highway employees alike shortly before the split in 1989. "We're not pulling away from our ODOT relationship," he promised highway personnel just after the new Division was formed in 1990. And it *was* a relatively amiable separation, with ODOT and OPRD continuing to work closely together through the 1990s and beyond, as they figured who would get assets, and where OPRD would have to begin spending independently for services they once shared with ODOT. But the die was cast. Later executives were less starry-eyed. "It's taken 13 years to finalize the divorce," Assistant Director Jana Tindall would announce in 2003, as the last of the shared administrative mechanisms fell away. The severance may have been friendly, but it was fundamental.[259]

---

258 Kathryn Straton, "Amended Speech Draft," Nov. 27, 1985, pp. 3, Folder: Governor's Conference on State Parks, 1985, Box: Meetings and Events, Oregon State Parks and Recreation Collection; Folder: Richard D. Dunlap, "Economic Benefits: State Parks Relation to State Highway Dept.," Box: Legislation and Statutes, Oregon Parks and Recreation Collection.

259 *Via: Oregon Department Transportation* 14:8 (Aug 1989), p. 3; *Via: Oregon Department of Transportation* 15:1 (Jan 1990), p. 5; Robert L. Meinen, "Interview Transcription," Interview with Elisabeth Walton Potter, Apr 28, 2000, p. 22, Folder: Kate Schutt Records, Oregon Parks and Recreation Digital Archive. Anita Lanning, State Parks and Recreation Commission Meeting Minutes, March 25, 1993, pp. 7 – 8, Folder: Commission Meeting Notes [1990 – 2013], unfiled, Oregon State Parks and Recreation Digital Collection; *FYI* 489 (May 31, 2003).

The new Oregon Parks and Recreation Department (OPRD) was not much different from the old Division. The lines of authority were simpler. Superintendent Talbot had reported to both a Transportation Commission and a Parks Advisory Committee. Newly minted Director Talbot reported soley to the new State Parks Commission. But in practice, life on the ground in Parks remained the same. A few key members of the old Committee, like Loran Stewart and Lynn Newbry, stayed on to assist the new Commission. And though they had more power in theory, in practice they still left the day-to-day business of Parks largely in the hands of the Director and the Department.[260]

The first months of independence in 1990 seemed encouraging. Parks might not have been viewed as essential infrastructure in the same way highways were, but state parks remained generally popular on both sides of the still-growing urban/rural divide in Oregon. General Fund support for the ambitious goals of the 2010 Plan was still only a dream, and no separate source of funding had gained sufficient political momentum. But OPRD was at least set to get enough money for basic operations in this first year. Urban economies in Oregon had recovered, there was a plan in place for sustainable growth, and there was more measurable political and popular support for parks than there had been in years.[261]

Dave Talbot was at the apex of his career in 1990, seemingly preparing for golden years ahead. Twenty-six years into his 28-year career, he was at the time the longest-serving state park head in the country. He sat down for extended interviews about the past, present, and future of Oregon State Parks, which would shape every history of the institution to follow. And (like Boardman before him) Talbot was awarded the prestigious Pugsley medal, a recognition for outstanding accomplishments in U.S. parks and conservation. But he was too busy to travel across the country to receive this award in person. Trouble on the horizon was brewing.[262]

Foundations Seem to Be Eroding Beneath You:
Measure 5 Slashes State Funding

Passed in 1990, Measure 5 gutted state government. The state constitutional amendment capped property taxes throughout Oregon, reducing by tens of millions the amount of money that would be in the General Fund. Voted in primarily by residents of the greater Portland area dismayed at the effect rising housing costs might have on their tax burden, Measure 5 achieved a long-standing goal of the same anti-tax movement that had kicked Parks out of the gas

---

260 Anita Lanning, State Parks and Recreation Commission Meeting Minutes, Feb 20, 1990, esp. 3, Folder: Commission Meeting Notes [1990 – 2013].

261 Lanning, State Parks and Recreation Commission Meeting Minutes, Feb 20, 1990; Josh Leshner, "Oregon's Great Recession Update," *Oregon Office of Economic Analysis*, June 29, 2015.

262 Folder: Administrative History – Oral History – David G. Talbot, Director, 1964 – 1992 [entire], Box: Staff Biographies and Oral Histories, Oregon State Parks and Recreation Collection; John Crompton, David G. Talbot Pugsley Award Bio, ~1992?, **https://aapra.org/pugsley-bios/david-g-talbot**.

Measure No. 5 STATE OF OREGON

Proposed by initiative petition to be voted on at the general election, November 6, 1990.

BALLOT TITLE

5 STATE CONSTITUTIONAL LIMIT ON PROPERTY TAXES FOR SCHOOLS, GOVERNMENT OPERATIONS

YES ☐

QUESTION Shall constitution set limits on property taxes, and dedicate them to fund public schools and non-school government operations?

NO ☐

SUMMARY Amends constitution. Limits 1991-1992 property taxes for public schools to $15, and property taxes for non-school government operations to $10 per $1000 of market value. Schools limit gradually decreases to $5 per $1000 in 1995-1996 and after. Government operations limit remains same. Limits do not apply to government assessments, service charges, taxes to pay certain government bonds. Assessments, service charges shall not exceed cost of making improvements, providing services. General Fund to replace, until 1996, school funds lost due to school limits.

ESTIMATE OF FINANCIAL EFFECT—

AN ACT
Be It Enacted by the People of the State of Oregon:

PARAGRAPH 1. The Constitution of the State of Oregon is amended by creating a new section to be added to and made a part of Article XI and to read:

SECTION 11b. (1) During and after the fiscal year 1991-92, taxes imposed upon any property shall be separated into two

1990's Measure 5 "gutted state government," including the shoestring Parks budget. Anti-tax sentiment seemed firmly ensconced in Oregon politics.

tax in 1980. Tapping into deep wells of local discontent, bankrolled by wealthy interests within and beyond the state, anti-tax ballot measures were a crowning achievement of a broader anti-government political revolution in 1990s Oregon. Although a majority of Oregonians* saw little to no tax relief from Measure 5, it did sharply cut the tax burden on businesses and wealthier homeowners. The measure sent shockwaves through the state and sharply reduced the amount of tax income available for government services. The whole of government, not just parks, would now have to "learn how to live with less."[263]

The main focus of debates on Measure 5 was school funding, a huge portion of the state budget and the main reason repeated efforts at the same sort of measure in the 1980s had failed. Mechanisms that purportedly protected school funding were built into Measure 5. Nonetheless, school funding per capita did decrease for most K – 12 districts (and all state colleges) over the course of the 1990s—but

263 Richard J. Ellis, *Democratic Delusions: The Initiative Process in America* (Lawrence: University of Kansas Press, 2002), esp. 2 – 24; Lawrence M. Lipin and William Lunch, "Moralistic Direct Democracy: Political Insurgents, Religion, and the State in Twentieth-Century Oregon," *Oregon Historical Quarterly* 110:4 (2009): pp. 514 – 545; Richard A. Clucas, Brent S. Steel, and Mark Henkels, *Oregon Politics and Government: Progressives versus Conservative Populists* (Lincoln: University of Nebraska Press, 2005), chap. 18. *Determining who has received tax relief from a particular measure is difficult and contentious. Based on the gross homeownership rate and adjusting for second homes, non-dependent cohabitants, prisoners, etc., a little over half of all Oregonians were homeowners in 1990. Most saw little to no property tax relief until 1997, and even then many homeowners in populous Multnomah County saw none. U.S. Census Bureau, Housing and Household Statistics Division, "Historical Census of Housing Tables [1940 – 2010]," (Oct 2011); Jed Kolko, "Why the Homeownership Rate Is Misleading," *New York Times* Jan 30, 2014; Robyn L. Cohen, "Prisoners In 1990," *Bureau of Justice Statistics Bulletin* (U.S. Government Printing Office, May 1991); Tom Linhares, *Recent History of Oregon's Property Tax System, with an Emphasis On Its Impact On Multnomah County Local Governments*, ed. Elizabeth Provost (Self-published, 2011). It is true that *overall* Oregonian tax burdens went down significantly because of Measure 5, but only a (sizable) minority of wealthier Oregonians have enjoyed those reductions. Much of the coverage of the pros and cons of Measure 5 elides this distinction, and ignores all non-homeowning Oregonians: see for example the editorials written by wealthy Oregonian Mark Zusman, "Nov. 6, 1990: Voters approve Measure 5...," *Willamette Week* Nov 4, 2014 AND June 2, 2017.

then, funding for almost every department decreased. Parks were a tiny part of the budget compared to schools, but parks were like schools in that they were broadly popular. Anti-government advocates in the 90s thus tended to argue that OPRD should somehow be more efficient rather than arguing that they should reduce or change their services. Or advocates would bring up the much-feared power of eminent domain, which had stoked so much backlash against the Willamette Greenway—and which had not been used by parks since at least the 1970s.[264]

This was not the first time Oregon State Parks had run into anti-government sentiment. Within and beyond the department, from the "party bus" to the political committees, from boots on the ground to Talbot on the tables, park employees, managers, Commission members, and outside boosters had built support for state parks across many conventional political lines. Heading toward his retirement in 1992, Talbot thought that much of the anti-government sentiment could be countered through outreach:

> *Much of the negativism of many intelligent people who felt this way reflected their ignorance of the process. Most could not identify their elected representative, had no understanding of how they were taxed, how their taxes were spent, or how laws were made.*[265]

Whatever the truth (or condescension) of this assertion, it summed up the approach Oregon Parks and Recreation took under Talbot. This had been a central premise of the 2010 Plan. The solutions proposed there were not internal changes but external funding, with support built through outreach and education. Talbot and the other people at parks had reason to believe that outreach was working. Every survey they had taken indicated broad support for parks. The visitor surveys, particularly, indicated strong support for new taxes to keep and improve Oregon State Parks.

Faced with a gaping new hole blown in an already tight budget, parks supporters scrambling to find new money to fill the gap. In 1992, friends in the Oregon Legislature put forward two measures to fund parks for the present and (hopefully) support for the future that had been sketched out at the end of the 1980s. One measure proposed bonds for state park improvements, allowing infrastructure repair and creation through borrowing. The other proposed a potential restoration of the gas tax that had been lost in 1977 and severed

264 Rob Manning, "Oregon School Funding Still a Challenge, 25 Years After Measure 5," *OPB* Apr 15/19, 2016; Nancy McCarthy, "Ballot Measures Seek Funds for State Parks," *Oregonian* Sept 23, 1992, p. C07. By the 1990s, eminent domain was by unofficial parks policy a never-used tool. See Anita Lanning, State Parks and Recreation Commission Meeting Minutes, Feb 20, 1990, p. 6, Folder: Commission Meeting Notes [1990 – 2013]. The quotation at the head of this section comes from Gregory Smith, "Living with Oregon's Measure 5: The Costs of Property Tax Relief in Two Suburban Elementary Schools," *Phi Delta Kappan* 76:6 (1995): pp. 4452 – 4461. Measure 5 increased state control of local school districts, reduced the money available for schools per capita, and equalized unstable funding between urban and rural districts. This meant funding increased for some rural districts, decreased for others, and decreased substantially for most urban districts. Dee Lane and Erin Hoover, "School District's Cuts Nick Everyone," *Oregonian* March 20, 1994, p. A01.

265 John Crompton, David G. Talbot Pugsley Award Bio, ~1992?, **https://aapra.org/pugsley-bios/david-g-talbot**.

permanently in 1980: an additional 2 cents per gallon charge on gas. Either would have kept parks afloat. Both would have allowed them to move forward.

"[U]nlike most new government proposals, this one's already worked once," the *Oregonian* said in an editorial arguing in favor of the potential gas tax increase for parks. And it was "about the only state government contribution [tourists] make." Monte Turner, Oregon State Parks spokesman, warned that increased fees and/or closed parks would be inevitable without some increase of funding. But unlike the Good Roads organizations of the 1910s and 1920s, the Oregonians for Good Roads in 1992 campaigned against park funding through gas taxes. And the anti-tax forces seemed to be the driving force of the political moment.[266]

The proposed parks tax was shellacked. Almost three in four Oregonians voted against a fuel tax increase for parks. By a narrower but still clear margin, the bond measure was voted down too. Visitor surveys had shown strong support for both—but the enthusiasm of park visitors was not, in 1992, a match for the anti-tax instincts of Oregonians generally. Talbot had retired in June 1992, but he was far from gone. As the budget crunch increased and the costs of deferred maintenance towered ever larger, Talbot would be working outside of the department as a private citizen to help marshal the "army for parks" he'd hoped for as Director. His immediate successor was Nancy Rockwell, who had just transferred from the Department of Energy and took over as first Acting Director and then Deputy Director.[267]

Talbot's permanent replacement was Robert "Bob" Meinen, who had managed state park systems in Idaho and Kansas before coming to Oregon. He had been a young Business major drawn to Natural Resources (and then state parks) by his love of the outdoors. Perhaps it was that start in business that inflected Meinen's focus on partnership, public relations, and above all the bottom line. The need for a "stable, long-term funding source" had been his mantra when in Idaho and Kansas, and the search for stable funding would be at the core of Meinen's mission throughout his time at Oregon Parks and Recreation.[268]

266 "Yes on Measure 2," *Oregonian* Oct 17, 1992, p. B06; McCarthy, "Ballot Measures Seek Funds for State Parks."

267 Anita Lanning, State Parks and Recreation Commission Conference Call Meeting Minutes, July 1, 1992, p. 1, Folder: Commission Meeting Notes [1990 – 2013]; Anita Lanning, State Parks and Recreation Commission Meeting Minutes, May 9, 1991, p. 8, *ibid*. Judging by some internal documents, many parks staff struggled with the disconnect between the desires of self-selecting survey respondents and those of the average Oregon voter. See especially the description of the 1992 proposed gas tax in "Long-Term Stable Funding Options" [internal memo, 1996], Folder: Administrative – Park Issues – Park Closures – Resolution, Box: Park Issues – Park Closures and Funding Crisis, Oregon Parks and Recreation Collection.

268 Meinen, "Interview Transcription," 20 – 21; "Local Man Shares Story of Saving Mesa Falls," *Rexburg Standard Journal* Aug 25, 2017; United States Senate, *City of Rocks National Reserve Act of 1987: Hearing Before the Subcommittee on Public Lands, National Parks, and Forests of the Committee on Energy and Natural Resources…*, (Washington, D.C.: U.S. Government Printing Office, 1988), pp. 17 – 19; Rick Just, "Robert Meinen and Idaho State Parks," Interview with Marc James Carpenter [phone], July 15, 2020, unfiled, Oregon Parks and Recreation Digital Collection; Mary Kay Spanbauer, "Kansas & The President's Commission On Americans Outdoors," *Kansas Wildlife & Parks* 45:6 (Nov/Dec 1988): pp. 39 – 43, quote on 40.

A More Business-Driven Organization:
Turning Visitors into Customers

Bob Meinen was the most divisive leader Oregon Parks and Recreation had in a hundred years. He took over a dilapidated, demoralized, and defunded department late in 1992. When Meinen left under a cloud of controversy in 2000 (see Chapter 7), the department was on firmer financial footing than it had been since the 1970s. The years in between marked existential crises for Oregon state parks. The economic crises that had plagued parks intensified. In the lowest points of 1996 it appeared that much of the system might simply shut down. And within and between economic shocks, there was a cultural crisis. Meinen and his leadership team ran Oregon state parks more like a business, and with that pivot came tectonic cultural and economic shifts.

The shift toward business didn't come out of nowhere. The calls from the 1900s and 1910s on to recognize the extent to which parks brought tourist dollars to the state had been a business-minded strategy. Armstrong had highlighted business potential in the 1950s. The Citizen Committee that created the 2010 Plan in 1988 had paid significant heed to business trends, including the creation of a mission statement. Like those of the corporate world it emulated, this statement was more comprehensive than catchy. State parks would, they declared:

> provide, protect and enhance sites and areas of outstanding natural, scenic, cultural, historic or recreational value for the enjoyment and education of present and future generations of Oregonians and their visitors.[269]

Meinen—and the executive team he quickly assembled—rebranded "visitors" to "customers," and parks to products. "Customer service" was now the watchword in communications with staff, and "put[ting] out a better product" the preoccupation of management. The reverence for nature Boardman had preached would be still be maintained—at precisely the level customers and the "brand identity" of Oregon state parks demanded.[270]

This new focus on business-mindedness was a form of (re)branding in and of itself. A master goal of Meinen's management team in their first few years was to "[d]evelop a lean, well-managed agency that is mission-drive[n] *and is viewed as such* by the public and the Legislature" [emphasis added]. The popularity of parks had not been enough to spur new funding in part because opponents had

---

269 2010 Citizen Advisory Committee, "Oregon State Parks 2010 Plan" (Salem: Oregon Parks and Recreation Division, Department of Transportation, 1988), p. 4, Box: Strategic Plans 1956 – 2012, Oregon State Parks and Recreation Collection.

270 *FYI* 56 (1994); *FYI* 103 (July 21, 1995); Robert L. Meinen, "Interview Transcription," Interview with Elisabeth Walton Potter, Apr 28, 2000, Folder: Kate Schutt Records, Oregon Parks and Recreation Digital Archive. Meinen and his team referred to "customers" rather than "visitors" practically from the start, but for the updated mission statement they eliminated "Oregonians and their visitors" altogether (along with the goal of "enhancement").

painted the department as too bureaucratic or too spendthrift. Under Meinen, the department intended to show that it meant business.[271]

The cultural pivot to a more business-oriented atmosphere was vivid in the minds of those who lived through it. Talbot had mourned the loss of family feeling in parks when interviewed in 1990. But survey respondents in 2013, including those who had been with parks since the 1970s, nearly all identified the Meinen era, rather than the times of Talbot, as when the culture shifted away from a parks family and toward a parks business. They might disagree on the effects of the change, but not on the substance. For many personnel, like the three quoted below, the sense of a "parks family" was irrevocably altered:

> *[Department culture] was more family oriented, but tightly dictated/control[l]ed in the early years... It has turned more [into a] business driven organization with the guidance being left to the individual, but more freedom in that work.*

> *It used to be a big family, Dave Talbot knew everyone's name, and your kids['] names... Now everyone is too busy to even make a trip out to the field from Salem [Headquarters]... We have employees that haven't been to hardly any parks, they sit in their cube and work on putting stuff from the in basket to the out basket, go home and don't visit parks on their time off.*

> *The culture[e] was a "family" when I started[,] with lo[n]g-term employees and a closely held executive level. Transitioned to less of a family and more to a team and partnership of internal and external members.*[272]

And those were the opinions of park workers who *didn't* lose their jobs amidst the cutbacks of the 90s.

There had been significant job losses under Talbot. Under Meinen, layoffs went from last resort to logistical routine. He and his team framed the elimination of positions as an advance rather than a failure. Under euphemisms like "salary savings" and "reorganization," OPRD put forward the perhaps-unavoidable staff reductions as proof that they were a "lean, well-managed agency" that could not afford further cutbacks.[273]

---

271 Anita Lanning, Oregon Parks and Recreation Commission Workshop Minutes, Feb 23, 1995, Folder: Commission Meeting Notes [1990 – 2013]. The "lean, well-managed agency" was mentioned as a carried-over goal, one that went back to at least 1994 and perhaps earlier.

272 Because of the sensitivity of the data and the method of collection, identifiers for the 2013 survey of parks employees are not used here. "Draft OPRD History Questionnaire, 1990 – Present [2013]," p. 29, Folder: Kate Schutt Records – More Kate Schutt Records, Oregon Parks and Recreation Digital Archive.

273 Davan Maharaj, "In The 1990s, Layoffs Become A Business Strategy," *L.A. Times* Dec 13, 1998; Anita Lanning, Oregon Parks and Recreation Commission Workshop Minutes, Feb 23, 1995, esp. 4, Folder: Commission Meeting Notes [1990 – 2013].

The most dramatic set of layoffs came in May of 1994. A reorganization had been underway since January. Facing a formidable budget gap, park managers were summoned to the Silver Falls conference center, a building that was beginning to crumble from years of deferred maintenance. They took part in a three-day workshop and brainstorming session, discussing how to reorganize, reinvent, and reinvigorate Oregon state parks using business principles.

Then they were all fired.

Meinen and his team eliminated a layer of management, and created a smaller number of jobs managing multiple parks that the original managers could now reapply for. Interviews were "like the Spanish Inquisition," one of the managers who survived recalled. "It was just short of waterboarding," another reflected. Most people were not rehired for management positions. Many retired, or quit. These and other reorganizations (with smaller but still significant layoffs) shook the whole department throughout 1994 to 1996—"They were all scared they were next," as one senior parks person put it a decade later. These staff shake ups were perhaps always part of the plan. Meinen had overseen a similar series of reorganizations and layoffs when he was in charge at Kansas State Parks back in the late 1980s.[274]

Brian Booth, Chairman of the Parks Commission, voiced concern at the beginning of 1995. Given "all of the changes over the past year," how did Meinen "perceive... staff morale"? According to the minutes of the meeting:

> *Meinen said he believes morale is good within the department and that there seems to be a sense of excitement within the new management team created out of the reorganization. He reported at an all-managers meeting held in December, managers welcomed the idea of entrepreneurial budgeting with enthusiasm.*
>
> *Meinen said it was also necessary at this time to advise the Commission of the potential strike in the early summer.[275]*

The two-week strike, part of a broader statewide labor issue, suggested that perhaps morale wasn't *universally* "good within the department." But Meinen was no doubt correct about the "sense of excitement" expressed by the new management team. Those who might still have hesitated or expressed reluctance about "entrepreneurial budgeting" had already been purged before 1995. Back in the

---

274 Annual [OPRD] Chronology 1990 – 2013, Folder: Kate Schutt Records, Oregon Parks and Recreation Digital Archive; "OPERATIONS DIVISION/AREA MANAGER MEETING Silver Falls May 17 – 19," *FYI* 42 (May 1994); *FYI* 43 (1994), pp. 3 – 5; "OPRD History Panel Discussion," Interviewer - Kathy Schutt, pp. 3 - 4, December 2012, Folder: Kate Schutt Records, Oregon Parks and Recreation Digital Collection. *Kansas Wildlife and Parks* 45:5 (Sept/Oct 1988), p. 23. This pattern may have held in Idaho as well. One of Meinen's first acts after moving from Deputy Director to Director of Idaho State Parks in 1984 was to eliminate the deputy director position he had ascended from entirely. Just, "Robert Meinen and Idaho State Parks."

275 Anita Lanning, Oregon Parks and Recreation Commission Workshop Minutes, Feb 23, 1995, p. 4, Folder: Commission Meeting Notes [1990 – 2013].

1960s, Talbot had wrestled with a culture clash between the opinions of old guard and the new direction in which he wanted to take the department, slowly integrating the new and the old over a couple of decades. Meinen fired anyone not on board, transforming the management of the department in the course of only a few years. It was just business.

Revenues… Are Everyone's Burden!:
New Fees and New Ideas

With General Fund contributions sputtering out and no dedicated source of funding available, OPRD under Meinen imposed new fees and searched for new revenue streams. Day use parking fees, long perceived as poisonous by park backers, were rolled out in many parks by 1993 and expanded in the years to follow. Camping fees increased, sometimes putting campsite costs above those of private campgrounds. Rangers were provided with brochures to hand out to anyone protesting these increases, explaining the loss of General Fund money and comparing park recreation costs to the price of dinner and a show. These were added to a suite of other promotional brochures, pointing out the many budget concerns and benefits of Oregon state parks. The push for parks to market themselves that had been suggested by the Citizen Committee in 1988 was now institutional. Such brochures, employees were told, had "been used by Disney Corp. and other companies to promote better customer service." In the newly business-oriented parks, that was practically a benediction.[276]

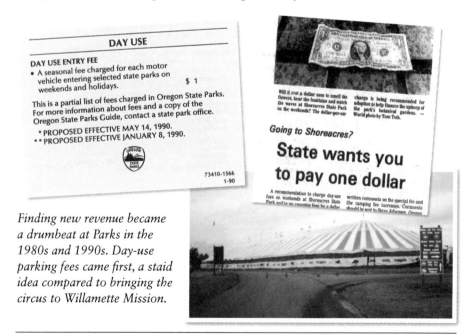

Finding new revenue became a drumbeat at Parks in the 1980s and 1990s. Day-use parking fees came first, a staid idea compared to bringing the circus to Willamette Mission.

---

276 Anita Lanning, State Parks and Recreation Commission Conference Call Meeting Minutes, July 1, 1992, Folder: Commission Meeting Notes [1990 – 2013]; *FYI* 98 (June 19, 1995); *FYI* 56 (1994).

Park staff at every level were asked to find cost savings and new ways of bringing in money. As Nancy Rockwell wrote in a typically chipper all-staff message:

> *If we are going to operate more business-like then we have to take responsibility for both sides of the ledger – expenditures and revenues. Revenues have been the burden of a selected few in the past. Now they are everyone's burden!* [277]

"It went," as one participant later recalled, "from a rigid system to the Wild West." A few parks opened espresso stands. One sold beanie babies.[278] There were implementations of modern conveniences once shunned by Boardman-esque park personnel—cable TV hookups, say.[279] And there were massive technological undertakings, like the move to a two-state phone reservation system that centralized reservations (see Chapter 7).

Many changes were minor efficiency improvements, ideas that might come from above or below to reduce redundancy or shave off unnecessary services. Messages from management tended to mix praise with menace. "[M]ost staff found they were well equipped to think like business people trying to squeeze the most from the least," Rockwell announced in the intradepartmental newsletter *FYI* late in 1994. "In some cases we will need to evaluate staff skills and abilities in order to determine how we will alter staffing to meet these new needs," Meinen menaced a few months later, in 1995. "One of the keys to the department's financial survival," Meinen wrote during the worst of the crisis in 1996, "will be our ability to take one dollar and turn it into two." Jobs were on the line. [280]

This might have given Craig Tutor an extra thrill of relief when his zany notion to build Mongolia-inspired fixed-frame tents in parks turned out to be a marquee moneymaker for the department.

YURT ALERT!:
Expansions in Camping

The wordplay was almost irresistible. From the moment Craig Tutor first introduced yurts to Oregon state parks in 1994, visitors and staff alike had fun with the rhyme schemes. "YURT ALERT!" was the title of the first *FYI* article announcing the installation of new round tents in several state parks.[281]

---

277 Nancy Rockwell, "Director's Corner," *FYI* 115 (Nov 2, 1995).

278 "OPRD History Panel Discussion," Interviewer - Kathy Schutt, p. 6, December 2012, Folder: Kate Schutt Records, Oregon Parks and Recreation Digital Collection.

279 Anita Lanning, Oregon Parks and Recreation Commission Meeting Minutes, Jan 12, 1995, p. 7; *FYI* 89 (Apr 7, 1995).

280 *FYI* 138 (Apr 6, 1996); *FYI* 73 (1994); Bob Meinen to All Salem Managers, March 20 1995, *FYI* 87 (March 24, 1995).

281 *FYI* 56 (1994). In later years more strained rhymes like "yurtin' for certain" were suggested, only to be killed in the editorial stage. Jean Thompson, personal communication, July 24 2020.

As the new lodgings took off among visitors, so did the rhymes, include whole stanzas of doggerel verse:

> *With your walls and ceiling, nature's wrath you avert;*
> *rendering wind and rain powerless, inert.*
> *I can roam around inside in my boxers and shirt;*
> *Oh, how I do love my warm little yurt.*[282]

After the success of Tutor's pilot program at Cape Lookout State Park, yurts became a symbol of Oregon State Parks in the 1990s. The park information booth at the Oregon State Fair in 1994 was a yurt. The roll-out of yurts in seven new state parks attracted enough attention that Honeyman State Park hosted an "open yurt" event that October, where press and the public could walk around the new structure. Attention went national, with a New York Times article on the Honeyman yurts inspiring people across the country to reserve a yurt in Oregon. Other press coverage, local and national, followed. Securing a loan through the newly-created Oregon State Parks Trust, the department put up fifty more yurts—and counting—by the spring of 1996. They filled too. Yurts became the success story of Oregon parks in the mid-90s, earning innovation awards, national attention, and (vitally) bringing in profits at a time when park budgets were desperate for pennies.[283]

Why yurts? Charming design elements and the potential for wordplay undoubtedly played a role in news coverage, but the new lodgings also suited the needs of the moment. As state parks had to rely more and more on user fees in the 1990s, park officials and commission members agreed that camping needed to go year-round wherever possible. Discounted rates for off-season camping would both bring in more visitors and soften the blow of necessary fee hikes that came in the mid-90s. But the off-season was off for a reason; many tent campers were reluctant to go camping amidst sleet, rain, and snow. Yurts provided a possible answer. Originally engineered for the driving winds and cold winters of the Mongolian steppe, they provided a way for would-be campers to enjoy state parks at times when "nature's wrath"—or at least nature's distemper—might otherwise have prevented a visit. And once they were on the scene, they became even more popular in the summers, filling a niche between primitive camping and motorized recreational vehicles.[284]

Yurts unlocked a flood of alternative camping arrangements. Back when the 2010 Plan was first developed, the 1988 Citizens Committee had identified a need to "do some innovative testing of new ideas, such as tent cabins or other rustic facilities." The runaway success of yurts proved the potential effectiveness of

---

282 *FYI* 205 (Aug 8, 1997). The original poem has five stanzas, with another five in the sequel.

283 *FYI* 56 (1994); *FYI* 66 (1994); Susan G. Hauser, "A Bit of Mongolia In Oregon," Jan 1, 1995; *FYI* 72 (Jan 6, 1995); *FYI* 137 (March 29, 1996); *FYI* 317 (Nov 26, 1999).

284 *FYI* 90 (Feb 14, 1995); Helen Caple, "Playing with Words and Pictures: Intersemiosis In a New Genre," PhD diss., University of Sydney, 2009, chap. 4; *FYI* 62 (1994); Bob Meinen to All Salem Managers, March 20 1995, *FYI* 87 (March 24, 1995); Nancy Rockwell, "Deputy Director Comments," *FYI* 105 (Aug 4, 1995); "Yurts Make Winter Camping Easy in Oregon and Washington," *Seattle Times* Nov 16, 2008.

Make your own yurt!

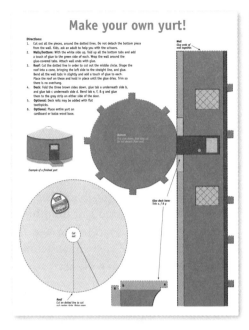

Yurts were so popular that volunteers got in on the action, creating a paper yurt cutout for kids.

"rustic" arrangements. Farewell Bend State Recreation Area installed two covered wagons that had been transformed into cabins in 1995. How did staff explain the feasibility of these new rustic options? "The wagons are tent structures, built similar in concept to yurts." The next year, they installed rentable "tepees," with a few other parks following their lead. How rustic yurts really were is debatable— many yurts had not only electricity but TV hookups (where "junior and squirt" could "sit... down to watch Ernie and Burt"). But they demonstrated that there was a market for what Tutor called "no-fuss camping facilities," which gave at least the impression of rusticity.[285]

Yurts were not a cure-all. Although they quickly became a critical and profitable part of the park system, significant upfront prices plus substantial maintenance and cleaning costs made them only one part of a desperate puzzle. Yurts expanded at a time when "turbulence and change" were reaching new heights at Oregon Parks and Recreation, with churning layoffs, low morale, and a stark budget cliff looming. Along with a critical fresh funding source, yurts allowed OPRD a new narrative. The yurt stories painted Oregon state parks as innovative, quirky, adventuresome, and successful. As parks leadership took the fight for public relations and message discipline to new heights in the 90s, this was a cherished narrative to have.[286]

285 2010 Citizen Advisory Committee, "Oregon State Parks 2010 Plan" (Salem: Oregon Parks and Recreation Division, Department of Transportation, 1988): 8, Box: Strategic Plans 1956 – 2012, Oregon State Parks and Recreation Collection; *FYI* 113 (Sept 29, 1995); *FYI* 141 (Apr 25, 1996); *FYI* 205 (Aug 8, 1997); Kristin Jackson, "Oregon Coast — Shelter from The Storm — Staying In A Yurt In Fort Stevens State Park," *Seattle Times* Oct 8, 1997.

286 Jean Thompson in Becky Kemery, *Yurts: Living in the Round* (Salt Lake City: Gibbs Smith, 2006), pp. 82 – 84; Doug Beghtel, "Yakking about Yurts," *Oregonian* Nov 15, 2007; Jamie Hale, "How Yurts Helped Save Oregon State Parks," *Oregonian* Dec 15 2019 AND Jan 23, 2020.

To Keep the System Alive:
Free and Unfree Labor for Oregon State Parks

Volunteers had been a vital part of Oregon state parks since before the beginning. Volunteers and donors had carried the system through the 1980s. As funding got even scarcer in the 1990s, parks people pushed for more assistance. In the 1990s, volunteer programs were expanded, new donor networks were built, and work-hours were solicited from other government-funded entities. One of the best ways to "turn one dollar into two" was to get work or land for no dollars at all.

Donor management had been a central part of the job for Boardman and Talbot alike. The shadow mission of the old Parks Committee had been fund-raising and the cultivation of donors. The same held true for Meinen and the new Parks Commission. From the start, Meinen was aggressive about acquisition. Even in times of extraordinary financial stress, when layoffs seemed unavoidable and maintenance was turning critical, Meinen focused on continuing at least some level of acquisition, largely or entirely through donations of land and money.

Meinen had a tool that the Superintendents of years past did not. Talbot had retired from the job, but not the fight for funding. In 1995, the Oregon Parks Trust was formed with Talbot at the head. Meinen had facilitated a similar Idaho Heritage Trust for historic preservation in that state, and Talbot had long dreamed of an umbrella organization coordinating park boosters. A legally separate entity from OPRD, the Parks Trust acted as a fundraiser and advocate for park issues. They raised hundreds of thousands of dollars from organizations and individuals, some of which would have been unlikely to support a government agency directly. They bought land for parks, covered budget gaps, and purchased yurts. The Parks Trust also quarterbacked many of the fights for funding from 1996 to 1998 [see below]. At times the Parks Trust was too close to the department: a later audit found that their entanglement had bordered on illicit, citing in particular a sweetheart yurt leasing deal Meinen had brokered to provide the trust with much of its early operating capital. But whatever its initial indiscretions, the Parks Trust enabled a greater coordination of donor and supporters than had previously been possible.[287]

Existing volunteer programs continued and expanded. The budget crisis was getting worse, and the outcry against it getting organized. This new attention brought new volunteers and partnerships to parks. "In the face of ebbing financial support for state parks," one new family of volunteers said, "all Oregonians

---

287 Just, "Robert Meinen and Idaho State Parks"; It bears noting that the Audits division found "the courtesies and cooperation extended by the officials and staff... commendable and much appreciated." No punitive action was recommended, and auditors agreed that none of the indiscretions had been in pursuit of personal gain. Oregon Audits Division, "State of Oregon Parks and Recreation Department: Review of the Department's Relationship with the Oregon State Parks Trust," John N. Lattimer, Director, No. 1999-27 (Aug 5, 1999), pp. viii, 16 – 17, 28.

need to become advocates for their public recreational areas." More people than ever would be needed, another said, just "to keep the system alive."[288]

In addition to expansions of scale, there were also expansions into new kinds of volunteering and workshares. In 1996, Safety Coordinator Mary Bachurin made official the program that placed Oregon State Police cadets in parks for on-the-job patrol training. OPRD also worked with the Oregon State Police to develop "an all-volunteer state park patrol program." Citizen volunteers with official Parks jackets would patrol beaches along Highway 101 and "assist patrol officers in the detection of crimes," while still doing much of the same work with the public as other volunteers.[289]

OPRD collaborated with many other government agencies to get parks work done without parks monies. One area of growth was with the Oregon Youth Conservation Corps (OYCC). Patterned after the Civilian Conservation Corps of the 1930s (see Chapter 2), the Youth Conservation Corps movements attempted to give young people (especially those deemed at-risk) temporary jobs in outdoor settings. The Oregon Youth Corps had done work in state parks practically since its inception in 1987. Indeed, there had been a similar and more troubling program as far back as 1951, when "delinquent boys from Woodburn Boy's School" had been compelled to do park work for about one-sixth of the minimum wage for child laborers at the time.[290]

Unlike the "delinquent boys" of prior years, the young workers of all genders at the OYCC were paid a fair wage with government funds—but, importantly, not park funds. Using grants from other agencies and donations from the Parks Trust, Friends groups, and other organizations, Oregon youth worked in parks in many of the same ways the CCC had in years past. They built trails, crafted playgrounds, and took up small parts of the massive maintenance backlog. Some OYCC programs even delved into interpretation.[291]

The popularity of state parks made it easier to get help from other programs. The Oregon Youth Conservation Corps wasn't the only body to make the leap. The dislocated farm workers who got relief and jobs from the Oregon Human Development Corporation (OHDC) also ended working in parks, particularly in disaster relief after flooding in 1996 wrecked parks along with much of the rest of the state. "We knew the parks were a mess," OHDC director Jeanette Ewald said, "and when we called, OPRD seemed to jump with excitement." And indeed, parks management jumped at any chance to get parks work done without

288 Jackie Scott, "Volunteers Pitch in for the Gorge," *Oregonian* May 15, 1997; Joyzelle Davis, "Trail's End," *Oregonian* Sept 15, 1996, p. D01.

289 *FYI* 136 (March 22, 1996); *FYI* 169 (Nov 15, 1996).

290 C.H. Armstrong, "The Oregon State Parks in 1951," p. 1, Folder: Annual Report to NPS – Statistics, Acreage and Expenditures, Box: Chester H. Armstrong Papers; *Monthly Labor Review* 73:1 (Washington, D.C.: U.S. Government Printing Office, 1951), p. 687. It is unclear when the sub-minimum wage labor by incarcerated children in Oregon state parks ended.

291 *FYI* 86 (March 17, 1995); *FYI* 94 (May 19, 1995); *FYI* 239 (Apr 24, 1998). More recently the Oregon Youth Corps dropped "Conservation" from their title, to reflect the wider array of jobs now undertaken. We have kept the acronym here OYCC to reflect what the organization was called at the time.

blowing new holes in the smoldering crisis that was the budget. One of the bigger financial opportunities came in 1994, when Oregon voters demanded a vast expansion of the prison system in the state. Measure 11 introduced mandatory minimums, which rapidly increased the number of people incarcerated. Measure 17 attempted to turn this newly expanded pool of prisoners into a resource. [292]

Measure 17 required that prisoners in Oregon work full-time, and barred them from receiving pay for their labor. Compelling prisoners to work without pay in this manner was the only form of slavery specifically permitted by the 13th Amendment to the U.S. Constitution. It is unclear how many of the 71% of Oregonians who voted in favor of the measure realized it mandated slavery. The debate around Measure 17, and the abbreviated text on the ballot, was only about making prisoners work, and how much it would cost—though proponents did use the language barring inmates from being paid as a positive feature when pressing for the measure in some media.

Measure 17 was one of many Oregon ballot initiatives amidst the national "tough on crime" movement, which rested on the theory that crime rates could be reduced and society improved by locking up those convicted of crimes for as long as possible in conditions as harsh as possible. In practice, Department of Corrections (DoC) officials quietly avoided the mandate to enforce slavery, which they viewed as infeasible. Instead, the DoC attempted to obey the voter mandate to force prisoners to work, but indirectly continued to give prisoners wages—equivalent to one-tenth or less of the Oregon minimum wage.[293]

Oregon Parks and Recreation was the first state agency to take advantage of this new source of labor. There had been prison labor in the parks in one form or another since at least 1966, but not at this scale or with this much of the cost covered. After a slow start Meinen directed all managers "to evaluate projects that might be suitable for inmates in the parks, such as roof repairs, trail maintenance and the like…. [as well as] at work projects that might be suitable for work inside the prisons such as, making signs, picnic tables, and fire rings." [294] By 1996, prison work crews were taking care of long-neglected maintenance and

---

292 *FYI* 136 (March 22, 1996); Phil Manzano, "Oregon Voters Solidly Back Crime Initiatives," *Oregonian* Oct 13, 1994, p. B04. Measure 11 originally extended to juvenile offenders who were 15 years of age, amidst of a broader move in the 1990s to imprison children even for "relatively minor infractions" to "keeping budding criminals from blooming." See Nena Baker, "Criminal Kids: Who Goes to Jail?," *Oregonian* Dec 18, 1994, B01. See also Jaron Browne, "Rooted in Slavery: Prison Labor Exploitation," *Race, Poverty & the Environment* 17:1 (2020), pp. 78 – 80; Heather Ann Thompson, "Why Mass Incarceration Matters: Rethinking Crisis, Decline, and Transformation in Postwar American History," *Journal of American History* 97:3 (2010), pp. 703 – 734;

293 Dan Pens, "Oregon's Prison Slavocracy," *Prison Legal News*, May 15, 1998; Phil Manzano and Nena Baker, "Officials Await Fallout, Cost of Sentencing Measure," *Oregonian* Nov 10, 1994, p. C09; Rick Bella, "Corrections Director Blasts Get-Tough-On-Crime Measures," *Oregonian* Oct 25, 1994, p. D05; Phil Manzano and Ashbel Green, "Kitzhaber Accepts Resignation of State's Corrections Director Mark Wilson," *Oregonian* Jan 12, 1995; Michelle Roberts, "Fight Brews Over Inmate Work Program," *Oregonian* Dec 22, 1998, p. D01; "Oregon Prison Industry Program Nets Record $28.5 Million as Prisoners Earn $1.25/Hour," *Prison Legal News* Apr 2, 2019. This was not the first time enslaved felons had built parkland in Oregon—the early waysides along the Columbia River Highway were built by uncompensated compelled prison laborers. It bears mentioning that the "tough-on-crime" laws, in Oregon and nationally, had a disproportionate impact on people of color generally and Black people specifically. See also Michelle Alexander, *The New Jim Crow: Mass Incarceration in the Age of Colorblindness* (New York: The New Press, 2010).

294 *FYI* 118 (Nov 3, 1995).

repairs at several parks.[295] There was a backlash among some park employees on the ground, who feared an upcoming "replacement of parks staff with prisoners" that would mirror or exceed the replacement of paid labor with volunteers in the 1980s. Meinen denounced such speculation as unfounded rumor, and invited any employee with misgivings about the prison program to call him up if they "want[ed] the facts."[296]

The largest and most lasting move toward acquiring prison monies for park purposes was the Parks and Prisons Partnership program. This program brought millions of dollars of prison-manufactured goods to a cash-strapped OPRD. "Foundations, furniture[,] and 8 x 8-foot decks for the yurts" were the first marquee delivery, since prison labor allowed for a much quicker expansion into the hot item of the 1990s. Prison workers also constructed new fire rings, picnic tables, and signs, just as had been suggested. In a budget crunch brought on by both tax cuts and unfunded mandates, it made sense to park leaders to try and use money earmarked for prisons to pursue park goals.[297]

Fire rings and picnic tables made by prison labor rounded out the yurt package in the 1990s.

295 *FYI* 120 (Nov 16, 1995); *FYI* 132 (Feb 23, 1996); *FYI* 135 (March 15, 1996).

296 Oregon State Parks and Recreation Department, "Oregon State Parks in Peril: Public Forum 1996," p. 5 (pamphlet, 1996), Folder: Administrative – Park Issues – Park Closures – News Articles, Box: Park Issues – Closure and Funding Crisis, Oregon Parks and Recreation Collection; Robert L. Meinen, "Director's Column," *FYI* 166 (Oct 25, 1996).

297 *FYI* 225 (Jan 16, 1998). Prison labor also built the bookshelves upon which the Oregon Parks and Recreation Collection sits.

Prison labor is a thorny issue. Critics stress the harsh working conditions, substandard wages, the class and race biases that shape who goes to prison for how long, and practices that stray near—or sometimes into—slavery. Advocates assert the value of work, preach the potential to gain job skills, and point to the testimony of many prisoners who prefer underpaid work to idleness. Prison labor for Oregon parks was one of the better jobs available to the incarcerated, with a higher-than-average one-tenth of Oregon minimum wage as pay and (sometimes) a chance to work outside. For OPRD management in the 1990s, it was never a debate, at least not in public. There was too much to be done for not enough money, and any source of unpaid labor, free or unfree, was pounced upon.[298]

"You Need to Show Some Blood": The Threat of Park Closures

"Things are going to get even more intense," Bob Meinen warned in one of his messages to staff in 1995. "To survive, let alone flourish, in the years ahead, it will take each and every OPRD employee's effort." Acquisitions had been restarted with the help of the Oregon Parks Trust. The department had been rebranded with the help of yurts and business speak. But a "stable source of funding" seemed more remote than ever. In 1996, Oregon Parks and Recreation would turn to an option long contemplated but never enacted. Without more money, they warned, state parks would have to close. And this threat of closure would spark a sea change in the politics of parks.[299]

Park budgets in 1996 looked especially grim. The fee hikes of previous years had, as critics had warned, driven down visitor numbers. With the General Fund struggling to cover voter-mandated investments in schools and prisons, legislators had whittled away the money going to parks practically to nothing. And then there was the flood.[300]

In February of 1996, torrential downpours collided with historic snowpack to create the worst flooding in Oregon since at least the 1960s. Usually placid rivers raged, mudslides claimed whole neighborhoods, and flooding was everywhere. State parks were ravaged along with the rest. What remained of Rooster Rock State Park's beaches was a "myriad of twisted debris and dead trees," and many of the other parks with river frontage had issues just as severe. Millions of dollars of repairs were needed, with a budget already millions underwater. Park personnel managed to patch the system back together with FEMA funds, volunteer hours, and additional prison labor. But even with clean-up costs

---

298 David Leonhardt, "As Prison Labor Grows, So Does the Debate," *New York Times* March 19, 2000, p. A01; Chandra Bozelko and Ryan Lo, "The Real Reason Prisoners Are Striking," *Reuters* Sept 6, 2018; Sarah Shemkus, "Beyond Cheap Labor: Can Prison Work Programs Benefit Inmates?," *The Guardian* Dec 9, 2015; *FYI* 217 (Nov 7, 1997).

299 Robert L. Meinen, "Director's Corner," *FYI* 119 (Nov 9, 1995)

300 Bob Meinen to All Salem Managers, March 20 1995, *FYI* 87 (March 24, 1995).

(partially) covered, income from the flooded months of February and March was a total wash. Oregon Parks and Recreation entered the summer of 1996 an extra half million dollars in the hole.[301]

Parks leadership had been considering closures since the end of the gas tax. In December of 1981, the Parks Advisory Committee had contemplated park closures as a means of spurring the public into action. "You need to show some blood," committee member George Bell had argued, to shock the public into recognizing the funding crisis. In end, though, a coalition led by Lu Beck voted down the possibility of park closures. Better, they said, to avoid "'punishment cuts' to the public" that might raise ire rather than money, and better instead to find ways of "shortening our stirrups." Fifteen years of budget cuts, layoffs, and deferments followed.[302]

The new Parks Commission had also contemplated park closures. In Nancy Rockwell's first meeting as Acting Director in July, 1992, the Commission accurately predicted that the funding measures for that year were going to fail. If that happened, it was agreed, the Commission would "have to raise fees or close down parks." And "if the department threatens they intend to close parks based on budget decreases," Chairman Booth had cautioned at a later meeting with Meinen, "it must follow through and not be left with the image of crying wolf for no real cause."[303]

By June of 1996, the fees could go no higher, the stirrups could get no shorter, and the wolf was at the door. As Meinen and Rockwell put it in a letter to staff:

We have feared this day… we [have] tried to impress on you the serious problems we face. No matter how we cut the deck we still come up short. There simply are no more rabbits to pull from the hat. The reservoir of quick fixes is empty.

Staff layoffs and park closures are the only way we can curb the deficit problems we face.[304]

Facing a grim budget and a hostile legislature, Meinen, Rockwell, and the Parks Commission went nuclear. Closing down some parks to preserve the rest was a "last resort," Commission member (and future chair) Betsy McCool insisted. But the last resort had, at last, arrived. The idea of closures

301 Brian Meehan *et al*, "Too Much Rain, It's Plain," *Oregonian* Feb 7, 1996, p. A01; Dionne Peeples-Salah, "Little Left to Crow About at State Park," *Oregonian* Feb 20, 1996, p. B01; Peter Farrell, "Torrent of Figures Tote Flood's Costs and Keep On Rising," March 2, 1996.

302 State Parks and Recreation Advisory Committee Meeting Minutes, Dec. 3 – 4, 1981, pp. 8 – 9, Folder: Advisory Committee Minutes & Actions 1981 – 1989, Oregon State Parks and Recreation Collection.

303 Anita Lanning, State Parks and Recreation Commission Conference Call Meeting Minutes, July 1, 1992, Folder: Commission Meeting Notes [1990 – 2013]; Anita Lanning, Oregon Parks and Recreation Commission Workshop Minutes, Feb 23, 1995, p. 5, *ibid*.

304 Robert Meinen and Nancy Rockwell to All OPRD Staff, June 10, 1996, Folder: Administrative – Park Issues – Park Closures – Internal Communication, Box: Park Issues – Park Closures and Funding Crisis.

began to seem inevitable, with sad acceptance announced from Governor John Kitzhaber's office and cautious approval from Majority Leader Brady Adams in the state legislature.[305]

On June 19, 1996, the Parks Commission dropped the boom. No fewer than 60 parks across Oregon would close in September, with 11 more moving from year-long to seasonal service. And they warned that even more parks—between 17 and 30—were likely to close without further funding by the end of the year. "We have kind of done the easy one," Meinen primly noted to the press following the announcement. "The next round will probably have to take some serious looks at some of the major parks."[306]

Meinen and the Commission repeatedly asserted that they weren't "closing parks to outrage the public." And they certainly did not want to be perceived as trying to "outrage the public." Some in the Salem office were sure it was a "political strategy.... meant to force the public's hand." Many in the field saw the closures as real, a prelude to another devastating round of layoffs. Whether they were meant to provoke outrage or not, the announced closures set off an immediate firestorm. To paraphrase Talbot: *everyone* could smell the toast burning now.[307]

By June 20, Governor Kitzhaber was convening emergency meetings with the legislature to find the money to keep parks open. Senator Adams, as one newspaper phrased it, "reversed his support of the closure once he saw the hit list." And he wasn't alone. Once the threat of closures moved from abstract government cuts to the loss of specific parks, many state legislators were suddenly getting an earful from their constituents. [308] As one among the raft of editorials put it:

> *Perhaps the announced closures will do what the prospective threat didn't: Give political leaders and the public the message that wishful thinking has failed and concrete steps are needed to put the parks system on a stable financial base. We need to regain the quality system we had and want to have again.*[309]

The gambit had worked. Editorials in newspapers across the state declared that "Oregonians should be outraged" and "[s]tate parks desperately

---

305 Ashbel S. Green, "State May Fold Tent on Some Parks," *Oregonian* June 6, 1996.

306 Oregon Parks and Recreation Department, "Parks Placed on Future Closure List," Press Release June 19, 1996, Folder: Administrative – Park Issues – Park Closures – News Articles, Box: Park Issues – Closure and Funding Crisis, Oregon Parks and Recreation Collection; Ashbel S. Green, "State Closes 65 Parks, Eroding Beach Access," *Oregonian* June 20, 1996, p. A01. Ashbel Green counted campgrounds within those parks that were closing as separate parks when enumerating for his headline, and excluded parks that would close without partnerships entirely.

307 "State Park Closures" [internal report] (Nov. 18, 1996), Folder: Administrative – Park Issues – Park Closures – Internal Communication, Box: Park Issues – Park Closures and Funding Crisis; Suzanne Richards, "Parks and Piqued Public," *Oregonian* June 21, 1996, p. C02. Meinen asserted throughout this period that if the threatened closures had been primarily political, he would have "picked some major parks" to close. He also, it must be noted, warned that the closure of major parks remained an inevitability if the department did not receive financial relief. Green, "State Closes 65 Parks, Eroding Beach Access"; "OPRD History Panel Discussion" Interviewer - Kathy Schutt, Dec. 2012, Folder: Kate Schutt Records, Oregon Parks and Recreation Digital Collection.

308 Richards, "Parks and Piqued Public"; "A Political Quick Fix," *Redmond Spokesman* June 26, 1996.

309 "Don't Take Parks Apart," June 21, 1996, p. C10.

need a new, long-term stable source of funding." The "stable source of funding" that had been Meinen's mantra and Talbot's focus was now part of the political conversation.[310]

The stakes were high. Governor Kitzhaber wanted to use the pressure of the threatened closures to push for a long-term solution to state park funding. Senator Adams and the state legislature asked for time to work out a solution, and promised to bring forward emergency funding at the end of the year to cover any budget gap that keeping the threatened parks open would bring. OPRD and the Parks Commission fretted that leaving a budget hole in an election year might result in that promise evaporating once the election was concluded—especially if the legislature that had made the promise changed. On the other hand, closing parks even when future funding to keep them open had been proffered might turn the public outrage toward OPRD.

As they had throughout the year, Meinen and the rest of the executive team issued orders to everyone to hammer home the crisis. Area managers, still shaken from mass layoffs, had already been informed that outreach to legislators was part of their job. But parks people on every level were told to reach out in every possible way to communicate that "parks [were] in peril." The summer of 1996 saw another set of tours like Talbot's Burnt Toast tours a decade prior—though they were if anything even more scripted under Meinen. The main purpose was to inform concerned citizens of the dire state of park finances, and to gauge which funding schemes might be the most acceptable.[311]

Less than a month before the deadline, the Parks Commission took a gamble and announced that the threatened parks would stay open. "There's plenty of risk, but I think we need to rely on the good-faith assurance of elected leaders and that we have their attention," Chairman Booth said. "It's a horrible thing for Oregon to close its parks — the parks and beaches are the soul of Oregon." If the gamble failed, the budget gap would be even worse—possibly big enough to take down the whole park system. [312]

Meinen and Rockwell refused to let the pressure abate. Some staff worried that pushing the message of closure too hard might backfire. As Monte Turner put it, "I know we want to keep the pressure on, but I'm not ready for another tempest." But the executive team wanted to keep the message of hazard ongoing:[313]

310 "Parks Are Wrong Target," *Roseburg News-Review* June 21, 1996; "Parks Decline Is a Crime," *Daily Astorian* July 23, 1996.

311 OPRD, "Oregon State Parks in Peril"; Monte R. Turner to OPRD Staff, "Guidelines for Answering Calls/Questions" [e-mail], Nov 20, 1996, Folder: Administrative – Park Issues – Park Closures – Internal Communication, Box: Park Issues – Park Closures and Funding Crisis Mabel Royce, "Parks Department Meeting Was a Sham," Bay Area Dispatch n.d. (summer 1996?), Folder: Administrative – Park Issues – Park Closures – News Articles, Box: Park Issues – Closure and Funding Crisis.

312 Matea Gold, "State Puts Off Park Closures," *Oregonian* Aug 8, 1996; Tony Davis, "Parks Will Stay Open 3 Months," *Statesman Journal* Aug 8, 1996.

313 Nancy L. Rockwell to Area Managers, "Closure Signs" [e-mail], Aug 9, 1996, Folder: Administrative – Park Issues – Park Closures – Internal Communication; Monte Turner to Frank Howard, Nancy L. Rockwell, and Craig L. Tutor, "Scheduled to Be Closed Signs" [e-mail], Aug 9, 1996, *ibid*.

In an effort to keep financial problems in the consciousness of residents, visitors, and volunteers, signs will be installed… read[ing] "This property is scheduled to be closed this fall due to a lack of state funding."[314]

The risk and the outreach paid off. In the elections of 1996, state parks were part of the conversation in a way they hadn't been for decades. Promising to protect a beloved local state park, as it turned out, was an easy political position. The state legislature followed through, pushing through the allocation of enough emergency funds to close the budget gap of 1996 and keep the state park system going. But a longer-term solution was harder. Parks were one among "[m]any… competing interests" that were "very attractive," Senator Adams said. "But we just don't have enough money for everything."[315]

June 24, 1996: ominous headlines and a map of 64 parks on the chopping block.

---

314 Anita Lanning, Oregon Parks and Recreation Commission Workshop Minutes, Feb 23, 1995, p. 8; Public Services Section, OPRD, "Parks in Peril," *Co-Op Update* 3 (Aug 19, 1996), Folder: Administrative – Park Issues – Park Closures – News Articles, Box: Park Issues – Closure and Funding Crisis.

315 Ashbel S. Green, "Legislators Say They Won't Fold Parks' Tent," *Oregonian* Nov 14, 1996.

As 1997 began, Oregon state parks were in the public consciousness more than they had been for a generation. One of the policy priorities in Governor Kitzhaber's "State of the State" address was, for the first time, a call to "rebuild and retain one of the nation's great parks systems." But though OPRD had political attention and enough money to survive the moment, emergency measures were not a source of stable funding. "We are gaining ground," Meinen told staff, but "[w]e can not ease our relentless push forward. We must continue our efforts at the park and local levels that inform the public of our plight and what it will take to stabilize our condition." In the next two years, parks boosters and personnel would have to use the hard lessons of the last two decades to push for a more permanent solution. Where *could* the money come from? At long last, could public support for parks once again extend to public funding?[316]

Fine Words Don't Operate Parks:
The Army for Parks Assembles

Where could the money come from? Talbot's "Burnt Toast" tours and the 1988 Citizens' Committee had brainstormed all kinds of funding ideas. Some suggested taxes along the lines of those used to fund parks in other states, like a tax on real estate transfers or an (extra) tax on cigarettes. Some hoped to link taxes to those businesses state parks most benefitted—restaurant taxes, hotel taxes, or (additional) gas taxes. A few schemes would have opened whole new categories of product to taxation, like the quickly-squelched proposed taxes on sporting goods or video rentals.

But the proposals that got the most traction in the 1990s were those that extended existing government funding sources to parks. There were perennial calls for parks to get a greater proportion of the General Fund, especially as Oregon's General Fund provided an unusually small percentage of the state park budget. Some pushed for parks to get a piece of state lottery revenues, either directly or through bonds. And there was, most of all, a push to fund parks through expansion of the Bottle Bill.[317]

Getting tax money from soda and beer had been long-time favorite for parks boosters. This was the option that had gotten the most support in the townhall meetings of the 1980s, and had been put forward as one of the best options by the 1988 committee. Oregon had passed the first Bottle Bill in the nation in 1971, requiring customers to pay a "deposit" on bottles that could be redeemed if they returned the emptied containers for recycling. Oregon customers who resisted sales taxes generally were thus already used to paying a little extra for bottled products. And this extra was already associated with nature, as the bill had initially been passed to reduce littering and was associated with

---

316   John A. Kitzhaber, "The State of the State: Keeping Oregon's Quality of Life," (Salem, OR: Office of the Governor, Jan. 13, 1997); *FYI* 170 (Nov 22, 1996).

317   2010 Citizen Advisory Committee, "Oregon State Parks 2010 Plan," 61 – 62, 73.

Oregon's image of livability. In 1988, the Citizens' Committee had found that the addition of a mere 1-cent bottle tax would be enough to pay for everything that state parks needed.[318]

In the early 1990s, bottle money seemed like the answer for parks problems. Other states passed laws giving over a portion of bottle deposits to environmental causes in 1989 and 1990. By 1991, Dave Talbot was working Governor Barbara Roberts's staff to get a beverage tax through committee. "[T]his is our designated winner in terms of a parks funding source," he informed the Parks Commission. But that bill died before reaching the floor of the legislature. And despite strong support from parks boosters and a common-sense argument for success, similar bills in 1996 and 1997 followed suit. Soda taxes remained what park publications groan-inducingly referred to as the "stable funding source… 'Pop'ular choice" among park boosters, but were unable to gain purchase with the legislature. Even with Governor Kitzhaber's support for a 3-cent fee in 1997, beverages taxes for parks couldn't even get on the agenda.[319]

There was some hope in 1997 of an even older parks budget idea: more money from the General Fund. This was always a part of what parks boosters were pushing, and now, with parks in the public conversation again, Talbot's long-dreamed-of army of park supporters was taking shape. The Oregon State Parks Trust, coordinating with OPRD, spurred the development of a new umbrella organization. "SOS Parks!" coordinated a rally for state parks (and especially parks funding) in Salem on March 17, 1997.[320]

> Promises to keep the keep the parks open and running well raised cheers from the 400 placard-carrying parks boosters, including heavily badged Girl Scouts, buckskin-clad mountain men, Eddie Bauer-garbed mountaineers, hikers and canoers, and even the lady RVers in fashion print rain-coats."[321]

The parks rally was striking for its political breadth as much as its size. Buses brought in supporters from major population centers across the state, but folks from smaller communities also drove in to participate. It was, as newspapers at the time pointed out, a movement that sprang from popular demands

318 "CHAPTER 745: AN ACT [HB 1036] Relating to beverage containers; and providing penalties," *Oregon Laws and Resolutions: Enacted and Adopted by the Regular Session of the Fifty-sixth Legislative Assembly Beginning January 11 and Ending June 10 1971* (Salem, Oregon: Oregon Legislative Assembly, 1971); Richard J. Bacon, "Oregon's Bottle Bill: A Battle Between Conservation and Convenience," (Eugene: University of Oregon Scholars' Bank, 2005); 2010 Citizen Advisory Committee, "Oregon State Parks 2010 Plan," 62.

319 Brent Walth, "No Deposit, No Return: Richard Chambers, Tom McCall, and the Oregon Bottle Bill," *Oregon Historical Quarterly* 95:3 (1994): 278 – 299; Anita Lanning, State Parks and Recreation Commission Meeting Minutes, May 9, 1991; *FYI* 172 (Dec 13, 1996); Gail Kinsey Hill, "State Parks Could Be Rolling in Clover," *Oregonian* Jan 4, 1997, p. C01; Steve Suo and Gail Kinsey with Steven Carter and Nancy Mayer, "GOP Budget Cuts 280 Million," *Oregonian* March 6, 1997, p. A01.

320 *FYI* 183 (March 7, 1997); John Henrikson, "Oregon Park Lovers to Rally for More State Funding," *Statesman Journal* Aug 17, 1997. Some charged that the Oregon State Parks Trust and OPRD coordinated too closely. Oregon Audits Division, "State of Oregon Parks and Recreation Department: Review of the Department's Relationship with the Oregon State Parks Trust," John N. Lattimer, Director, No. 1999-27 (Aug 5, 1999).

321 Diane Dietz, "Politicians Take Parks Pledge," *Statesman Journal* March 18, 1997.

rather than business interests or political machinations. Speakers at the event crossed the political spectrum, with leaders from both sides of the political divide pledging to keep parks open. "It's obvious that more legislative members are recognizing the problems that exist today as a result of increased usage and reduced budgets," Dave Talbot said of the event and an ongoing letter-writing campaign that he helped coordinate. Talbot was gracious enough not to publicly dwell on the fact that he'd been saying as much for 20 years.[322]

All parties agreed on the merit of parks, but no single agreement on how to fund them emerged, at the rally or afterwards. "We've heard a lot of fine words," Chairman Brian Booth said of the vague political promises made at the rally. "But fine words don't operate parks." With the urging of the Parks Trust, SOS Parks!, and many others on what was colloquially known internally as the "Stable Funding mailing list," park people inside and outside of the program tried to keep the pressure on. The threat of closure had been delayed, not extinguished.[323]

Thousands of letters and petitions poured in from 1996 to 1998, to legislators across the state, to the governor, and to the Oregon Parks and Recreation Department. Some came from visitors who had used the state parks for decades, others from new arrivals. Particularly piquant letters were saved, like this one to Governor Kitzhaber:

> *This is my 5th year of girlscouts and almost every year I have gone to this campground which we call The Big Tree Campground [at LaPine State Recreation Area]. We have alot of fun with all the girlscouts that can come....*
>
> *I'm asking is just please don't shut down the Big Tree Campground*
>
> *If you do shut it down where do we all go? Will we all get to be together?*
>
> *PLEASE!*
>
> *We are willing to do anything to keep this Park open!!!*
>
> *PLEASE*
>
> *PLEASE Don't shut it down!!!*[324]

Most letters were answered, often by management figures. The message was always about the same: the legislature *must* "find a stable funding mechanism for the agency" to avoid a shutdown.[325]

---

322 Ashbel S. Green, "It's No Day at the Beach for Parks," Oregonian March 23, 1997, p. C02; FYI 189 (Apr 18, 1997).

323 Green, "It's No Day at the Beach for Parks;" Monte R. Turner to Nan E. Evans and Robert Meinen, "RE: Letter from Bob" [e-mail], Dec 5, 1996, Folder: Administrative – Park Issues – Park Closures – Internal Communication, Box: Park Issues – Closure and Funding Crisis.

324 Savanna Marsala to Governor Kitzhaber, [received] Oct 31, 1996, Folder: Administrative – Park Issues – Park Closures – Visitor Letters [but see entire folder], Box: Park Issues – Closure and Funding Crisis. Spelling errors preserved to maintain the twee character of the original.

325 Quotation in Craig Tutor to William Burnett, Feb 20, 1997, Folder: Administrative – Park Issues – Park Closures – Visitor Letters [but see entire folder].

In 1997, they didn't. But it was still the best year for Oregon state parks in a generation. Confronted by the "army for parks," the legislature doubled the General Fund contribution for the year, closed a few loopholes, and allowed for infrastructure bonds to be taken out against the profits of the Oregon State Lottery. For the first time in a long time, OPRD could begin to pick at the edges of a two-decade maintenance backlog. But there were concerns that the budget successes of 1997 would fade in future years, when public pressure for parks inevitably began to ease. What the department did not yet have was a source of *stable* funding.[326]

And despite the successes, there were still budget shortfalls in 1997, and with them the looming threat of layoffs. "We may not be flush, but we have a history of rising to challenges like these," Meinen proclaimed to surviving staff in Salem. "We won a battle, but we did not win the war."[327]

> [T]he truth is, without an appreciable, stable funding source, our parks don't have a positive future. Their existence will continue to be hardscrabble, and our ability to keep a viable park system will be compromised....
>
> Doing more with less will be our modus operandi for the next two years—some would say, "business as usual." [328]

Public outcry might not have been enough to push the legislature to impose a new tax for parks—even the relatively popular bottle tax, which was not put before the voters themselves. But shifts in public opinion did make proposals for mass closure of parks political poison. A legislative move in May of 1997 to divest from or close non-profitable state parks lasted less than a day—the idea of closing that many state parks couldn't make it into committee, much less onto the floor of the legislature. Faced with the refusal of the legislature and governor to agree on a source of stable funding for the department, park boosters decided to pursue it through the same mechanism that had hamstrung parks in 1990 and 1994. Direct ballot measures had just taken another swipe at state budgets in 1997, further reducing the property taxes allocated for state programs. But park proponents had hope that the newly energized movement could convince the electorate to vote in a source of funds. The gas tax of 1992 had been a sharp failure. But the lottery bonds newly available for park infrastructure suggested a possible path forward.[329]

---

326 Jeff Mapes, "Voters Willing to Use Their Green on Parks," *Oregonian* June 24, 1997, p. C05; Brian Meehan, "Legislature Comes to the Aid of State Parks," *Oregonian* July 12, 1997, p. A01.

327 "Budget Deficit Forces Reality Check," *FYI* 217 (Nov 7, 1997).

328 *FYI* 213 (Oct 10, 1997).

329 Ashbel S. Green, "GOP Plan: Privatize or Close Parks," *Oregonian* May 7, 1997, p. A01; Ashbel S. Green, "GOP Drops Park Closure Plan," *Oregonian* May 8, 1997, p. A01.

This Bite Is Minimal:
Lottery Dollars for Parks

The idea of dedicating Oregon Lottery funds for parks had been around longer than the lottery itself. As parks scrambled for funding in 1981, Chairman of the Parks Advisory Committee "Stub" Stewart had encouraged research and development into a "lottery for park and recreation purposes to be divided 75 percent to the State; 12 percent to the Counties and 12 percent to the Cities."[330] Initial attempts by the 1983 legislature to create a state lottery bill directed the money "State Parks, tourism, and Economic Development." [331] But by the time the lottery was voted in by direct ballot measure in 1984, funds were to be wholly devoted to economic development and job creation.[332] This did not necessarily have to exclude parks—after all, OPRD had half a century of data showing that state parks promoted both. And in practice, the lottery dollars for "economic development" were routed wherever legislators pleased. The push to put lottery funds into parks remained on the back burners through most of the budget brainstorming of the 1980s and 90s.[333]

In 1995, lottery dollars for schools went from a matter of custom to a matter of law. In practice, a significant portion of the profits from the state lottery already went to schools. But the legislature and the public made this a part of state law, by overwhelming margins. "Stub" Stewart continued to push for more park involvement in the lottery—including, he suggested, installing video poker machines at some of the more built-up facilities like Wolf Creek or Cove Palisades. "[I]t is important," he said, "not to rule out any potential revenue source."[334]

As parks boosters at the end of 1997 searched for a way to transform public sympathy into financial support, "Stub" Stewart and Brian Booth were among those who led the push for a lottery amendment. Seeing the success of the lottery bonds for infrastructure in 1997 AND the failure to get the same in 1996, they proposed that parks and waterways split a dedicated 15% cut of lottery dollars. The Campaign for Parks and Salmon, as the coalition in favor of the measure came to be known, included a spectrum of politicians (including multiple former governors), conservationists, recreation interests, and even

---

330 State Parks and Recreation Advisory Committee Meeting Minutes, Dec. 3 – 4, 1981, p. 7, Folder: Advisory Committee Minutes & Actions 1981 – 1989, Oregon Parks and Recreation Collection.

331 State Parks and Recreation Advisory Committee Meeting Minutes, April 1, 1983, p. 2, Advisory Committee Minutes & Actions 1981 – 1989, Oregon State Parks and Recreation Collection.

332 Office of the Secretary of State, *Oregon Blue Book: 1983 – 1984* (Salem: Oregon State Archives), pp. 395 – 396.

333 Don MacGillivray, "History of the Oregon Lottery," *Southeast Examiner* Jan 1, 2014. Legislation dedicating state lottery funding to parks in Arizona (1990) and Colorado (1992) may also have influenced conversations about the possibilities of lottery funding for state parks in Oregon. Alia Beard Rau and Macaela J Bennett, "Where Does Arizona Lottery's Revenue Go?," *Arizona Republic* July 1, 2016; Colorado Lottery Board, "Colorado Lottery—Thirty Years of Play: FY13 Annual Report," (Denver: Colorado Department of Revenue), 14 – 15.

334 Gail Kinsey Hill, "House Votes to Let Schools Hit State Lottery Jackpot," *Oregonian* Feb 3, 1995, p. D01; Ashbel S. Green, "Oregon Has Shakes Over Dependency on Gambling Money," *Oregonian* Dec 13, 1995, p. D01; Anita Lanning, Oregon Parks and Recreation Commission Workshop Minutes, Feb 23, 1995, p. 4.

timber consortiums (possibly due to Stewart's position in the forestry community). Measure 66, the Oregon Lottery Revenues for Parks and Conservation Act, would in concert with General Fund support bring in just enough money to pursue park goals.[335]

Passage of Measure 66 was a walk in the park. Boosters raised money and attention, supporters came out in droves, and there was little organized opposition from monied interests. Because the lottery was most closely associated with school funding, there were concerns among some education advocates that 15% for parks and salmon might end up eating into school budgets. Proponents of Measure 66 argued that the amount parks was asking for was miniscule compared to school funding—"this bite is minimal," as one editorial put it. Some organizations were tepid about adding yet another spending mandate, pointing to the raft of required spending that already bound the state legislature. Only a few voices brought up the issue of funding parks on the backs of gamblers. The one "Argument Opposed" that made the ballot was from an environmentalist in favor of parks spending, but unwilling to facilitate "preying on the weak to abdicate our moral responsibility to fund these very legitimate programs." But with the state lottery already an institution upon which state budgets relied, this argument fell on deaf ears.[336]

Chastened by criticisms of a too-close relationship with the Parks Trust in preceding years, Oregon Parks and Recreation avoided taking too direct an official role in the fight for lottery dollars. "While the initiative certainly would help our cause," Bob Meinen told staff, "the department is not, and cannot be, involved in campaigning for the proposal." says Director Bob Meinen. But that did not prevent them from passing on calls from the media or the public to those fighting for the initiative. Nor did it prevent individual parks personnel from campaigning for parks money. The department officially took no part in the campaign—but managers still felt pressure to spend hours each week working the phone banks to drum up support.[337]

Measure 66 passed easily, with over two-thirds of the vote. As Meinen said, "The significance of the election results was that Oregonians, with their votes, showed they support their parks, beaches, open spaces and natural resources." Indeed, this was most unequivocal show of support from Oregon voters in the

---

335 Jonathan Nicholas, "Your Last Chance to Save the Soul of Oregon," *Oregonian* Apr 22, 1998, p. B01; *FYI* 172 (Dec 13, 1996); Steve Mayes with Jeff Mapes, "Former Governors Want to Park a Proposal on Ballot," *Oregonian* July 2, 1998, p. B01; Steve Mayes, "Parks Seek Lottery Help to Dismay of Educators," *Oregonian* July 14, 1998, p. B01.

336 Steve Mayes, "Parks Seek Lottery Help to Dismay of Educators," *Oregonian* July 14, 1998, p. B01; "For Parks and Salmon[,] Measure 66 Would Give Much-Needed Help to Maintaining and Restoring Oregon Treasures," *Oregonian* Sept 24, 1998, p. B08; City Club of Portland, "Ballot Measure 66: Lottery Funds for Parks and Watersheds," *City Club of Portland Bulletin* 80:21 (Oct 23, 1998); Steve Mayes, "Schools Face Competition for Lottery Dollars in Vote to Support Parks, Salmon," *Oregonian* Oct 14, 1998, p. A11; Richard L. Lippke, "Should States Be in the Gambling Business?," *Public Affairs Quarterly* 11:1 (1997): pp. 57 – 73; Ramona DeNies, " Is Oregon Addicted to the Lottery?," *Portland Monthly* June 25, 2019.

337 *FYI* 233 (March 13, 1998); "OPRD History Panel Discussion," Interviewer - Kathy Schutt, p. 8, December 2012, Folder: Kate Schutt Records, Oregon Parks and Recreation Digital Collection.

history of the Oregon state parks. Notably, the measure did not increase taxes, as the rejected gas tax or the never-voted-upon-by-the-public bottle tax would have. Guaranteed lottery funds brought Oregon Parks and Recreation closer to a source of stable funding. Lottery dollars fluctuated, but they were less susceptible to conventional economic distress than many other forms of funding.By itself lottery funding was not enough for park priorities, but it was a lifeline that pulled parks out from underwater.

The "army for state parks" had at last succeeded in a campaign. Lottery funds might not have been a cure-all, but they were a nationally-recognized success for Oregon state parks. Never one to rest on laurels, Meinen compelled staff to "continue to keep the public aware of the financial problems that face state parks and the ways we are using our funds." But as 1998 came to a close, even he was happy to proclaim that "[i]t was a very good year for state parks."[338]

But as always, there was trouble on the horizon. OPRD had turned around the budget, but not without cost. Parks were now reliant on gambling and prison labor to stay afloat. Staff were still stretched from years of austerity. Department leadership was politically wounded by the clashes over closures. Approaching the new millennium, parks would have to try and hang on to stability amidst an avalanche of backfill, backhands, and backtracking from political figures still smarting from the bruising battles of the mid-90s.

---

338 Just, "Robert Meinen and Idaho State Parks"; *FYI* 267 (Nov 20, 1998); *FYI* 272 (Jan 8, 1999).

Cottonwood Canyon construction, 2013

CHAPTER 7

Brace and Take on the Task:
Parks for the Past,
Parks for the Future (1999 - 2014)

The 1990s left Oregon Parks and Recreation worn down. Those staff left standing were exhausted by funding battles, political problems, new programs, and constant calls to do more with less. Bob Meinen, a savvy if unpopular leader, was left with too many bruises to adequately recover, and no one what sure what the next decade would bring. Compared to the declaration of park independence in 1989, the passage of Measure 66 brought only a small amount of fanfare, and no giant cake. Parks were falling apart, and even a temporary end to budget shortfalls didn't shake feelings of fatigue. In this new century, parks would continue to fight for their place in Oregon's government and live up to the mandate of Measure 66—to make parks thrive. But the legislature, and the economy, wasn't going to make it easy. Still, OPRD grew in unexpected ways in the new millennium. Embracing new programs, new technologies, and new policies, the department worked to be more "for the people" than ever before. Despite obstacles and obstinance, Oregon State Parks struggled toward a better future.

Meinen Knew How to Manage Parks but Not Politicians:
Fights in the Legislature

Parks boosters had hoped that the passage of Measure 66 in 1998 would solve the struggle for funding. Adding lottery money to the other funding sources for parks would be enough to put them on firm financial footing. However, threatened shutdowns, demands for relief, and grim state budgets took their toll. Although the Oregon Parks and Recreation Department gained a critical source of funding, they lost much of their financial support from the General Fund and political support in state government. The department emerged from the budget battle better funded but bruised—and Meinen bore the brunt of it.

In what some parks boosters believed was bipartisan betrayal, Governor Kitzhaber and the Republican-dominated legislature both supported "backfilling" the lottery dollars earmarked for parks by Oregon voters. Much of what had been intended to add to park coffers would instead replace the General Fund contributions of previous years. There was some back-and-forth over how much to take from Parks. Eventually, the state legislature decided to take it all. The General Fund contribution for Oregon Parks and Recreation in the 1999 – 2000 budget was $0 dollars, when it had at one point provided nearly a third of the park budget.[339]

Meanwhile, the perception that parks would now be flush with lottery cash led many legislators to try and shove programs new and old into the parks budget, and reassert control over lottery funds. Much of the Measure 66 money mandated for park use was stripped from OPRD's general budget and put into a "reserve fund," with any spending from the fund subject to the "greater oversight" of the legislature. A legislative demand requiring OPRD to build a series of "scuba dive parks" was not successful, but administration of "pioneer cemeteries" (broadened to "historic cemeteries" in 2004) was shifted to parks without an attendant shift of money to pay for them. Parks were also given the All-Terrain Vehicle program (which at least came with its own source of funds). The department had hoped to focus on land acquisition and deferred mainte-nance—difficult enough, as many of the experts needed for maintenance and repairs had been let go amidst the layoffs. But now OPRD also had to scramble to fund and staff new non-park programs on a budget smaller than projected. And, as Meinen juggled these new responsibilities, the eyes of a hostile legisla-ture were on him.[340]

The state legislature responded to outrage over their cuts to OPRD in the face of popular will by blaming parks leadership. Questioned about whether these cuts reflected the desires of voters, Senator Lenn Hannon of the Ways and Means committee deflected: "I've been disappointed, quite frankly, with Mr. Meinen's leadership." Weary of the threat of park closures and stung by popular outrage over (the lack of) park funding, legislators redoubled the critiques of park management that had been a mainstay of the 1990s—and launched a new audit of OPRD aimed at financials. [341]

Unlike the earlier audits of lobbying efforts (see Chapter 6), the 1999 au-dit of park management was grounded in differences of philosophy rather than violations of the law. The recommendations made in many cases matched with those that had previously been considered and rejected by OPRD. The report suggested broader implementation and enforcement of day use fees, but did not include consideration of whether those fees would reduce visitation. Nor

---

339 Steve Suo, "Governor's Critics Say State Parks Are Being Shortchanged," *Oregonian* Feb 1, 1999, p. E08; Steve Suo, "Measure 66 Supporters Attack $30 Million Parks Budget," *Oregonian* Apr 15, 1999, p. D07.

340 *FYI* 286 (Apr 16, 1999); *FYI* 297 (July 2, 1999); "Draft OPRD History Questionnaire, 1990 – Present [2013]," p. 19, Folder: Kate Schutt Records – More Kate Schutt Records, Oregon Parks and Recreation Digital Archive; "An Act Relating to Cemeteries…," Chapter 731 Oregon Laws 1999; "Relating to the Oregon Pioneer Cemetery Commission," Chapter 173 Oregon Laws 2003.

341 Suo, "Measure 66 Supporters Attack $30 Million Parks Budget."

did this recommendation consider political feasibility—a growing concern, as the same legislature that ordered and endorsed the report had moved strongly against new day-use fees at beachfront recreation areas. The report assumed fees from state park campgrounds could be brought into rough parity with private campgrounds, and rejected long-held studies and concerns by the OPRD and Parks Commission that the comparative lack of amenities in state parks would make raising fees to that extent infeasible. The last major revenue idea in the audit suggested replacing seasonal workers with temporary ones, operating under the assumption that seasonal work positions needed little to no experience or training.[342]

But though the critiques in the audits were mild, the attacks from legislators were devastating. Reporting transformed the decorous "opportunit[ies] for improvement" in the audit into a more attention-grabbing "mismanagement." Senator Eugene Timms, joint chair of Ways and Means in the legislature, responded to the audit with exasperation. "Why do we keep having a problem with the parks division? We've got to get someone managing that department better. It makes me sick." Meinen responded coolly: "When I hear there are management problems, I don't hear specifics."[343] The Parks Commission urged Meinen to work on his relationships with the legislature. Commissioner Betsy McCool suggested the immediate implementation of opening ceremonies for parks receiving maintenance to showcase the work parks were now able to do with new lottery funding. This sort of public performance was in line with the culture of public relations Meinen had been trying to instill since his arrival. But he was exasperated with demands and insults from the legislature:

> [It is] important to keep in perspective [that] the agency has come from almost closing parks, laying off staff and almost starving to death in the last 20 years and then as soon as there is money they expect the plans to be all finalized and ready to roll out.

The Commission offered to help smooth things over with the legislature, but soon found that they, too, were viewed skeptically. In 2000, they came in for legislative critique—both because it was unclear if they were active enough in policy decisions and because the Commission was not "as inventive as they should be" in fundraising efforts. Demands to "do more with less," it seemed, would continue. [344]

---

342 Oregon Audits Division, "State of Oregon Parks and Recreation Department: Management of State Park Resources," John N. Lattimer, Director, No. 1999-28 (Aug 5, 1999).

343 Lisa Grace Lednicer, "Audit Finds Mismanagement in State Parks," *Oregonian* Aug 6, 1999, p. A01.

344 Odie Vogel, State Parks and Recreation Commission meeting minutes, April 29, 1999, p. 6, Folder: Commission Meeting Notes [1990 – 2013], unfiled, Oregon State Parks and Recreation Digital Collection; Odie Vogel, State Parks and Recreation Commission meeting minutes, January 13, 2000, p. 5, Folder: Commission Meeting Notes [1990 – 2013], unfiled, Oregon State Parks and Recreation Digital Collection.

The Recent Events Have Tested our Resolve and Broken our Hearts:
Attack at Oswald West State Park

As Director Meinen fought the legislature in Salem on issues of funding, the Parks system suffered an immeasurable tragedy in the field. On April 27, 1999, two rangers on duty at Oswald West State Park were shot while checking the restrooms. Danny Blumenthal died instantly, Jack Kerwin survived and was able to assist police in locating the assailant, who was arrested later that day. Danny Blumenthal, described as quick to smile and a lover of the outdoors, was 51 years old. He was a "big kid at heart," trying to instill in visitors of all kinds a respect for the trees and amazing Pacific coast views that brought people to Oswald West State Park. He and Jack Kerwin worked together for two years before the shooting, doing the work all rangers knew well, trail maintenance, handling visitors, cleaning, and education. Jack Kerwin recovered from his injuries and returned to the work that he loved. Bob Meinen wrote at the time, "the recent events have tested our resolve and broken our hearts." Rangers gathered at Oswald West State Park for a memorial, and, in uniform, stood with the family of Blumenthal as they mourned. Soon after, two of the major creeks at Oswald West State Park were named after Kerwin and Blumenthal. Blumenthal Creek empties over a cliffside beach view, one of the many oceanside vistas Blumenthal had urged visitors to savor.[345]

The attack sent shockwaves through the organization as park rangers grappled with the loss of a colleague and questioned their own safety in the field. Perversely, the state legislature had slashed the proposed budget for parks safety almost to nothing just two weeks before the shooting. Governor John Kitzhaber said in a prepared statement, "We take for granted the safety of our roads, streets, parks and public places. We should not." Washington State had just begun arming some park personnel after a ranger was grievously wounded in a vehicular assault. Rangers in California state parks had been permitted to carry firearms since 1986. Oregon had resisted this measure. In the aftermath of the shooting, this decision was hotly debated. Director Bob Meinen wrote in a staff newsletter directly after the attack,

> I… believe, that as we move ahead in the weeks and months to come, that our reaction to how and why this tragedy occurred needs to be responsive, but not one of overreaction. Our approach needs to be thoughtful and measured. The work of our task force looking into equipment and safety for our employees needs to continue with objectivity and intensity. If we need to make changes, we will make changes.

345   "Director's Corner," *FYI* 289 (May 3 – 7, 1999), p. 1; Oregon Parks and Recreation Department, "Oswald West trail guide" [Online Brochure], n.d., **https://stateparks.oregon.gov/index.cfm?do=v.publications**, accessed July 20, 2020; "Blumenthal Falls, Tillamook County, Oregon," Northwest Waterfall Survey [online], updated March 19, 2017, **https://www.waterfallsnorthwest.com/waterfall/Blumenthal-Falls-3884**.

In an editorial days after the attack, the *Oregonian* urged state parks not to arm their officers, despite this act of violence. The difference between Oregon and Washington, the editorial noted, was that Oregon rangers were not law enforcement officers, nor should they become them. Oregon State Parks historically relied on assistance from Oregon police to handle any serious infractions, and, the editorial noted, this arrangement was largely successful. By requiring rangers to wear firearms, the job would move away from its role as interpreter and visitor support, and towards a role of enforcement. With this change, the tenor of parks would change as well, shattering the innocence of recreation in Oregon's scenic spaces.[346]

Reporting to the Oregon State Parks and Recreation Commission, Meinen stressed that this tragedy was not directed at the rangers specifically, but was rather a random act of violence that did not signify a danger unique to park employees. He urged the committee to consider the issue of arming rangers, but to keep the issue in perspective. Stub Stewart agreed with the *Oregonian* editorialist that rangers should not be armed, but he noted that many people had voiced support for arming rangers during his recent trip to Salem. Other Commission members agreed a patient and cautious approach to the issue should be taken— and pointed out the sharp reduction in the safety budget that the legislature had just imposed.[347]

A friend of Kerwin's noted that Jack, a Vietnam veteran and US Marine Corps Colonel, was not in favor of rangers carrying guns. The taskforce convened under Meinen agreed: rangers would not be permitted to carry weapons of any sort while on duty. Government risk management staffers pointed to data that suggested arming park personnel would make serious injury and accidents more likely. Instead, the slow-growing pilot program training parks staff in how to deescalate dangerous situations would now be made a part of ranger training. Park Officer Safety Training was created to prevent further violence without the use of force. The safety of parks would not be maintained through the arming of parks personnel.[348] ⚔

346 *FYI* 286 (Apr 16, 1999); Bryan Denson, Hal Bernton, and Jonathan Nelson, "Attack on Park Rangers Leaves 1 Dead, 1 Injured," *Oregonian* Apr 28, 1999, p. A01; Seabury Blair, "Olympia: Parks Panel Takes Aim at Issue of Rangers and Guns," *Kitsap Sun* Dec 18, 1998; Pieter M. O'Leary, "A Walk in the Park: A Legal Overview of California's State and Federal Parks and the Laws Governing Their Use and Enjoyment," *Natural Resources Journal* 52:1 (Spring 2012), p. 257; "Director's Corner," *FYI* 288 (Apr. 26 – 30, 1999), p. 1; "Friendly, Helpful, Unarmed: The Brutal Random Attack on Two Park Rangers Is Frightening, but Oregon Should Not Arm Its Park Employees with Handguns," *Oregonian* Apr. 29, 1999, p. D12.

347 Odie Vogel, State Parks and Recreation Commission meeting minutes, April 29, 1999, p. 1, Folder: Commission Meeting Notes [1990 – 2013], unfiled, Oregon State Parks and Recreation Digital Collection

348 Denson, Bernton, and Nelson, "Attack on Park Rangers Leaves 1 Dead, 1 Injured."; *FYI* 299 (July 16, 1999); *FYI* 119 (Nov 9, 1995); *FYI* 283 (March 26, 1999); Tim Wood, "Looking Back from 2013: Synopsis and Commentary by Director Tim Wood," 13, Folder: Kate Schutt Records, Oregon State Parks and Recreation Digital Archive Collection.

Assuming Nothing Goes South on Us:
OPRD Tackles Technology

One key new line item for parks safety in the 1990s was the purchase of cellphones. An expensive and exotic technology that worked even less often at the time, it took several years for mobile phones to become a standard item for park rangers to carry. Among the many changes of the 1990s, career rangers often mentioned the sudden dependence on technology for a job that was once entirely removed from computer systems. The first mention of technology of any sort was in a 1971 staff newsletter, in which the office marveled over the new equipment in the Engineering department, a Monroe 990—essentially a glorified calculator. Perhaps a touch tongue in cheek, the newsletter boasted,

> *The Engineering staff is proudly sporting an electric computer, a Monroe 990, which literally produces answers in the twinkling of an eye. It has a square-root key, a memory bank, and even a floating decimal point! Truly a magical aid. The Recreation staff is experimenting with a printing electric calculator. Stop by for your own amazement.*

Computer systems wouldn't be mentioned again until the mid-1990s, and rangers were hesitant to engage with them even then. The job of a ranger was not based at a desk, and any suggestion that it should be was met with jeers. [349]

Park reservations, started under Dave Talbot early in his tenure, were one example of the analog procedures that dominated the park system prior to 2000. Before a telephone reservation system, people mailed in their reservation requests, which were collected in a 50-gallon drum, and opened on "Black Monday," the second Monday in January. It would take until March to process them. The pile of requests was sorted, one by one, and campsites were assigned.

Field staff began to see more indoor work, courtesy of the PC revolution that ramped up in the 1990s.

---

349   *FYI* 176, (Jan 17, 1997); "The Office" *Oregon State Park Times* 9:2[?] (Aug 1971), p. 24.

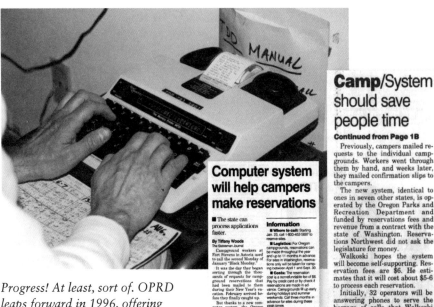

Camp/System should save people time

Continued from Page 1B

Previously, campers mailed requests to the individual campgrounds. Workers went through them by hand, and weeks later, they mailed confirmation slips to the campers.

The new system, identical to ones in seven other states, is operated by the Oregon Parks and Recreation Department and funded by reservations fees and revenue from a contract with the state of Washington. Reservations Northwest did not ask the legislature for money.

Walkoski hopes the system will become self-supporting. Reservation fees are $6. He estimates that it will cost about $5-6 to process each reservation.

Initially, 32 operators will be answering phones to serve the barrage of calls that Walkoski anticipates. He said during the first days, callers will likely receive busy signals. Georgia, which has an identical system, reported 50,000 attempted calls per hour on the opening day of its system.

Later in the season, 12 to 18 temporary operators will answer phones. Operators will be contracted through Goodwill Temporary Services.

Computer system will help campers make reservations

■ The state can process applications faster.

By Tiffany Woods
The Statesman Journal

Campground workers at Fort Stevens in Astoria used to call the second Monday of January "Black Monday."

It was the day they began sorting through the thousands of requests for campground reservations that had been mailed to them during their New Year's vacation. February arrived before they finally caught up.

But thanks to a new computer system, the Oregon Parks and Recreation Department will be able to process campground reservations faster, and campers will have their reservations confirmed in minutes, instead of weeks as before.

Starting Jan. 23, campers can call 1-800-452-5687 to reserve sites at 25 Oregon and 35 Washington campgrounds or to receive information about state campgrounds.

The Portland-based reservation system, called Reser-

Information
■ **Whom to call:** Starting Jan. 23, call 1-800-452-5687 to reserve sites.
■ **Logistics:** For Oregon campgrounds, reservations can be made throughout the year and up to 11 months in advance. For sites in Washington, reservations only will be taken for camping between April 1 and Sept. 30.
■ **Costs:** The reservation cost is a nonrefundable fee of $6. Pay by credit card or by check if reservations are made in advance. Campgrounds fill up early during holidays and summer weekends. Call these months in advance for sites during these peak times.
■ **Hours:** 8 a.m. to 5 p.m. weekdays. Closed on holidays.
■ **Further information:** A brochure with information about the new system is available by calling Reservations Northwest at 1-800-452-5687.

vations Northwest, was installed because the previous manual system was inefficient, director Richard Walkoski said.

Please see **Camp**, Page 2B

Progress! At least, sort of. OPRD leaps forward in 1996, offering a computerized telephone reservation system that suffered some spectacular, early glitches. Eventually, things improved.

Although a call center existed, they usually could do no more than inform customers of which campsites might be available. But "that all changed on Tuesday, January 23, 1996 when OPRD stepped into the modern world of centralized reservation systems." Helping to build a single system to handle reservations for both Oregon and Washington, Oregon State Parks spent almost $3 million dollars to step into the modern era. They went through 300 reservations employees in the first year. The system was plagued by busy signals, double bookings, and the slow crawl of early computer systems. One unlucky soul answering phones, Kristi Granberg, remembered of one customer, "She stopped just short of threatening bodily harm. And at the end of the call, I raised my head up above the cubicle wall for some air, much like a periscope on a submarine. It was hard to go back for more of that punishment." Field employees suffered as well, with double bookings causing a flood of angry campers that would end up in hotels, on the park's dime, instead of at camps.[350]

The new phone reservation system was a shock to a department that relied on pen and paper. By the late 1990s, park staff were faced with more

---

350 "OPRD History Panel Discussion," Interviewer - Kathy Schutt, Dec 2012, p. 7 Folder: Kate Schutt Records, Oregon Parks and Recreation Digital Collection. Hereafter "OPRD History Panel Discussion [2012]."; *Oregon State Park Times* 8:1[?] (April, 1970), p. 26; Richard Walkoski, "Happy Anniversary: Twenty Years of Central Reservations" *FYI 2.0* January 22, 2016, p. 1; "OPRD History Panel Discussion [2012]."

technological challenges. The rough implementation of phone reservations made it clear to park administrators that OPRD was behind the curve on technology upgrades, especially in parks. This problem became all the more urgent at the decade progressed. The Y2K frenzy, centered on the fact that many computers did not have the capacity to recognize the year 2000, required Oregon Parks to reluctantly thrust themselves into the 21st century. A 1999 *Oregonian* article noted at the time that the United States spent over $100 billion dollars on preparing computer systems to recognize the year 2000. Staff worked frantically not only to upgrade computers, but to force a reluctant staff to train on new systems. [351]

Staff newsletters in 1999 tried to ease the fears of staff, not only of the potential upheaval from Y2K, but also on the changing roles of technology in parks. Rangers with 20 years of experience in the field were now spending more time on computers, whether they liked it or not. Even a small software change seemed insurmountable. A 1999 FYI article noted that OPRD was going to standardize software to Microsoft suite products, and the IT pros in charge were readying themselves for the panic that this would cause among the staff. That year, OPRD owned 486 computers, which were recently upgraded to 64 MB of memory and a whopping 3 GB hard disk. A decade later cell phones would have roughly the same processing power. Money earmarked to prepare for Y2K allowed Meinen's staff to complete necessary system upgrades, get everyone using the same software, and start the long process of training staff. This diligence led to an uneventful switch to the year 2000. [352]

Equipping staff with computers was only the beginning. Park websites, online reservation systems, and even a MySpace* page were implemented the late 1990s and 2000s. OPRD got its first mention on a website in 1995. According to a staff newsletter, "Internet users can now find OPRD information through accessing Oregon Online, an internet information service." This early website only had phone numbers of parks and camp descriptions but promised that it would grow over time. A standalone website for OPRD was introduced in 1998. Chris Havel, the project coordinator, was cautiously optimistic about the launch, saying "We'll be placing the files online this weekend. Assuming nothing goes south on us, you should be able to reach the site with web browsing software by Sunday." Five years later, the first *FYI* internal newsletter with embedded pictures was sent out to staff, using the magic of html. [353]

---

351 "Happy New Year: Here Comes the New Millennium—Ready or Not," *Oregonian* Dec 31, 1999, p. C06.

352 "Conversion to Microsoft Office Coming New Year," *FYI* 311 (Oct 11 – 15, 1999), p. 1. 1; "Y2K Update," *ibid*, 2; There was one incident reported: A rock climber that bought a day pass at Smith rock did received a ticket with the wrong date. This was resolved when staff arrived on site and updated the day use ticket machine. Odie Vogel, State Parks and Recreation Commission meeting minutes, January 13, 2000, Folder: Commission Meeting Notes [1990 – 2013], unfiled, Oregon State Parks and Recreation Digital Collection; see also Francine Uenama, "20 Years Later, the Y2K Bug Seems Like a Joke—Because Those Behind the Scenes Took It Seriously," *Time* Dec 30, 2019.

353 "OPRD's on Oregon Live," *FYI* 85 (March 6 – 10, 1995); "Editor's Note," *FYI* 500 (Aug 17 – 23, 2003), p. 1. MySpace was an early social networking platform that rose meteorically around 2005 then fell a few years later. Nicholas Jackson and Alexis C. Madrigal, "The Rise and Fall of MySpace," *Atlantic* Jan 12, 2011.

Online reservations also quickly grew. In 1999, 12 people reserved a campsite online. The next year, 7,200 did. In 2008, online reservations outnumbered reservations by phone for the first time, signaling a shift in how Oregonians chose to interact with park personnel. These accommodations continued when wireless internet hotspots were set up along some coastal parks in partnership with the Oregon Travel Information Council in 2006. State parks also took to social media, creating MySpace, Facebook, and, later, Instagram pages to connect more directly with visitors. These technological upgrades, though slow to implement, allowed parks to function more cohesively, using networks and direct marketing to better meet the needs of the department. For the first time field staff and Salem staff were easily connecting online and sharing information across networks. This signified an improvement in efficiencies, but it also drastically changed the role of rangers. Computers, once a strange anomaly, were now necessary to the job duties of all staff. Technology also permeated the ways visitors engaged with parks, from online reviews to social media posts. Just as camping changed the physical layout of Oregon parks, technology changed how, and why, visitors came to see the landscape.[354]

I Carried my Load: Meinen's Legacy

The Y2K success was one of the last acts of the Meinen administration. He announced in January, 2000, that he was stepping down from his position, hopeful that a new Director, without the baggage of the fight for Measure 66, may have more luck in securing sustained funding. After his retirement, the *Oregonian* noted that "Meinen knew how to manage parks but not politicians. Ultimately, it led to his departure." Democrats in Salem saw Meinen in a different light, arguing that he had dealt with the mess he was handed admirably. Representative Randell Edwards praised Meinen as "cautious and prudent." Oregon Parks staff would remember these years as unsteady and dizzying, a mix of hope for the future of parks and fear that OPRD, and their own jobs, were precariously bound up in political maneuvering. Meinen would end up finishing his parks career in Idaho, where he had begun. There, he was "well-known... for getting the lottery money for State Parks in Oregon" and "[f]amous for getting kicked out of the state for having that success." [355]

Meinen headed the park system through funding disasters, staff layoffs, immense tragedy, and rapid technological advancement. But for all his success,

---

354 "Internet Camping Reservations Escalate," *FYI* 322 (Jan 10 – 14, 2000), p. 2; "Online Bookings Lead to Changes for Reservations Northwest," *FYI* 726 (Apr 20 – 26, 2008), p. 1; "Wireless Internet Access Installed at Central Coast Parks," *FYI* 646 (Sept 10 – 16, 2006), p. 3. Facebook and Instagram, like MySpace before them, are social networking programs.

355 Robert L. Meinen, "Interview Transcription," Interview with Elisabeth Walton Potter, Apr 28, 2000, p. 8, Folder: Kate Schutt Records, Oregon Parks and Recreation Digital Archive; Steve Mayes, "State Parks Hunts for New Director," *Oregonian* March 13, 2000, p. E01; Rick Just, "Robert Meinen and Idaho State Parks," Interview with Marc James Carpenter [phone], July 15, 2020, unfiled, Oregon Parks and Recreation Digital Collection.

most state legislators couldn't wait to see him leave. Staff were still scarred and distrustful from years of layoffs, and Nancy Rockwell had already departed a few years before. After Meinen's retirement, he continued to work with OPRD on a temporary basis, under Acting Director Laurie Warner, to ease the transition and wrap up a few acquisition projects. Although multiple heads of the state park system, including Sam Boardman and Dave Talbot, had done similar part time work after their resignation to transition projects, this arrangement enraged the legislature. Watchdog groups claimed that Meinen was being given the state equivalent of a golden parachute. Meinen commented on the backlash from the legislature, now a very familiar occurrence, by saying simply, "I carried my load." A leader of state parks during its most tumultuous eight years, Meinen wished his successors luck, knowing full well that they would need it. He believed that the lottery funds would help stabilize the budget, but he also knew that revenue outside of the unstable flow of lottery funding would be necessary. In an interview, he said, "You can put sugar coating on it, and you probably can have some freedom over the next biennium from severe cuts and things like that, but the reality is that our system needs a certain level of operational money to be a success."[356]

More than the need for money, Meinen also came to understand that "Oregonians are not going to tolerate compromise." There was an expectation of high caliber recreational facilities, and any compromise or cuts to those services would be met with anger on the part of the visitor. The way to avoid these cuts to services, Meinen believed, was for the voting public to maintain a watchful eye on park funding, and, just as they had with Measure 66, continue to advocate for parks. To create advocates OPRD needed to educate the public on the importance of these parks. Meinen said, "if we don't make them familiar with the outdoor resources that they have, they won't treasure them." Despite the conflict with staff and legislators that would be the defining legacy of this era, Meinen believed that he made a tough situation better, sometimes at a great cost. He said, "I came into the organization when it needed a change in vision and set a positive course... I've accomplished a lot of what I set out to do." Meinen also offered something his successor should keep in mind. No matter what a Director does, or how tightly the parks are managed, "you are going to run into issues that are going to make legislators unhappy."[357]

And this was certainly the case for Laurie Warner, who took over as Deputy Director when Rockwell stepped down in 1999, and Acting Director when Meinen resigned in 2000. Most of her brief time in charge was spent trying to keep all of the plates in the air. "The major challenge... was the political side," she remembered. Being Meinen's successor left her under a cloud. But she also had to balance the needs of the environment with the desires of ATV users, freshly put under OPRD purview and a "very focused and vocal group advocating

356 Harry Esteve, "Workers Leave with Golden Handshakes," *Oregonian* Feb 12, 2001, p. E01; Meinen, "Interview Transcription," 11.

357 Meinen, "Interview Transcription," 11-13; Mayes, "State Parks Panel Hunts for New Director."

for their interests." And she had to deal with the "backlog on every front," from preservation to planning to purchasing to the growing beast that was maintenance. The department was "still for the most part a work in progress." Warner spent most of her time making sure the wheels didn't fall off the bus before the department could be handed off to a permanent successor.[358]

The Box is Big Enough:
Carrier Calms the Storm

Michael Carrier was approached by Bob Meinen at the National Association of State Parks Directors board meeting in Portland, where Meinen asked Carrier if he would be interested in his job. Despite the tenuous position of Oregon parks, Carrier chose to throw his hat in the ring. Previously the Division Administrator for Iowa State Parks and Recreation, Carrier remarked that he was ready for a new professional challenge. In his conversations with Meinen, he was no doubt informed of just the sort of challenge he was likely to face. A disgruntled legislature, new budget constraints, and a staff still reeling from the restructuring shake ups five years prior, Carrier would either be a breath of fresh air or a lightning rod. Legislators were pleased that the Commission chose someone from out of state and removed from the recent events at OPRD. They hoped that this would give everyone a fresh start, separating the growing pains of the 1990s from the (hopefully) smooth sailing into a new century. "I think it's good that they went outside the state and brought in someone fresh," Senator Lenn Hammond, a long-time critic of Meinen, said. "We can move on from here and forget the past." [359]

During his tenure, Carrier focused on a "positive and transparent" relationship with both legislators and staff. He hoped to mend fences that had necessarily been broken during the 1990s. To do this, like many directors before him, Carrier logged a lot of "car time" meeting with local Friends groups, volunteers, and park staff. Carrier also worked to rebrand the Oregon State Parks and Recreation Department as a natural and cultural resource agency, not just one focused on recreation, which had been the emphasis in the 1960s through the 1990s. The newly created Stewardship Division handled these programs, ranging from habitat protections to historic preservation. Carrier's education and professional experience focused on the importance of these initiatives. He ushered in a new era of natural resources professionalization, but he was aware that these projects wouldn't gain any traction without the support of staff, the

---

358 Laurie Warner, "Written Interview with Laurie Warner, Deputy Director & Director," [Kate Schutt], 3 – 4, Folder: Kate Schutt Files— Guided Interview Questions with Directors, Dept. Directors, and Commission Chairs, Oregon State Parks and Recreation Digital Collection .

359 Michael Carrier, "Written Interview with Michael Carrier, Director," [Kate Schutt], Folder: Kate Schutt Files— Guided Interview Questions with Directors, Dept. Directors, and Commission Chairs, Oregon State Parks and Recreation Digital Collection; Steve Mayes, "State Commissioners Tap Iowa Man to Run Oregon's Park Department," *Oregonian* May 20, 2000, p. B01.

public, and the still-fuming state legislature. One staff member remembered that Carrier urged staff to "find ways to say yes" to both legislators and the pubic as an effort to combat the negativity of the previous decade.[360]

Carrier attempted to create an atmosphere of openness, but OPRD was far more rigid and "by the book" than it had been under Meinen. Claude Crocker remembered, "Carrier was about stewardship. He was not interested in camping or being entrepreneurial. He was tired of hearing about thinking outside of the box. He would say, 'The box is big enough. Stay inside it.' " This outlook extended to the slush funds, campaigning, and other rogue activities that had kept the park system afloat during the leaner years. Carrier was a rules follower and he expected the same from his staff. Dave Wright echoed this sentiment, remembering a shift away from "commercializing the system." "To me," Wright said, "I felt like the darkness of the growing years was lifting."

As the darkness lifted and long-term planning became an option again, it became apparent that years of backlogged maintenance would need immediate action. At the same time, the public and legislators that fought for parks wanted to return to an era of land acquisition after a long period of the status quo. Laurie Warner remembered, "the Parks Commission wanted to [do] as much as quickly as possible." Carrier had to balance the need for infrastructure updates and more public-facing park development. He had modest successes in historic preservation, and modest failures in yet another attempt to jumpstart the perennially stalled Willamette Greenway. Although Carrier laid the foundation for broader changes, it would be his successor that would be called on to see them to completion. [361]

Michael Carrier's tenure was one of quiet redirection, out of the fire of funding debates and into the business of glad-handing the political forces that had brought the organization to task for mismanagement real and perceived. Carrier believed his success was in his transparency. He was open with staff, the public, and the men and women in Salem that held the purse strings. This cordial relationship with the government led to Carrier's appointment as the Natural Resources Advisor under Governor Kulongoski. His tenure at OPRD was short, only four years. Like Harold Schick, who saw the department through the tumultuous beginnings of professionalization, Carrier's tenure can be viewed as a moment of transition. But where Schick had been disruptive, Carrier was restorative. The mission remained the same, but the pressure dropped several notches.[362]

---

360   "OPRD History Panel Discussion [2012]," p. 8.

361   Warner, "Written Interview with Laurie Warner, Deputy Director & Director," p. 3; "OPRD History Panel Discussion [2012]," p. 8; **Dave Wright, "Written Interview with Dave Wright, Deputy Director" [Kate Schutt], Folder: Kate Schutt Files— Guided Interview Questions with Directors, Dept. Directors, and Commission Chairs;** Gerry Frank, "Silverton Offers Great Burgers, Scenery," *Oregonian* Oct 25, 2002, p. A18; Stuart Tomlinson, "Vista House Project Allowed to Resume," *Oregonian* Jan 23, 2004, p. B02; Jonathan Nicholas, "An Idea Whose Time Just Came," *Oregonian* Aug 13, 2004, p. E01; "OPRD Given Action Plan to Revitalize Greenway," *FYI* 602 (Oct. 2 – 8, 2005), p. 1.

362   "Commission Bids Mike Carrier Farewell; Taps Tim Wood as Acting Director," *FYI* 546 (Aug 1 – 7, 2004), p. 1.

After a nationwide search for Carrier's replacement, the Parks Commission decided to go with a known entity to lead the parks system, Tim Wood. Wood had been with the agency since 1998, and under Carrier, held the role of Field Operations Manager. Previously, Wood worked with the US Army and the Army Corps of Engineers, including a posting as chief operating officer for the greater part of Oregon and Washington, where he gained local and national recognition for his response to the floods of 1996. A man known to the department as steadfast in his dedication to the mission and able to take on large and complex projects, Wood seemed like a steady hand for a department that had experienced its share of shakeups over the previous decade. Wood's tenure would see the highs of new park openings and a push to inclusivity in both staff and visitors, and the lows of an economic downturn that again threatened park funding. [363]

All of These Demands Added Up:
Tim Wood and the Cost of Saying Yes

In 2007, OPRD's annual revenue from the Lottery Fund peaked at $65 million. The same year, the recession took hold in Oregon and throughout the nation. Until 2013, the Lottery Fund suffered losses each year, proving that this funding source lacked the stability the department desperately required. In addition to economic downturns, OPRD inherited multiple money-draining programs that strained their financial and administrative capacities. Legislators

Taking on the responsibility—and debt—of the State Fair and Expo Center was an unpleasant surprise to Parks leadership, and strained staff capacity for years.

---

363 "Acting No Longer… Tim Wood Appointed Director," *FYI* 558 (Oct 24 – 30, 2004), p. 1.; *FYI* 220 (Dec 5, 1997).

offered fee waivers for certain groups using the park system, which cut into a budget already stretched thin. New programs included the State Capitol grounds and the financially disastrous State Fair and Expo Center—dubbed by parks advocates a "30-mile-high stack of manure." [364]

In July 2005, Governor Kulongoski let House Bill 3502 pass into law "without the benefit of his signature." This piece of legislation abolished the Oregon State Fair and Exposition Center as a separate entity and transferred its management to OPRD. The governor felt that this move challenged the intent of Measure 66 by unloading another struggling program onto the state parks system and that there was not an appropriate amount of public debate, but he wouldn't stop its passage. During an August Commission meeting, Commission Chair John Blackwell began discussion on this issue with, "The day isn't long enough to vent all of our emotions about the Oregon State Fair." Both poorly managed and not financially viable, the State Fair was, to the Commission, just another responsibility that would siphon off money that should go to the real business of operating parks. Commissioner David Kottkamp tried to look on the bright side: "I think we have to note that in a backhanded way this is a compliment to the staff—and maybe in a small measure the commission, that we've done a good job running our business." But, he continued, diverting resources and time to this project, "distresses me to no end." Disgusted by the new law, Kottkamp very publicly quit just a few weeks after sounding his distress. The Commission hoped that the State Fair would be a temporary addition to the park's portfolio, but, while it was under the parks umbrella, staff would be asked to "brace and take on the task."[365]

Carrier's mandate to "find a way to say yes" increased the expectations placed on parks, and as Bob Meinen had warned, working to please politicians was a zero-sum game. The more that the State Parks system seemed to be economically responsible and well-managed, the more programs OPRD was "asked" to take on. The public also clamored for a more involved and diverse park system, requiring OPRD to take on scenic bikeways and cultural heritage projects, in addition to more traditional parks focused on camping and boating. Wood wrote "All of these demands added up to millions and millions of dollars of new commitments OPRD was expected to make, on a shrinking revenue stream, and with mounting maintenance and staffing costs for the existing sprawling State Park System."[366]

Perhaps the flashiest of these new park programs was Governor Kulongoski's Park-A-Year mandate, announced in 2004 while Mike Carrier was still Director, in which one new park would be purchased, built, and opened each year of Kulongoski's term. This focus on acquisition, rather than the less glamorous work of maintenance and staffing, has long captured the imaginations

---

364 Wood, "Looking Back from 2013," p. 3; "Oregon's Newest Park: The Fair," *Oregonian* Aug 26, 2005, p. D10.

365 Jo Bell, State Parks and Recreation Commission meeting minutes, August 4, 2005, pp. 12-13, Folder: Commission Meeting Notes [1990 – 2013], unfiled, Oregon State Parks and Recreation Digital Collection.

366 Wood, "Looking Back from 2013," p. 4.

of visitors, advisory boards, and legislators. One of the key complaints levied against Chet Armstrong in the 1950s, as he had struggled to introduce camping amenities to former waysides, was the dearth of new acquisition. One of the key arguments made by Talbot and Meinen in their quest for funding had been the lack of new acquisitions. Looking back on his tenure, Tim Wood saw the Park-A-Year mandate, however successful it was from a public relations perspective, as a shortsighted policy that ignored the still-sizable maintenance backlog that threatened existing parks.

Governor Kulongoski, however, remembered a different financial situation. When a representative from his office was asked about the program, they responded,

> *Thanks to ballot Measure 66... OPRD has been given a wonderful opportunity for adequate funding and expansion at a time when parks in other states are closing... [the Governor's] love for parks and the value they add to the lives of citizens was a powerful motivator to ensure that the significant investment that citizens made in 1998 and 2010 was represented by several new parks to serve future generations.*

With the Park-A-Year program, Measure 66 had taken on new political meaning. Rather than an effort to protect the parks from closure, this wellspring of money was now meant to grow a system already frayed at the edges. [367]

"Stub" Stewart State Park was perhaps the shiniest example of Governor Kulongoski's "park a year" program that celebrated the largesse of Lottery funding.

367 Office of Ted Kulongoski, "Written Interview with Ted Kulongoski, Governor" [Kate Schutt], Folder: Kate Schutt Files— Guided Interview Questions with Directors, Dept. Directors, and Commission Chairs. "New" parks were sometime developed from existing acquisitions—Chris Havel, personal communication, Oct 1 2020.

The most symbolic opening was L.L "Stub" Stewart State Park in 2007. This was billed as the first new "full service" park—a park that included a campground—since 1972. Located in Washington County, the park, originally named Hares Canyon, was aptly renamed for the man known as "Mr. Oregon State Parks," "an unwavering, untiring advocate and promoter of Oregon's state park system." Stewart had served on the State Parks Advisory Board as well as the Commission before stepping down in 2000, the longest-serving advisory member, remembered for his push to bring more women on as voting members and his relentless respect for the bottom line. He had died in early 2005, still setting up new endowments for the good of Oregon practically with his last breath. Wood noted that "Stub" had been key in "forging the Department into a system of state parks and outdoor recreation programs that has gained national recognition." This park, it was hoped, could signify the end of dark times within the Oregon State Parks system, the important role of volunteers (especially volunteers with money) in the history of parks, and a new era of growth and prosperity. The park was dedicated in 2007, mere months before the Great Recession hit.[368]

To accomplish this mandate, Wood had to pull resources from other parks, delay maintenance projects, and compound resentments among park employees. Manager Kevin Price remembered,

> [The] Park a Year program… fostered the "them and us" feeling. When Stub Stewart was being built managers had to ask for help from each region and they were told "guess what, you are paying for your staff to work at Stub Stewart." That caused more resentment.

The new parks opened during this period became valued additions to the parks system, but the mandate also highlighted the strings attached to the lottery funding. Saying no to one's bosses in government, as Meinen had learned, could bring swift and terrible budgetary retaliation. But saying yes came with its own costs. [369]

We Need to Move Forward:
Steps Toward Inclusion

The 1990s required park staff to look inward, handling the immediate needs of money and staffing that threatened the organization. As the dust cleared, more staff started to see that Oregon State Parks and Recreation was walking out of step with the rest of the state. Since the beginnings of park surveys in the 1950s, there was an assumed "ideal" park visitor: Young families

---

368 Alice Tallmadge, "'Stub' Stewart, Timber Baron, Lawmaker, Dies at 93," *Oregonian* Jan 4, 2005; Jo Bell, State Parks and Recreation Commission meeting minutes, January 27, 2005, p. 2, Folder: Commission Meeting Notes [1990 – 2013], unfiled, Oregon State Parks and Recreation Digital Collection.

369 "OPRD History Panel Discussion [2012]," p. 3.

or retirees, middle or upper middle class, and avid recreationist, whether it be boating, swimming, or the ever popular "loafing" of the 1960s. It went unsaid in these early surveys, but these ideal guests were also largely White and able-bodied, in addition to appropriately well-off. By the 1980s, Parks took a look at those people that were being knowingly or unknowingly excluded from their parks. But finding remedies would be a long and faltering process.

New attempts at inclusion sometimes came from below. In 1973, long before accessibility became a matter of national law in 1990, the volunteer program at Tryon Creek State Park created interpretive programs tailored to people with disabilities. Parks leadership quickly saw the utility and morality of such programs. By the early 1980s, the Oregon State Parks Guide listed accessible parks and waysides, and there were moves to consider accessibility when building and remodeling. Accessibility goals were integrated into park plans and guidelines formally in 1988. In 2004, the issue of accessibility came face to face with the issue of historic preservation. Vista House, a historic structure and landmark of the Columbia River Gorge, was in the midst of a years-long restoration when the issue of accessibility features was brought to Carrier's attention.

Many groups—ODOT, the Historic Columbia River Highway Advisory Committee, some among the park staff—grew concerned that plans for wheelchair access to and within all levels of the building would significantly detract from the exterior and interior features of the building. Mike Carrier, meeting with the concerned parties, held firm that access to the building would be a mandatory feature of any restoration work, and that only the specifics of the design could be negotiated. Remembering this altercation years later, park staff recalled that it was "an unpopular but principled decision." Tim Wood continued the fight over ramps at Vista House, acknowledging that it was important to strike a balance between the architectural beauty of the building and the needs of visitors. He would strive to strike a balance "between all interested persons and competing interests," But he also stressed that "we need to move forward." Eventually, OPRD found a pragmatic third way. A semi-concealed lift with period-appropriate accents was installed in 2006, making the whole structure accessible to those with mobility issues without mortally offending preservationists. [370]

Moves toward accessible buildings, larger campsites for handicap vehicles, and other amenities geared towards visitors with disabilities began in the 1970s, but programs geared toward more culturally diverse Oregonians would not follow until the 2000s. In 2006, the Oregon Statewide Comprehensive

---

370 State Parks and Recreation Advisory Committee meeting minutes, April 1, 1977, p. 2, Advisory Committee Minutes & Actions 1971 – 1981, Oregon State Parks and Recreation Collection; John Elliott, "Questions and Answers Regarding State Parks" (Aug 26, 1982), p. 3, OPRD Digital Archive [unfiled]; 2010 Citizen Advisory Committee, "Oregon State Parks 2010 Plan" (Salem: Oregon Parks and Recreation Division, Department of Transportation, 1988), p. 7, Box: Strategic Plans 1956 – 2012, Oregon State Parks and Recreation Collection; "OPRD History Panel Discussion [2012]," p. 8; Jo Bell, State Parks and Recreation Commission meeting minutes, December 16, 2004, Meeting Brief # 17, Folder: Commission Meeting Notes [1990 – 2013], unfiled, Oregon State Parks and Recreation Digital Collection; Jo Bell, State Parks and Recreation Commission meeting minutes, December 16, 2004, p. 10, Folder: Commission Meeting Notes [1990 – 2013], unfiled, Oregon State Parks and Recreation Digital Collection; **https://vistahouse.com/accessibility/**.

Outdoor Recreation Plan (SCORP) looked specifically at two growing Oregon populations, retirees and minorities, and speculated about activities that might drive these groups to more regularly visit parks. In the resulting report it was noted that "the results of a statewide SCORP mail survey of Hispanic and Asian-American households show that members of the two minorities engage in fewer outdoor recreation activities, and in fewer numbers, than the general population."

The "Let's Go Camping" program taught families camping know-how and was designed to make parks more freely accessible to those less familiar with the outdoors. In 2006, the Oregon State Parks guide was printed in Spanish for the first time. Still, these efforts fell short in making parks more representative of the state as a whole. By 2017, it was clear that a more seismic shift would be necessary, after that year's "Let's Go Camping" event when "visitors from another group directed racial epithets toward program participants who were using the restroom facilities." The same year, park staff debates over the appropriateness of a confederate flag during Civil War reenacts at Fort Stevens State Park began to confront racism more directly (see below).[371]

These small advances ignored larger issues of stereotyping and a lack of representation that made parks unwelcoming spaces for minority populations. Focus groups conducted on the heels of the 2006 SCORP noted that it was stereotyping rather than a lack of interest that kept Black communities from using Oregon parks. Kevin Price, the first and at times only African American park manager in the first 100 years of Oregon State Parks, added that there was no education or marketing of parks to people of color. "People come from all over the world to see the scenery in the Columbia River Gorge, yet we've found that kids living only 20 miles away don't know it exists." Price worked with Black communities to open the door for more diverse visitors. One of his more famous programs brought students from Martin Luther King Jr. School in Portland to state parks along the Columbia Gorge. Price believed that experiencing the outdoors on guided tours with Black rangers eased the fears of some school children who were taught or internalized a certain discomfort with wild spaces. This program drew new visitors to Gorge parks, and OPRD made a glossy video praising Price and his program. But this was not followed by any systematic statewide equivalent that might directly engage with minority populations to encourage visitation. [372]

371 "SCORP to Target Social Issues," *FYI* 616 (Jan 29 – Feb 4, 2006), p. 3; "Potential Camping Interest Emerges in Latest Minority Recreation Survey," *FYI* 695 (Sept 2 – 8, 2007), p. 1; "State Parks Guide Now in Español," *FYI* 716 (Feb 10 – 16, 2008), p. 1; "Director's Office: Recent Incidents Shed Light on What It Means to Be Inclusive" *FYI 2.0* Sept 22, 2017, p. 1; Jean Thompson, Personal Communication, July 24 2020.

372 "Black History Observance, SCORP Research Target Barriers," *FYI* 665 (Feb 4 – 10, 2007), p. 1; Jennifer Anderson, "Boosting Diversity at Oregon State Parks," *Sustainable Life* Aug 1, 2017; "Park Manager Kevin Price reflects on his 35-year career with the Oregon State Parks" [video], ~Aug 2018, **https://www.oregon.gov/oprd/emp/Pages/EMP-overview.aspx**; Jean Thompson, Personal Communication, Aug 26 2020.

It Is Natural as Anything:
Continued Fights for Affirmative Action

As staff took a long look at the lack of representation in park visitors, the SCORP also recommended that Oregon State Parks needed to diversify their staff which would, it was hoped, create an environment of inclusion on all levels. The lack of representation among rangers and Headquarters staff was something that Dave Talbot noted in the 1990s. Kevin Price, when reflecting in 2007 on more than 20 years of service with OPRD, said "I still attend too many meetings where I'm the only Black person there... Some days, the only person of African American descent I see in our parks, let alone meetings, is Lavern Watson, our office manager. I'd like to see that change." Price suggested that staffing should to reflect Oregon's population: in 2007, he was one of only four Black OPRD employees statewide. OPRD had kept a passive eye on these racial disparities among staff since the era of Dave Talbot, but it became clear in the 2000s that OPRD needed to take an active role in education, training, and advocacy for more diverse staff and visitors in park spaces. In 2014, executive leadership identified inclusion, both among employees and park visitors, as a key strategic initiative of the coming years. Director Van Laanen (see below) acknowledged that parks were failing in "our ability to reach the full spectrum of Oregon citizens, regardless of race, ability, economic background, geography, or affinity for what we see as traditional recreational pursuits." So a committee was formed.[373]

Inequalities in representation were brought to the forefront in the era of Affirmative Action, but discrimination in the workplace was an issue of Oregon State Parks from its inception (see Chapter 4). In 1983, Maureen Kurtz, the Affirmative Action Coordinator reported to the Advisory Committee that "women and minorities are underutilized in certain jobs within State Parks." Four years later, Kurtz reported some improvement in the hiring of women and that "minority representation in Office/Clerical and Service/Maintenance categories remains above parity." It is unclear from the source whether the fact that minoritized people held a high number of clerical and maintenance positions was meant to applaud the efforts of the Affirmative Action program or to highlight the fact that minoritized people were being hired for blue and pink collar positions rather than more elevated roles. By 1989, only 16 percent of the 140 Oregon State Park rangers were women. The racial background of employees was not noted.[374]

373 "Black History Observance, SCORP Research Target Barriers," p. 1; "Director's Column" FYI 2.0 (Dec. 12, 2014), p. 1.

374 State Parks and Recreation Advisory Committee meeting minutes, Dec. 9, 1983, p. 8, Folder: Advisory Committee Minutes & Actions 1981 – 1989, Oregon State Parks and Recreation Collection; State Parks and Recreation Advisory Committee meeting minutes, Dec. 4, 1987, p. 9, Folder: Advisory Committee Minutes & Actions 1981 – 1989, Oregon State Parks and Recreation Collection; There were multiple park employees with Spanish names and surnames employed by Oregon Parks and Recreation by the 1980s; it is unclear how many of them were Hispanic or Latinx. "Changes Transform ODOT Workforce," *Via News: Oregon Department of Transportation* 9:10 (Oct 1984).

A 1989 article in *Via*, published through the Oregon Department of Transportation, noted that sexual harassment claims were on the rise in Oregon, though they blamed the uptick on "more men and women working side by side" rather than on the toxic norms of abusive masculinity many employees still embraced. In ODOT, 12 allegations of sexual harassment were investigated in 1989, though the Parks and Recreation Department had no formal sexual harassment investigations in 1988 or 1989. Operations analyst Deb Schallert was quick to note that the lack of formal complaints did not mean that Parks were without issues, "It's not that sexual harassment isn't a problem at Parks. It's just that things aren't escalating." The two complaints made in 1989 were "resolved at the local level."[375]

Unlike workers in earlier eras—the "girls with pretty eyes" regularly ogled and demeaned by coworkers—those facing sexual discrimination and harassment during this period had recourse. In 1987 a "seasonal employee at Wallowa Lake State Park was charged with sexual misconduct by the division, based on allegations by fellow employees. Concerns for employee and park visitor safety resulted in his removal from employment and investigation of charges." Despite the complaints of multiple employees, the removal could not be "justified," and the man who was fired sued on the grounds of emotional distress. This case, brought to the attention of the Advisory Committee, showcased a new effort on the part of the Parks system to investigate claims and act swiftly to protect employees. But it also demonstrates how difficult such changes can be in a hostile cultural climate. The man had been accused by multiple employees, and those accusations had purportedly been taken seriously. But apparently multiple witnesses and allegations were not enough to "justify" the complaint, and the man was able to bring a lawsuit credible enough that the Advisory Committee needed to know about it.[376]

Changes among staff were stilted and largely tactical. The 1960s culture of parks, the old jokes and the boys' club mentality, stayed largely intact into the next decades. Affirmative action and sexual harassment policies were brought into the organization through federal and state mandates. Unlike the old *Oregon Park Times*, the new internal newsletter *FYI* did not feature regular stories making light of sexual harassment by perpetually ogle-some male employees. But below the surface of officialdom, the fraternity of workers went unchallenged. "I'm afraid our organization is guilty of some 'good ol' boy' mentality," Dave Talbot said in 1990. "It is natural as anything." And that societal presumption about what was "natural" haunted all attempts at inclusion or representation in parks.[377]

375 "Sexual Harassment on the Rise," *Via News: Oregon Department of Transportation* 15:1 (Jan. 1990), p. 1.

376 State Parks and Recreation Advisory Committee meeting minutes, Dec. 4, 1987, pp. 13 - 14, Folder: Advisory Committee Minutes & Actions 1981 – 1989, Oregon State Parks and Recreation Collection.

377 David G. Talbot, "Personal Views on the Development of Oregon State Parks," May 16, 1990, Interview with Lawrence C. Merriam and Elisabeth Walton Potter, p. 118, Folder: Administrative History – Oral History – David G. Talbot, Director, 1964 – 1992, Box: Staff Biographies and Oral Histories, Oregon State Parks and Recreation Collection.

For decades, women were almost never considered for field management jobs. By the 2000s, that picture was beginning to change.

Lisa Van Laanen (later Sumption) was interviewed by the *Statesman Journal* in 2015, after a year as the Director of State Parks. An employee of the parks department since 2007, Van Laanen was already familiar with the Parks system before she had been tapped to lead it. When asked if she faced any hardships as the first woman serving permanently in the role, she replied:

> *This is honestly the first time I've thought about it ... I've never felt like I have to show up different because I'm in a male-dominated organization. I work with people who love what they do, who know that I love what I do, and that's the most important thing. So, thank goodness no, it hasn't been a hurdle at all.*

Others working within OPRD saw the positive changes from earlier eras but still urged the organization to strive for more. As one employee said in 2013:

> *Initially, in the '90s, OPRD was a male dominated, hierarchical agency. New, strong, qualified women brought a sense and reality of equality... However, the culture was still fairly closed as far as acceptance went.... The "good 'ol boys" network was slow to change and open.*

Women were able to rise through the ranks of the parks system, and staff training on sexual harassment gave marginalized workers opportunities for advancement and legal recourse for any claims of harassment. But disparities still existed and exclusion would still partially define working within parks.[378]

---

378 Zach Urness, "Parks Leader Charts New Direction for Oregon," *Statesman Journal*, March 5, 2015; "Draft OPRD History Questionnaire, 1990 – Present [2013]," pp. 29 – 30, Folder: Kate Schutt Records – More Kate Schutt Records, Oregon Parks and Recreation Digital Archive. As is often the case with more subtle forms of discrimination, it can be difficult parse potential sexism in records from the 2000s and 2010s. Many of the mostly male participants in a 2012 group oral history of the turbulent 1990s described Nancy Rockwell as an especially divisive and aggressive member of the executive team. But it is unclear the extent to which those descriptions reflected her role and attitude as Meinen's enforcer, and to what extent they reflected sexist biases (unconscious or otherwise) among participants. "OPRD History Panel Discussion [2012]"; Deborah A. Prentice and Erica Carranza, "What Women and Men Should Be, Shouldn't Be, Are Allowed to Be, and Don't Have to Be: The Contents of Proscriptive Gender Stereotypes," *Psychology of Women Quarterly* 26:4 (2002): pp. 269 – 281.

You're in Our Country:
Indigenous Nations Working with Parks

Although progress in the realm of inclusivity came slowly, efforts to include and honor Indigenous nations within the park system leapt forward in the 2000s. In 1990, the federal government enacted the Native American Graves Protection and Repatriation Act (NAGPRA). Although specifically relevant to gravesites and only mandated for organizations that received federal funding, this legislation encouraged states to examine their treatment of Indigenous peoples, cultures, and objects. Prior to NAGPRA, the treatment of Indigenous remains and objects was left largely unregulated and no clear-cut legal recourse existed for Indian nations in the event that burial sites were found, looted, or destroyed. A 1969 Oregon State Parks newsletter highlights the confusion over handling of remains:

> Elisabeth Walton has three boxes of bones in her room
>
> On October 9 Joe Davis of Champoeg brought the three boxes of skeletal remains (presumed to be Indian) unearthed during construction on private land, about 12 miles north of Champoeg. The bones were offered to the park after having been offered to OMSI and the Oregon Historical Society. She is transferring them to the University of Oregon Museum of Natural History for study.

Walton had reason to believe that the remains in her office were Chinook, but it didn't occur to any of the people who handled these boxes to contact anyone of Chinook descent to weigh in. NAGPRA was designed to avoid instances like this. [379]

In 2019, Nancy J. Nelson, Oregon State Parks archaeologist, determined that most state park properties had at least one precontact archaeological site. To respectfully handle these sites and train staff on appropriate management, OPRD held its first archaeological training in 2005 and the first archaeologist for OPRD was hired in 2006. This signified a shift in the relationship between Indian nations and Oregon State Parks. OPRD for the first time acknowledged their role as stewards for lands that were violently taken (see Chapter 1). [380]

The purpose of the trainings was to bring Indigenous people into discussions of appropriate use of lands, help staff understand the importance of certain natural resources to cultural identity, and create reciprocal relationships between park employees and tribal nations. Most importantly, staff were

---

379 "MEANWHILE BACK AT THE OFFICE," *Oregon State Park Times* 7:3[?] (Nov. 1969), p. 18, Folder: Staff Newsletter – Park Times – 1969, Box: Publications – Staff Newsletters, 1963 – 1994, Oregon State Parks and Recreation Collection.

380 Nancy J. Nelson, "Tribes and the Oregon Parks and Recreation Department—Partnerships in Training, Repatriation, and Traditional Plant Gathering," in Dennis G. Griffin *et al*, "The State of Oregon and Nine Federally-Recognized Tribes Forge a Path Forward," *Journal of Northwest Anthropology* 55:1 (2021), pp. 173 – 184, esp. p. 2.

given clear guidelines on when and how to involve tribal leadership in the decision-making process on state park land. In 2003, a policy was drafted that "permit[ed] Native Americans to conduct traditional plant collecting and ceremonial activities on OPRD owned or managed property." Programs extended to include appropriate training for law enforcement when looting is discovered, a problem that was once common among park visitors and park staff alike (see chapter 4). In 2008, OPRD began the process of repatriation more than 5,000 artifacts looted from lands belonging to the Klamath and housed at Collier Memorial State Park. The slow process of cataloguing and returning these objects took nearly a decade to complete. Going beyond the requirements of NAGPRA to attempt the spirit, not just the letter, of the law, this repatriation effort signaled the changes that could be made when ongoing relationships are developed between OPRD and Indigenous communities. [381]

The return of physical objects and open communications between OPRD and Indian nations was one step. Another was acknowledging Oregon State Parks' own history of erasing Indigenous nations from the narrative of the Oregon. At Champoeg State Heritage Site, a traveling exhibit titled "Oregon is Indian County" designed by the Oregon Historical Society and the nine recognized Indigenous nations of Oregon was brought in. Together with new interpretation linking Champoeg to its Kalapuya origins, the exhibit helped to dispel some of the White pageantry usually associated with Champoeg as the seat of a new territorial government. During the restoration of Vista House, the Parks Commission requested that Indigenous history be featured in any new interpretive displays and, more importantly, that local Indigenous nations be consulted in the creation of that exhibit. These small acts in re-framing Oregon history showcase the very tentative steps State Parks took in the 2000s, and highlight that there is still much more to be done.[382]

In 2009, Oregon State Parks and Recreation opened the first park that explicitly acknowledged the location's ties to Indigenous history. Named Iwetemlaykin, Nez Perce for "at the edge of the lake," this was the first park created with input from multiple Indigenous councils at the onset. The Umatilla Indian Reservation, Nez Perce Tribe, and Confederated Tribes of the Colville Reservation all partnered with Oregon State Parks in the acquisition and development of this park. Located in the Wallowa Lake Basin, this site is adjacent to the Nez Perce National Historical Park. [383]

---

381 Angie Springer, State Parks and Recreation Commission meeting minutes, January 23, 2003, p. 7, Folder: Commission Meeting Notes [1990 – 2013], unfiled, Oregon State Parks and Recreation Digital Collection; Nelson, "Tribes and the Oregon Parks and Recreation Department—Partnerships in Training, Repatriation, and Traditional Plant Gathering"; "Site Stewards Sought to Keep an Eye on Park Archaeological Treasures," *FYI* 802 (Dec 6 – 12, 2009), pp. 3 – 4.

382 Traveling Historical Exhibit at Champoeg Focuses on Native American Heritage," *FYI* 802 (Dec 6 – 12, 2009), pp. 4 – 5; Angie Springer, State Parks and Recreation Commission meeting minutes, June 19, 2003, p.2, Folder: Commission Meeting Notes [1990 – 2013], unfiled, Oregon State Parks and Recreation Digital Collection; David G. Lewis, "The Spirit of Colonization of Indian Country: Vista House and American Nationalism," *Quartux Journal* Sept 4, 2017.

383 "Iwetemlaykin Timeline on Pace for September Opening," *FYI* 765 (March 1 – 7, 2009), p. 1.

The Parks Commission met with representatives of the tribal nations of the Wallowa Lake Basin in 2005 to discuss the potential of a park in the area. Joseph McCormack, speaking on behalf of the Nez Perce General Tribal Council, appealed to the Commission for the protection of certain key lands in the area:

> We feel that we need help in this and we approach this Board to help collaborate in the securing of this area for the future of the tribal people and also for the citizens of Oregon. It's very imperative that our people continue to be able to come here and celebrate this area knowing that our ancestors had always done so... We are not a people that has vanished. We continue to revere this lake.

Bobbie Conner, speaking on behalf of the Confederated Tribes of the Umatilla Indian Reservation and a retiring member of the State Parks Commission, urged not just the protection of sacred spaces, but also a rethinking of how state parks handled notions of "ownership" and "cultural significance."

> I find it ironic that you're in our country, from which we were dispossessed—for anyone else to possess it now required dispossession from us—and you're asking us to prove what we know to be true.... It is strange that a people whose history is no-impact and low-impact camping are now being required to dig holes to prove that we know that there is something there. Again, we're not talking about the rules that exist, because you only have the responsibility for making sure that they're carried out. But I would like to challenge one of the rules.... modify the regulation so that it does not use the word 'site,' but instead 'landscape or 'area.'

Requiring a "site," Conner argued, meant that Native people had to comply with a potentially violating act of archaeology just to prove, in the eyes of American law, what they already knew—that their homelands were their homelands. Iwetemlaykin was eventually made into a cultural area as requested, with the financial assistance and collaboration of the three Indigenous nations most closely tied to the lake, and despite contentious meetings characterized by racial tensions. It was, as Nez Perce Vice Chair Brooklyn Baptiste said at the dedication, a way to "bring a little peace," and perhaps to serve as an "example... of what can be done to heal those wounds, what can be done to make amends in some way.... to work together toward a common goal." But the issue Bobbie Conner raised remained. OPRD had taken significant steps towards inclusion, particularly when it came to Indigenous issues. But what about when inclusion isn't enough? [384]

---

384   Jo Bell, State Parks and Recreation Commission meeting minutes, September 22, 2005, pp. 1-5, Folder: Commission Meeting Notes [1990 – 2013], unfiled, Oregon State Parks and Recreation Digital Collection; Terry Richard, "Memorize Iwetemlaykin: It Will Be Famous," Oregonian March 9, 2009; "Iwetemlaykin: At the Edge of the Lake, a State Park Is Born," La Grande Observer, Oct 15, 2009; Brooklyn Baptiste, "Iwetemlaykin Grand Opening - Part 5" [video], Oregon Parks and Recreation Department, uploaded Dec. 16, 2009.

Exterminate Every One:
Reckoning with a Problematic Past

Oregon Parks and Recreation has long approached the creation of history collaboratively. From Champoeg onward, most historical sites in the state parks system came from dedicated individuals on the ground excited about a particular site or aspect of history. Interpretation, so often on the budgetary chopping block, has frequently been the purview of enthusiastic amateurs, invested volunteers, or rangers with a particular passion. This has spurred expansions and changes in interpretation. In 1994, for example, Ranger Kelly Brady and the Confederated Tribes of the Umatilla put on a tribal living history event at Emigrant Springs State Park—the very spot where President Harding had celebrated the violent conquest of Native America some 70 years before (see Chapter 1). But although individual passions could lead to positive changes, they could also mean that popular historical narratives would become ingrained in the state parks system, even when scholarship has moved past or challenged them.[385]

In the 2000s and 2010s, efforts were made to bring forward previously excluded narratives. Kam Wah Chung, a vital site for the history of people of Chinese descent in 19th century Oregon, went from afterthought to a prized jewel of the historic park system. During the restoration of Vista House, the Parks Commission asked that Indigenous history be featured in any new interpretive displays and, more importantly, that local Indigenous nations be consulted in the creation of that exhibit. In 2004, the Parks Commission approved an updated policy that "allows for Tribal consultation in the naming process if there is a tribal cultural affiliation with the property."[386]

This new naming policy was a tangible move toward avoiding repetition of the mistakes of the past. But it did nothing to redress them. Naming practices for parks in the past have celebrated colonialism and violence. In 1979, Dexter State Park was rededicated as Elijah Bristow State Park, meant to honor Bristow as the "first white settler in Lane County." Following the recommendations of the Lane County Historical Society and the subsequent approval of the Advisory Committee, Parks and Recreation overlooked the fact that they were naming a park after a settler who was known to have shot a Klamath man in the back, threatened to "exterminate every one" of that Klamath man's friends and companions, and a little later beat a visiting Klickitat person half to death for no clear reason other than "to show courage." These anecdotes were indisputably known to the Lane County Historical Society, which had published them as part of a celebratory history of Bristow in 1968. Whether Oregon Parks and Recreation was aware of this history at any level is unknown—they were, after all, just

---

385 *FYI* 51 (1994). This was far from the only such partnership—see for example the Confederated Tribes of Warm Springs involvement in Lake Billy Chinook Days, *FYI* 208 (Sept 5, 1997).

386 Angie Springer, State Parks and Recreation Commission meeting minutes, February 26, 2004, p. 7, Folder: Commission Meeting Notes [1990 – 2013], unfiled, Oregon State Parks and Recreation Digital Collection; Angie Springer, State Parks and Recreation Commission meeting minutes, June 19, 2003, p.2, Folder: Commission Meeting Notes [1990 – 2013], unfiled, Oregon State Parks and Recreation Digital Collection

listening to the experts. But the racist renaming showcases the ease with which "pioneer" history continues unchallenged. [387]

By design, inclusion adds to, rather than replaces, existing narratives. While it was at Champoeg, the "Oregon Is Indian Country" exhibit may have been a counterpoint of sorts. And there have been other moves to bring the Indigenous history of Champoeg to the forefront. In 2018, for example, OPRD co-hosted a "Champoeg Celebration" with the Confederated Tribes of the Grand Ronde. Harkening back to the Indigenous and etymological roots of the site—Champoeg's name is derived from a Chinook word for the edible roots cultivated and gathered there—the event was yet another result of the carefully built partnerships between OPRD and Oregon's Indigenous communities.[388]

But "history" at the site in the 2010s was still dominated by the historical narratives that were popular at the time of its foundation in the 1900s. "Living history" reenactments, which can do so much to engage visitors, also run the risk of repeating harmful historical narratives. Volunteers dressed up as "pioneers" or "mountain men" in multiple parks have typically ignored the racism, theft, rape, murder, and genocide that typified the conquest of Oregon in the 1840s and 50s, focusing instead on demonstrations of trapping, farming, and "pioneering" unencumbered by the historical reality of violence (see Chapter 1). Native people continued to be largely absent from the events and the narrative—except for the redface portrayals of largely Euro-American women pretending to be the Metis/Native wives of fur trappers in re-enactments. The racism of the pageantry billed as "what life was like in the 1800s" most likely sprang from ignorance more than malice. And formally ending it at Champoeg might even require legal action, as OPRD has arguably been mandated by law to "encourage the further development of the pageant and promote increased attendance at its performances." But whatever their ultimate fate, "pioneer" reenactments illustrate the thornier issues of history in state parks. Adding new stories is generally popular. Removing racist narratives can be harder.[389]

This issue came to a head over the Confederate flag. At least as early as 1990, Civil War reenactors were performing in Oregon State Parks, especially

---

387 State Parks and Recreation Advisory Committee meeting minutes, March 22, 1979, pp. 2 – 3, Advisory Committee Minutes & Actions 1971 – 1981, Oregon State Parks and Recreation Collection; Fannie Leggett, "A Short Historical Sketch of a Part of the Bristow Family," *Lane County Historian* 13:3 (Fall 1968): 63 – 68; Marc James Carpenter, "Pioneer Problems: 'Wanton Murder,' Indian War Veterans, and Oregon's Violent History," *Oregon Historical Quarterly* 121:2 (Summer 2020): pp. 156 – 185. These stories of violence were the ones Bristow bragged of publicly; there is no reason to believe that he did not commit other acts of violence deemed less suitable for public consumption. The "Dexter" in what was Dexter State Park purportedly came from the name of a cookstove.

388 Danielle Frost, "Champoeg Celebration Attracts 100 Attendees Interested in Native Plants," *Smoke Signals* Oct 18, 2018.

389 Oregon State Parks and Recreation, "Champoeg State Heritage Area Trappers Camp, 2017" (video), uploaded July 26, 2017; Collin Ellis, "Founders Day Celebrates History of Champoeg," *Newberg Graphic* May 2, 2019; ORS 186.30, "Champoeg Historical Pageant as Official Statehood Pageant," *CHAPTER 186—State Emblems; State Boundary* (Legislative Counsel Committee, 2019); Ann Virtu Snyder, "Location, Location, Location: Reflections of an Itinerant Practitioner," *NWSA Journal* 17:2 (2005), pp. 142 – 149; Patrick McCarthy, "'Living History' as the 'Real Thing': A Comparative Analysis of the Modern Mountain Man Rendezvous, Renaissance Fairs, and Civil War Re-Enactments," *ETC: A Review of General Semantics* 71:2 (2014): pp. 106 – 123. C

Milo McIver and Fort Stevens. The mock battles, which took place over multiple days, drew thousands to Oregon state parks in the 1990s. The Northwest History Association was in charge of most of these events. They dabbled in other wars, once putting on a WWII demonstration at Fort Stevens that included pitting those dressed as US servicemen against those dressed as Nazi soldiers. But the Civil War was their focus. Like other "living history" re-enactors they focused on the attention to material conditions that could be brought to life. Like other "living history" reenactors they glossed over the violent racism (though not the other violence) that was so central to the history they were playing with. And like other Civil War re-enactors, those roleplaying as Confederates flew the Confederate battleflag, which retains its visceral power as a symbol of violent racism for many people of color *and* White supremacists in the Pacific Northwest. The Northwest History Association has always asserted that the use of Confederate iconography has been meant to reflect history rather than celebrate it—whether in flying the flag of slavery during their re-enactments on the grounds of state parks, or when wearing replicas of the uniforms of those who fought against the United States when they march in Veteran's Day parades.[390]

In the September 2017 issue of *FYI*, unnamed "people of color in the agency" raised concerns with OPRD leadership about the effect that flying of the Confederate flag on parks property had on themselves and potentially on visitors. Leadership responded with a commitment to examine the issue. There was no official announcement about what followed. But special treatment of reenactors ended. Previously, they had gotten fee waivers for visiting and camping—no more. The non-profit Friends of Fort Stevens were asked by people within OPRD to stop advertising or assisting with the events. "[S]tate parks no longer want us here," Northwest History Association Chairman Earl Bishop complained. And so the reenactors did not return to state parks in 2018, or after.[391]

A call to re-examine a problematic practice may have led the leadership to forego at least some profit in the pursuit of racial justice. Civil war reenactments had first been encouraged during the "Wild West" of the 1990s, when park profits were paramount. They were reconsidered at a time when priorities had changed, but money was once again tight. Budget difficulties, briefly warded off in the early 2000s, came roaring back. Budget problems *always* came back.

---

390 Northwest Civil War Council, "Who We Are," **https://www.nwcwc.net/who-we-are.html**; *FYI* 190 (Apr 25, 1997); *FYI* 237 (Apr 10, 1998); *FYI* 305 (Aug 27, 1999); *FYI* 825 (Sept. 10, 2010); Lizzy Acker, "White Nationalist Grad Student Responsible for Confederate Flag Hanging Across from Black Cultural Center in Corvallis, Police Say," *Oregonian* Jan 26, 2018; Bennett Hall, "Reenactors Rise Again at Parade," *Corvallis Gazette-Times*, Nov 11, 2019; James O. Farmer, "Playing Rebels: Reenactment as Nostalgia and Defense of the Confederacy in the Battle of Aiken," *Southern Cultures* 11:1 (2005): pp. 46 – 73; Tony Horwitz, *Confederates in the Attic: Dispatches from the Unfinished Civil War* (New York: Random House, 1998).

391 "Director's Office: Recent Incidents Shed Light On What It Means to Be Inclusive" *FYI 2.0* Sept, 22, 2017, p. 1; Jack Heffernan, "Ordering a Retreat," *Daily Astorian* Feb 20 2018 AND Dec 4 2018; Northwest Civil War Council, "To Avoid Further Confusion" Facebook post, March 31 2018; Bryn Stole, "The Decline of the Civil War Re-Enactor," *New York Times* July 28, 2018.

Everything They Asked For, and More:
Tim Wood Weathers Another Storm

Tim Wood began his directorship in 2004 focused on the growth of programs. By the time he stepped down in 2014, however, it was clear that his era would be defined by how OPRD handled the Great Recession. The recession hit at the end of a rare moment of optimism. Referring to the 2005 – 2007 budget, Tim Wood noted that parks received "everything they asked for, and more". Though the "and more" hinted at the tendency for the legislature to unload struggling programs onto the park system, the overall tenor of budget planning that year was one of cautious hope. The approved budget hinted that the financial storms that had wracked the department under Bob Meinen and washed in with each new troubled program under Carrier might be coming to an end. The calm, such as it was, lasted two years.[392]

In 2007, a cascade of disasters from subprime lending and the collapse of the real estate market had a swift and far-reaching impact on the finances of the United States and the world. These impacts rippled quickly through the financial sector, closing banks and putting mortgages underwater. As foreboding and fear swept Oregon, fewer people took a gamble on lottery games. In the summer of 2007, as the crisis was just unfolding, Director Tim Wood recruited Lisa Van Laanen for the role of Assistant Director. Van Laanen's background was largely in business management and customer service, and Wood knew that the money pits OPRD had been inheriting would require business savvy to weather. When she was recruited from among a pool of candidates to replace Tim Wood at his retirement in 2014, the *Statesman Journal* wrote, "In some ways, Van Laanen was an unusual choice. Although she'd worked at OPRD for seven years, her background was in internal auditing and business administration, not natural resources." Van Laanen's role, her involvement overseeing the team dealing with the State Fair mess, and her eventual promotion to lead OPRD signaled that those in charge were returning the "business" of managing parks to center stage.[393]

As the financial crisis deepened in 2008, Tim Wood tried to avoid the mass layoffs that had traumatized the department in the 1990s. The budget plan in May required hiring freezes, travel restrictions, and programmatic cuts, but not the mass destruction of jobs that had accompanied budget reductions in previous decades. In February of 2009, Wood warned that, depending on the economy projections, more cuts might be necessary. That summer, high gas prices challenged another revenue source—campsite rentals—and strained an already slim budget. Although people with planned trips still went camping, drop-in sites were often vacant. In November of 2009, Van Laanen presented the

---

392 "OPRD's 2005-2007 Budget" 'Everything asked for, and more'" FYI 595 August 14-20 2005 p. 1.

393 "New Assistant Director Assumes OPRD's Administration Lead," *FYI* 693 (Aug 19 – 25, 2007), p. 2; Zach Urness "Parks Leader Charts New Direction for Oregon," *Statesman Journal*, March 5, 2015.

financial situation to the Commission. The state of Oregon instituted 10 closure days in which staff would be furloughed, and an additional one to four furlough days would be instituted for management only. Parks would remain open, and the overall budget projections for parks seemed, if not promising, sustainable. Compared to the downturns of previous eras, this probably felt like a miracle. Lottery funding was not as resistant to economic downturns as gas or bottles would have been, but compared to those agencies solely reliant on the General Fund, Oregon Parks and Recreation weathered the Great Recession well.[394]

Wood urged optimism and a staff-wide focus on the mission of the organization, which was more important now during these times of uncertainty. He saw visitors still coming to parks, just choosing parks closer to home, as an example of parks' importance to the community. When livelihoods are threatened, he argued, the "respite and solace" found in state parks "improve[s] the daily lives of Oregonians." This was a lesson Sam Boardman had taught his own staff during the Great Depression: that people need parks more, not less, when times are tough. But despite the optimism of management and the dedication of the staff, the impacts of the Great Recession were keenly felt in parks. Hiring freezes and furloughs meant fewer hands on the ground to clean, lead programs, and maintain the landscape. Staff kept their jobs, but the work became harder. The 2009-2011 budget was nine percent less than requested, but, Wood said, most programs would thankfully remain intact. [395]

In 2010, Oregon Parks and Recreation sailed through another important milestone. With the economy still recovering from the Great Recession, Oregon voters were asked if they still wanted to fund Oregon state parks through the lottery. They answered with a resounding "yes!" The State Parks portion of lottery funds was made permanent, with a majority of Oregonians in every county, urban or rural, voting in favor.[396]

The larger financial crisis had largely passed by 2013, but lottery revenue for state parks was still in a decline—placing a spotlight on the dangers of relying on those funds for operational security. Wood saw this as an opportunity to take a hard look at the park system's viability. The 2012 Systems Plan, created in this era, was meant to guide OPRD's financial solvency through strategic downsizing of the park system. It also encouraged staff to consider revenue sources that would not sacrifice the integrity of the mission. In writing a history of the period, one staff member noted, "this [began] to sound quite a lot like the crisis

394 "Budget Proposals for 2009-2011 Receive Commission Approval," *FYI* 728 (May 4 – 10, 2008); "From the Director: Savings Plan Keeps Us in Control," *FYI* 761 (Feb. 1 – 7, 2009), p. 1; "From the Director: 2009 Brings Opportunities,"*FYI* 757 (Jan 4 – 10, 2009), p. 1; State Parks and Recreation Commission meeting minutes, November 18-19, 2009, p. 7, Folder: Commission Meeting Notes [1990 – 2013], unfiled, Oregon State Parks and Recreation Digital Collection.

395 "From the Director: 2009 Brings Opportunities," *FYI* 757 (Jan 4 – 10, 2009), p. 1; OPRD's Savings Plan: Communicating its Effects," *FYI* 763 (Feb 15 – 21, 2009), p. 1; "From the Director: OPRD Programs Intact as New Budget Period Begins," *FYI* 782 (July 5 – 11, 2009), p. 1.

396 Measure 76, which made the parks portion of the lottery permanent, got 69% of the vote overall—the most popular measure on the ballot in 2010. Craig Dirksen and John Isaacs, "Environmental Protection: A Resounding Call for Investing in Our Natural Assets," *Oregonian* Nov 19, 2010.

OPRD faced with proposing to close parks in the early 1990s." Closing parks in the 1990s prompted ire among visitors which created support for parks, but now this was more than a political ploy: it was the key, Wood believed, to remaining afloat. The report likened Oregon parks to other fundamental utilities, necessary for Oregonians and therefore, requiring of public support. "In many ways, recreational opportunity is like a public utility in Oregon. Similar to public education, water supply, and public safety, good outdoor recreation is an essential need of a healthy community." Public support, "right-sizing" the park system, and using business strategies to optimize resources would allow the park system to continue providing for Oregonians. If these strategies were ignored, the report warned, "people will be disappointed with worse service, sketchy parks, and nasty restrooms." Tim Wood announced his retirement in 2013 and would not be in the role of director as this latest scheme for solvency played out. Despite the hardship of his tenure, he looked back on the time with fondness for the staff and its mission, and a hope that the organization would continue to find new ways to adapt to the changing needs of Oregonians. [397]

In the year 2000, Mike Carrier wrote to his staff, "having stood on its own now for a decade – withstanding the hardest of times, strident criticism and shattered expectations – OPRD has matured into a fully-fledged, independent agency… Just imagine what we can accomplish in a string of years like 2000." He likely wasn't aware that he echoed Chet Armstrong's message nearly 50 years prior. Armstrong looked at the beginning of the park system as he would a baby learning to take their first steps. Both men saw growth and change and both men dreamed that these growing pains would soon pass, and that Oregon State Parks and Recreation would be fully realized. Though, as the new millennium saw the end to some uncertainties, it also saw change in ways that neither Carrier nor Wood anticipated. It was the organization's ability to adapt, rather than its ability to "mature," that let it survive. It was the dedication of those who loved parks, inside and outside of the department, that would allow it to thrive. Through the next crisis, and the next crisis, and the next. [398]

---

397 Oregon Parks and Recreation Department, "State Park Systems Plan," (Dec. 2012), p. 21, unfiled, Oregon State Parks and Recreation Digital Collection; Oregon Parks and Recreation Department, "State Park Systems Plan," p. 22; Wood, "Looking Back from 2013."

398 Carrier, Mike. "Director's Corner" FYI 369. December 18-22, 2000. Folder: Staff Newsletter – FYI – 2000, Box: Publications – Staff Newsletters, 1963 – 1994, Oregon State Parks and Recreation Collection.

So the Future Will Have a Place:
A Centennial Epilogue

by Chris Havel,
Deputy Director
Governmental Relations
Oregon Parks and Recreation Department
April, 2022

For people who have a strong connection to the Oregon state park system, the prior seven chapters will likely provoke a smorgasbord of reactions. Some of the stories—mainly successes—are well-known and have been repeated enough to become modern legends. The first Oregon state park superintendent, Sam Boardman, and his struggles to overcome enormous odds and sow the seeds of the system we enjoy today, features prominently. Likewise, the post-WWII boom and the spread of camping, especially under Chet Armstrong, became the Oregon State Park hallmark: state parks are the comfortable, accessible way to experience nature and explore Oregon history.

As reputations go, this is the kind of aura that attracts a talented, dedicated workforce and brings the community to the very doorstep of the state park system in a way no flashy marketing campaign or special event can.

When the cycle of funding crises reached a climax in the 1980s and 90s, the park system survived its most recent trial, and we now tell stories of the looming catastrophe and impending closure of dozens of parks, only to be rescued by voters who dedicated Oregon Lottery revenue to the cause. There may not have ever been a truly unfettered golden age for state parks in Oregon, but the relative boom that followed when the Lottery poured tens of millions of dollars into park repairs and improvements, community grants, and new parkland purchases likely seemed like one to agency employees and people who campaigned for the 1999 ballot measure.

We may have grumbled about it at the time, but the effort to build new parks from 2004-2014—even at a time when the maintenance load was still acute and depriving some parks of delivering service—created tremendous dividends. The coastal beach at Crissey Field near Brookings, rich history of Thompson's Mills south of Albany, expansive trails of "Stub" Stewart west of Portland, and arid wonderland of Cottonwood Canyon near Condon have served hundreds of thousands of visitors, and over their life, will probably benefit millions more. Lest we fall prey to this misconception that "as long as visitor numbers are high, we're doing good work," the true measure of success at each of these parks is in the quality of the experience, not the volume. It's a poorly-kept secret that most park rangers would prefer to spend an afternoon with a few dozen people who are deeply moved by their park experience than to hear that thanks to good parking management, their park hosted 10,000 people over the weekend.

When we told these stories, it was part pride, and part to cast a wary eye on the future in a possibly vain hope we could find a way to forestall the next inevitable funding crisis.

The pride is justified. When people like Jessie Honeyman, Stub Stewart, Carl Washburne, and Robert Sawyer acted, investing the assets of their privilege into what they viewed as betterment of their society, their efforts seem almost heroic to us now. Agency staff and volunteers can feel some linkage to them by doing their part to continue the work. Keeping 250-plus parks open and serving public needs is challenging, rewarding work and the signs of success come not from dollars earned or acres acquired, but in the life-affirming satisfaction experienced by its patrons.

We challenge the most callous soul to remain unsoftened by the gratitude of a family bonding over a sunset at Fort Rock or a solitary hiker proclaiming victory over their own weary legs atop Humbug Mountain. Those human moments are made possible by today's state park employees and volunteers drawing lines on a map, brushing a trail, cleaning a restroom, and emptying a trash can: arduous tasks that often obscure their glorious outcomes. Pride is, in a sense, a kind of compensation.

However, one of the reasons we directed the authors of this book to go wherever the tale led them was to leaven that pride with the complexity of history. We often speak of Governor Oswald West's horseback ride on a postal trail up over Neah-Kah-Nie Mountain, the lucky, or shrewd, or both, maneuver to have the legislature declare beaches a public highway in 1913, and how that set Oregon on a course to value public access to landscapes for recreation. We go to great lengths to remove obvious physical barriers that prevent people from enjoying the benefits afforded by access to natural landscapes, sometimes adding with a flourish, "This was Oswald West's dream, we think: working to help all people enjoy Oregon's beauty." We do not include in our stories the Governor's support for the monstrous eugenics movement, which declared that some people are more worthy and desirable than others and justified forced sterilizations in the name of genetic "progress." The concept found refuge in more than two dozen states, and the repercussions of the movement reverberated in Oregon until the 1980s.

The parks themselves are not, as Boardman imagined at the start, perfect jewels tasked with healing our wounds, delighting our senses, and connecting us with forces greater than ourselves. They do have beauty and adventure in abundance, and we believe our desire for the joy, peace, and unity with nature these attributes can inspire are among the many things all people have in common. That said, we do park landscapes a disservice if we ignore the fullness of their existence, because they also stand as testimony to wrongs suffered by tribal peoples, sometimes by merely existing within a landscape that sustained human cultures for millennia with virtually no acknowledgment of their existence. Kam Wah Chung State Heritage Site is a billboard, written in poetic yet cryptic verse, illustrating the journey from suffering inhumanity to celebrating acceptance for people from China who labored in Oregon. The Sumpter Dredge Valley Dredge converted lush riverside into a moonscape for what may as well be an eternity when viewed on human timescales.

So, no, not just perfect beauty: all public lands bear the marks of human history since time immemorial, and you'll find triumph, tragedy, crime, peace, joy, anger, and love, but not perfection. Likewise, the people who influenced state parks—governors, directors, commissioners, legislators, philanthropists—are neither purely heroic nor privileged despots. They, and the system they left in our care, are worth celebrating when their actions are judged virtuous, and rightly earn our dismay when in hindsight, they fall far short of even modest humane principles. To hear of racism, sexism, and other forms of disregard for basic humanity threaded into the cultural foundation of the state parks tradition does not diminish its accomplishments, but it prompts us to ask: how can we do better? It is extraordinarily difficult to judge our own attitudes and behaviors in the here and now, but dissecting our own legends is one way to both understand ourselves and make progress.

And that is the challenge. We can see in the most popularized words and deeds of our forebearers their aspiration to serve: "No local selfish interest should be permitted, through politics or otherwise, to destroy or impair this great birthright of our people," said Governor West, speaking of the beach highway legislation. One of the greatest difficulties anyone in public service can face is moving from the conception of a grand idea on paper to delivery of that service in reality, and through decades of buying and building public beach ac-

cesses, blunting development pressure, and protecting natural and cultural resources, it's easy to understand why most people regard the Oregon public ocean
shore as a marvel of public policy.

That does not mean, however, that all people are served equally by that
success. By definition, we cannot usually see our own blind spots, and questions
such as, "Whom are we leaving behind?" and "Whom does this help, and whom
does it hinder?" cannot be wholly answered by the same people who may have
unwittingly designed gaps in park services in the first place. The same can be said
of every systemic malfunction—bias, prejudice, narrow-mindedness—baked
into private and public institutional cultures, including state parks.

The purpose in studying history is not to judge our predecessors, but to
critique ourselves and our own leap from aspiration to service. Understanding
that these tumors exist in our body of work does not mean rejecting the wealth
the healthy parts have produced, but it presents a challenge we must be cou-
rageous enough to accept: we must go beyond merely building facilities and
presenting opportunities to enjoy outdoor recreation and Oregon history, and
instead fully embrace parks as a social endeavor that comes pre-loaded with the
benefits and barriers selected by a dominant culture.

The challenge before us has remained unchanged since the Boardman era:
protect Oregon's most special places, provide the greatest human experiences
possible in those landscapes, and do both in an enduring way. Each generation
has plumbed the depths of these seemingly bottomless pits in different ways,
though the need for money seems a central theme. As you've read up to this
point, Oregon seems to swing between sudden rushes of funding to accomplish
short term goals, to small changes in ongoing funding that incrementally increase
or decrease resources available for day-to-day operations. Gas tax, bonding, general tax funds, recreational vehicle license plate revenue, Lottery, visitor fees: the
shifting patchwork of finance schemes has contributed to past instability and
threatens the future ability to serve.

It seems like an obvious statement, but reliable, sufficient funding is and
will always be critical, because every mile of trail, campsite, restroom, trash
can, and access road has a price tag. Likewise, the park professionals who plan,
build, protect, and operate park services to meet higher-and-higher levels of use
deserve a fair wage. Even volunteers cost money.

The single greatest factor determining the present and future success of the
state park system may not be so practical, however. It is related to the tensions
described above: is there broad public agreement about the purpose of the park
system? Is it equally welcoming and capable of serving people without regards
to income, education, the color of their skin, whom they love, the language they
speak, how they style their bodies and clothing? Does the agency culture attract,

support, and encourage employees and volunteers with diverse backgrounds and viewpoints? Compared with the question, "But where will the money come from?" these questions may seem hopelessly abstract, or even academic.

They are intrinsically related. Backlash aside, people—visitors, people with tribal affiliation, employees, volunteers, and others—first deserve state parks that function well. "Function" is a complicated word, and runs the gamut from the personal, spiritual experience to "mere fun" to mental and physical health benefits to community economic strength and beyond. It also relates to the way our bureaucracy supports staff and volunteers. None of it is simple, and all of it requires negotiating a common understanding of the word. While it is possible to secure broadly-supported public funding without improving the functionality of agency services, doing so relies more on political persuasion campaigns based on what people already believe to be true, which does not always align with reality.

Past attempts to improve the state parks and recreation service have borne fruit, from the development schemes of the 1950s and 60s to the 2010 Plan, but have not attempted to examine some of the cultural and institutional barriers to success that exist within the agency, and between public servants and the people they serve. In a departure from the past, where issues of equity and bias were either ignored or given unenthusiastic treatment, as of 2022, the agency is taking a different tack to make progress against the headwinds of bureaucratic inertia. First, by holding open conversations internally among staff, and externally with communities that have felt unwelcome experiencing parks, we are following a structured approach: engage each other and those with diverse viewpoints in candid conversations about barriers, take the time to digest what we learn and relate to it on a personal level, then adapt how we work to incorporate an ethic of service to all people. Second, we are establishing a collaboration between agency human resource professionals and Oregon State University to recruit the expertise of social scientists, business leaders, and other human resource experts to review and recommend ways to develop a workforce that reflects the people we purport to serve.

These programs aim to lead to substantial change to the agency culture, a lofty goal that can take years, and even if improving service doesn't make it easier to pursue truly reliable, sufficient funding, it remains the correct course.

More practically, the state park system has grown opportunistically, through every director, every commission, every governor. The needs of the day, the availability and nature of funding, the public willingness to sell or donate property, have all combined to create a mulligan stew of properties. Past chapters have brushed against the issue—Should the state park system incorporate large tracts of old growth? Transfer property to local management? Discussions about what the state park system should embrace and where it should divest are part and parcel of a larger conversation about whom it serves and why. Ultimately, the state park portfolio will be shaped by both physical and social dimensions: locations that are either efficient or not for staff to operate, resources that are either closely associated with the recreation or not, history with state-level impact or not. To decide what "deserves" to stay in the state park system based merely on funding is a recipe for constant withdrawal down to our means, however. It is a far greater accomplishment, as a promise to our future selves, to pursue the means that live up to the vision of the state park system.

For all the shining victories and near-catastrophes since 1922, now we look ahead. To what end, and how will we get there? Our response will let slip what we have learned from our history: are we protecting special places to the best of our ability; are we providing opportunities for the great experiences to all people, including those who do not benefit from being heard as members of a dominant culture; can we make it last?

We are not completely surrounded by challenges, pushing in on us from all sides and preventing forward progress. We are supported from beneath and propelled forward by our history—the successes and mistakes—and by a general acceptance that outdoor recreation and history are valuable and necessary to the human experience. This forward motion is countered by resistance from the future: if parks are nothing more than leisure, and leisure is a luxury, how can we invest time, money, sweat, and space when we have yet to address existential threats from global climate change and economic inequities? It is possible the answer Oregon gives may be, "We cannot." If that happens, and there will be times it does, the people who care for parks will do their level best to help them endure until the answer changes.

Optimism is a defining characteristic among people who dedicated their lives to parks and history. Rather than mere luxury, we believe outdoor experiences and a deeper, personal understanding of history aren't just fun and useful on the smallest of scales, but also make us better people, capable of caring enough to be stewards not just of the places set aside with lines on a map and called "parks," but also of our communities, neighborhoods, state, nation, and planet.

So the future will have a place.

BIBLIOGRAPHY

Archive Collections, Unpublished

Advisory Committee Minutes & Actions, Oregon State Parks and Recreation Collection, Oregon State Parks and Recreation, Salem, OR.

Albin Walter Norblad Papers, Ax 680, Special Collections & University Archives, University of Oregon Libraries, Eugene, OR.

Cape Lookout Collection, Oregon State Parks and Recreation Collection, Oregon State Parks and Recreation, Salem, OR.

Chester H. Armstrong Papers, Oregon State Parks and Recreation Collection, Oregon State Parks and Recreation, Salem, OR.

Diaries and Reminiscences, Mss 1509, Oregon Historical Society Special Collections, Portland, OR.

Historic State Park Documents: Milo McIver State Park to Minam State Recreation Area, Oregon State Parks and Recreation Collection, Oregon State Parks and Recreation, Salem, OR.

John Minto Papers, Mss 752, Oregon Historical Society Special Collections, Portland, OR.

Legislation and Statutes, Oregon State Parks and Recreation Collection, Oregon State Parks and Recreation, Salem, OR.

Meetings and Events, Oregon State Parks and Recreation Collection, Oregon State Parks and Recreation, Salem, OR.

Oregon State Parks and Recreation Digital Archive Collection. Oregon State Parks and Recreation Collection, Oregon State Parks and Recreation, Salem, OR.

Oswald West State Park, Oregon State Parks and Recreation Collection, Oregon State Parks and Recreation, Salem, OR.

Park History, Oregon State Parks and Recreation Collection, Oregon State Parks and Recreation, Salem, OR.

Park Issues – Park Closures and Funding Crisis, Oregon State Parks and Recreation Collection, Oregon State Parks and Recreation, Salem, OR.

Planning – Interpretation and Bicentennial, Oregon State Parks and Recreation Collection, Oregon State Parks and Recreation, Salem, OR.

Progress Reports 1959 – 2003 Oregon State Parks and Recreation Collection, Oregon State Parks and Recreation, Salem, OR.

Progress Reports, 1951 – 1958, Oregon State Parks and Recreation Collection, Oregon State Parks and Recreation, Salem, OR.

Publications – Staff Newsletters, 1963 – 1994, Oregon State Parks and Recreation Collection, Oregon State Parks and Recreation, Salem, OR.

Publications – Rules, Surveys, and Reports, Oregon State Parks and Recreation Collection, Oregon State Parks and Recreation, Salem, OR.

Robert W. Sawyer Papers, Ax 100, Special Collections & University Archives, University of Oregon Libraries, Eugene, OR.

Samuel H. Boardman Papers, Oregon State Parks and Recreation Collection, Oregon State Parks and Recreation, Salem, OR.

Staff Biographies and Oral Histories, Oregon State Parks and Recreation Collection, Oregon State Parks and Recreation, Salem, OR.

Strategic Plans, 1956 – 2012, Oregon State Parks and Recreation Collection, Oregon State Parks and Recreation, Salem, OR.

W.A. Langille Articles—*The Oregon Motorist*, Oregon State Parks and Recreation Collection, Oregon State Parks and Recreation, Salem, OR.

Primary Sources, Published

"An Act Relating to Cemeteries…," Chapter 731 Oregon Laws 1999.

"Blumenthal Falls, Tillamook County, Oregon," Northwest Waterfall Survey [online], updated March 19, 2017, https://www.waterfallsnorthwest.com/waterfall/Blumenthal-Falls-3884.

"CHAPTER 745: AN ACT [HB 1036] Relating to beverage containers; and providing penalties," Oregon Laws and Resolutions: Enacted and Adopted by the Regular Session of the Fifty-sixth Legislative Assembly Beginning January 11 and Ending June 10 1971 (Salem, Oregon: Oregon Legislative Assembly, 1971).

"Garden Clubs and Roadside Beauty in Oregon," *The American Magazine of Art* 24:3 (1932): p. 228.

"Oregon Prison Industry Program Nets Record $28.5 Million as Prisoners Earn $1.25/Hour," *Prison Legal News* Apr 2, 2019.

"Oswald West, Governor of Oregon, to the Twenty-Seventh Legislative Assembly," (Salem: Willis S. Duniway, State Printer, 1913).

"Park Manager Kevin Price reflects on his 35-year career with the Oregon State Parks" [video], ~Aug 2018, https://www.oregon.gov/oprd/emp/Pages/EMP-overview.aspx.

"Relating to the Oregon Pioneer Cemetery Commission," Chapter 173 Oregon Laws 2003.

"The American Legion's 52nd National Convention," *American Legion Magazine* 89:5, Nov. 1970, pp. 23 – 25.

"The First National Park Conference," *Iowa Conservation* 5:1 (Jan/March 1921), p. 9.

"To Beautify Roads," *Oregon Voter* 24 (1921), 586.

Advanced Studies Unit, "The Economic Value of State Parks in Oregon, 1959," (Salem: Oregon State Parks & Recreation Division, Oregon State Highway Dept, 1959).

Anon, "Founding Story of Tryon Creek," https://tryonfriends.org/stories-of-tryon-creek/2020/3/founding-story

City Club of Portland, "Constitutional Amendment Limits Uses of Gasoline and Highway User Taxes (State Measure No. 1)," (Portland: City Club of Portland, 1980).

City Club of Portland, "Ballot Measure 66: Lottery Funds for Parks and Watersheds," City Club of Portland Bulletin 80:21 (Oct 23, 1998).

Cochran, Don, interview with Margie Walz, Oct 16, 2008, found in "Three Rivers District Oral History Project" (Plymouth, MN: Three Rivers District Administrative Center, 2008 [ongoing?]).

Cohen, Robyn L. "Prisoners In 1990," *Bureau of Justice Statistics Bulletin* (U.S. Government Printing Office, May 1991).

Colorado Lottery Board, "Colorado Lottery—Thirty Years of Play: FY13 Annual Report," (Denver: Colorado Department of Revenue), 14 – 15.

Crompton, John. David G. Talbot Pugsley Award Bio, ~1992?, https://aapra.org/pugsley-bios/david-g-talbot.

Galton, Francis. *The Art of Travel; or, Shifts and Conveyances Available in Wild Countries* (London: John Murray, 1855).

Guthrie, Jno. D. "Thirteen Million Acres of Recreation," *Oregon Motorist* Aug 1931, pp. 9 – 11, 19.

Highway Research News 34 (1969), pp. 10 – 11.

Journal of the Legislative Assembly... of the State of Oregon... 1913 (Eugene: The Guard Printing Company, 1913), pp. 555 – 556.

Journal of the Senate... of the State of Oregon, 1891 (Salem: Frank C. Baker, 1891), 204.

Kitzhaber, John A. "The State of the State: Keeping Oregon's Quality of Life," (Salem, OR: Office of the Governor, Jan. 13, 1997).

Kozer, Sam A., compiler. State of Oregon Constitutional Amendments... Together with the General Laws... (Salem: State Printing Department, 1921), Chapter 343 [S.B. 365], quotations from 654.

Leach, Florence. "The Old Oregon Trail: The Road That Won an Empire," *Oregon Motorist* Jan. 1925, pp. 12 – 13;

Legislative Council Committee, ORS 656.027 (2019), https://www.oregonlegislature.gov/bills_laws/ors/ors656.html;

Leshner, Josh. "Oregon's Great Recession Update," Oregon Office of Economic Analysis, June 29, 2015.

Manning, Rob. "Oregon School Funding Still a Challenge, 25 Years After Measure 5," *OPB* Apr 15/19, 2016.

Monthly Labor Review 73:1 (Washington, D.C.: U.S. Government Printing Office, 1951).

Northwest Civil War Council, "To Avoid Further Confusion," Facebook post, March 31 2018.

Office of the Secretary of State, *Oregon Blue Book: 1983 – 1984* (Salem: Oregon State Archives), pp. 395 – 396.

Olcott, Ben W. "Message of Ben W. Olcott to the Thirty-First Legislative Assembly, Jan. 10 1921" (Salem: State Printing Department, 1921), p. 17.

Oregon Audits Division, "State of Oregon Parks and Recreation Department: Review of the Department's Relationship with the Oregon State Parks Trust," John N. Lattimer, Director, No. 1999-27 (Aug 5, 1999), pp. viii, 16 – 17, 28.

Oregon Audits Division, "State of Oregon Parks and Recreation Department: Management of

Oregon Parks and Recreation Department, "Oregon State Parks Host Program," (Jan 2013), https://stateparks.oregon.gov/ckfiles/files/2013_parkhostprgmbasics.pdf.

Oregon Parks and Recreation Department, "Oswald West trail guide" [Online Brochure], n.d., https://stateparks.oregon.gov/index.cfm?do=v.publications, accessed July 20, 2020.

Oregon Parks and Recreation Department, Centennial Horizon: Shaping the Future of Oregon's Parks, Recreation, Conservation and Preservation (Salem: Oregon State Parks, 2008).

Oregon State Historic Preservation Office and Chrissy Curran, "The Look-Out on Cape Foulweather," NRIS No. 14001159, National Register of Historic Places Registration Form, Nov 20, 2014 (listed Jan 14, 2015).

Oregon State Parks and Recreation, "Champoeg State Heritage Area Trappers Camp, 2017" (video), uploaded July 26, 2017.

ORS 186.30, "Champoeg Historical Pageant as Official Statehood Pageant," CHAPTER 186—State Emblems; State Boundary (Legislative Counsel Committee, 2019).

Outdoor Recreation Resource Review Committee, "Public Outdoor Recreation Areas: Acreage, Use, Potential," (United State Government Printing Office, 1962): pp. 97 – 101.

Parks and Recreation Division, Department of Transportation, "Oregon State Parks Visitor Survey, 1984," (Winter, 1984),

Patterson, Governor Isaac L. "Oregon's State Parks," *Oregon Motorist* Aug. 1928, pp. 5 – 6, 19.

Pens, Dan. "Oregon's Prison Slavocracy," *Prison Legal News*, May 15, 1998.

Polk, James Knox. *Correspondence of James K. Polk*, ed. Herbert Weaver (Knoxville: University of Tennessee Press, 1969).

Samuel H. Boardman Grove, Angeline Boardman Kirk Grove, Walter W. Boardman Memorial Grove, https://www.savetheredwoods.org/donate/dedicate-a-redwood-grove-or-tree/dedicated-groves/.

Sawyer, Robert W. "Why Oregon Needs State Parks," *Oregon Motorist* May 1930, pp. 5 – 7.

State of Oregon... General Laws (Salem: State Printing Department, 1913), Chapters 47, 80.

"State Park Resources," John N. Lattimer, Director, No. 1999-28 (Aug 5, 1999).

Tyler, Timothy. "The Cooling of America: Out of Tune and Lost in the Counterculture," *Time* Feb 22, 1971.

U.S. Census Bureau, Housing and Household Statistics Division, "Historical Census of Housing Tables [1940 – 2010]," (Oct 2011).

U.S. Census of Housing, "Median Gross Rents By State, 1940 – 2000," https://www2.census.gov/programs-surveys/decennial/tables/time-series/coh-grossrents/grossrents-unadj.txt.

U.S. Government Printing "Compilation of the Domestic Volunteer Service Act of 1973 As Amended Through December 31, 1987," Serial 100-F (Washington, D.C.: U.S. Government Printing Office, 1988).

United States Bureau of the Budget, "The Budget of the United States Government: Appendix" (Washington, D.C.: U.S. Government Printing Office, 1954), 340.

United States Senate. City of Rocks National Reserve Act of 1987: Hearing Before the Subcommittee on Public Lands, National Parks, and Forests of the Committee on Energy and Natural Resources..., (Washington, D.C.: U.S. Government Printing Office, 1988), pp. 17 – 19.

Vista House Accessibility, https://vistahouse.com/accessibility/.

Wilson, Aileen. "The Amazing Journey: The Roosevelt Highway," *Oregon Motorist* June 1928, pp. 13 – 14, 30.

Newspapers

Arizona Republic

Atlantic

Boston Post

Corvallis Gazette-Times

Daily Astorian

Estacada News

Eugene Guard

FYI [Oregon Parks and Recreation Department News]

Guardian

Heppner Gazette-Times

Indian Country Today

Kitsap Sun

L.A. Times

La Grande Observer

New York Times

Newberg Graphic

Oregon Journal

Oregonian

Portland Monthly

Redmond Spokesman

Reuters

Rexburg Standard Journal

Roseburg News-Review

Salem Capital Journal

Seattle Times

Smoke Signals

Southeast Examiner

Statesman Journal

Sunday Oregonian

Time Magazine

Via – Oregon Department of Transportation News

Willamette Week

Secondary Sources

"Bohemia, Inc. History," *International Directory of Company Histories* 13, Tina Grant, Ed. (St. James Press, 1996).

"Loran L. Stewart" Biography, World Forestry Center Leadership Hall Exhibit (Portland, OR: 2003).

Abbott, Carl. "Greater Portland: Experiments with Professional Planning, 1905 – 1925," *Pacific Northwest Quarterly* 76 (1985): pp. 12 – 21.

Alexander, Michelle. *The New Jim Crow: Mass Incarceration in the Age of Colorblindness* (New York: The New Press, 2010).

Anderson, Jennifer. "Boosting Diversity at Oregon State Parks," *Sustainable Life* Aug 1, 2017.

Armstrong, Chester H. *Oregon State Parks: History, 1917 – 1963* (Salem: Oregon Highway Dept., 1965).

Bacon, Richard J. "Oregon's Bottle Bill: A Battle Between Conservation and Convenience," (Eugene: University of Oregon Scholars' Bank, 2005), http://hdl.handle.net/1794/2505.

Barber, Katrine. "⊠We Were at Our Journey's End': Settler Sovereignty Formation in Oregon," *Oregon Historical Quarterly* 120:4 (2019): 382 – 411.

Barber, Katrine. *In Defense of Wy-Am: Native White Alliances and the Struggle for Celilo Village* (Seattle: University of Washington Press, 2018).

Barnd, Natchee Blu. "A Lot to Ask of a Name: White Spaces and Indian Symbols," *Oregon Humanities* Aug 30, 2018.

Barron, Hal S. "And the Crooked Shall Be Made Straight: Public Road Administration and the Decline of Localism in the Rural North, 1870 – 1930" *Journal of Social History* 26 (1992): pp. 81 – 103.

Barry, J. Neilson. "Champoeg Park," *Oregon Historical Quarterly* 40:4 (1939): pp. 336 – 342.

Bauer, Webb Sterling. "A Case Analysis of Oregon's Willamette River Greenway Program," PhD Diss. (Oregon State University, 1980).

Belasco, F Warren James. *Americans on the Road: From Autocamp to Motel, 1910 – 1945* (Cambridge: MIT Press, 1979).

Boardman, Samuel H. *et al.* "Oregon State Park System: A Brief History, *Oregon Historical Quarterly* 55:3 (1954): pp.179 – 233.

Bone, Arthur H. and Walter M. Pierce. *Oregon Cattleman/Governor/ Congressman: Memoirs and Times of Walter M. Pierce* (Portland: Oregon Historical Society, 1981).

Boyd, Robert. "Strategies of Indian Burning in the Willamette Valley," in *Indians, Fire, and the Land in the Pacific Northwest*, ed. Robert Boyd (Corvallis: Oregon State University Press, 1999): pp. 94 – 138.

Brandt, Roger. "Auto Courts of the Illinois Valley, a Baseline Inventory: Southwest Oregon Highway 199 and Highway 46," (Self-published, 2013).

Brekas, Jeff. "The Daredevil Al Story," *Trail's End: News from Silver Falls* (Summer 1995).

Browne, Jaron. "Rooted in Slavery: Prison Labor Exploitation," *Race, Poverty & the Environment* 17:1 (2020), pp. 78 – 80.

Burnham, John Chynoweth. "The Gasoline Tax and the Automobile Revolution," *Mississippi Valley Historical Review* 48 (1961): pp. 435 – 459.

Cain, Eric. "Vortex I," *Oregon Experience* S4 E403 (original broadcast: Oct 28, 2010).

Caple, Helen. "Playing with Words and Pictures: Intersemiosis In a New Genre," PhD diss. (University of Sydney, 2009).

Carpenter, Marc James. "Pioneer Problems: 'Wanton Murder,' Indian War Veterans, and Oregon's Violent Past," *Oregon Historical Quarterly* 121:2 (Summer 2020): 156 – 185.

Carpenter, Marc James. "Reconsidering *The Pioneer*, One Hundred Years Later," report submitted to the Oregon Parks and Recreation Department, June 27, 2019, https://www.oregon.gov/oprd/OH/Documents/Fellow2019MarcCarpenterReconsideringThe%20Pioneer.pdf.

Chambers, Thomas A. *Drinking the Waters: Creating an American Leisure Class at Nineteenth-Century Mineral Springs* (Washington, D.C.: Smithsonian Institutions, 2002).

Christensen, Donald Watson. "An Evaluation and Criteria for Implementation of a Recreational Motorboat Educational Licensing Practice in Oregon," PhD Diss. (Oregon State University, 1978).

Claudy, C. H. "Federal Aid in Fighting Mud," *Scientific American* 116 (1917): pp. 14 – 15.

Clucas, Richard A., Brent S. Steel, and Mark Henkels. *Oregon Politics and Government: Progressives versus Conservative Populists* (Lincoln: University of Nebraska Press, 2005).

Conard, Rebecca. "National Conference on State Parks: Reflections on Organizational Genealogy," *The George Wright Forum* 14:4 (1997): pp. 28 – 43.

Cox, Thomas R. "The Crusade to Save Oregon's Scenery," *Pacific Historical Review* 37 (1968): pp. 179 – 199.

Cox, Thomas R. *The Park Builders: A History of State Parks in the Pacific Northwest* (Seattle: University of Washington Press, 1988).

Cronon, William. "The Trouble with Wilderness; Or, Getting Back to the Wrong Nature," *Uncommon Ground: Rethinking the Human Place in Nature*, William Cronon, ed. (New York: W. W. Norton, 1995): pp. 69 – 90.

DeBenedetti, Charles. *An American Ordeal: The Antiwar Movement of the Vietnam Era.* (Syracuse, N.Y.: Syracuse University Press, 1990).

Deloria, Phil. *Playing Indian* (New Haven: Yale University Press, 1998).

Deur, Douglas. "A Most Sacred Place: The Significance of Crater Lake among the Indians of Southern Oregon," *Oregon Historical Quarterly* 103 (2002): pp. 18 – 49.

Ellis, Richard J. *Democratic Delusions: The Initiative Process in America* (Lawrence: University of Kansas Press, 2002).

Evans, Gail E. "Promoting Tourism and Development at Crater Lake: The Art of Grace Russell Fountain and Mabel Russell Lowther," *Oregon Historical Quarterly* 116 (2015): pp. 310 – 343.

Fahey, John. "A.L. White, Champion of Urban Beauty," *Pacific Northwest Quarterly* 72 (1981): pp. 170 – 179.

Fahl, Ronald J. "S. C. Lancaster and the Columbia River Highway: Engineer as Conservationist," *Oregon Historical Quarterly* 74 (1973): pp. 101 – 144.

Fallen Fortress at Cape Lookout (film), Dir. Tim King, Oregon Public Broadcasting, 1993.

Farmer, James O. "Playing Rebels: Reenactment as Nostalgia and Defense of the Confederacy in the Battle of Aiken," *Southern Cultures* 11:1 (2005): pp. 46 – 73.

Figart, Deborah M. and Lonnie Golden. "Introduction and Overview: Understanding Working Time Around the World," *Working Time: International Trends, Theories and Policy Perspectives.* Deborah M. Figart and Lonnie Golden, Eds. (New York: Routledge, 2000): pp. 1 - 18.

Forby, Rev. Robert. *The Vocabulary of East Anglia..., v. 2* (London: J.B. Nicholas and Son, 1830): p. 158.

Freegood, Seymour. "The Hotels: Time to Stop and Rest," *Fortune* 68 (July 1963).

Gifford, Laura Jane. "Shared Narratives: The Story of the 1942 Attack on Fort Stevens," *Oregon Historical Quarterly* 116 (2015): pp. 376 – 383.

Gilson, Leland. "Willamette Valley Pyroculture," *Current Archaeological Happenings in Oregon* 17 (1992): pp. 9 – 11.

Green, F. B. "Recreation Vehicles: The Economics of Ownership," *Journal of Consumer Affairs* 12:2 (1978): pp. 364 – 372.

Grier, Katherine C. *Pets in America: A History* (Chapel Hill: University of North Carolina Press, 2006).

Hampton, Bruce. "The Airstream Brand at 75: Born On the 4th of July, Wally Byam Went on to Create an American Icon," *RV Business* 57:2 (2006): p. 32+.

Harcourt, William. "To Camp Indian Style," *Boy's Life* June 1952, 12 – 13.

Higgens-Evenson, R. Rudy. "Financing a Second Era of Internal Improvements: Transportation and Tax Reform, 1890 – 1929," *Social Science History* 26 (2002): pp. 623 – 651.

Horwitz, Tony. *Confederates in the Attic: Dispatches from the Unfinished Civil War* (New York: Random House, 1998).

Howe, Sharon M. "Photography and the Making of Crater Lake National Park," *Oregon Historical Quarterly* 103 (2002): pp. 76 – 97.

Hoyt, Jr., Hugh Myron. "The Good Roads Movement in Oregon, 1900 – 1920," PhD diss., (University of Oregon, 1966).

Hugill, Peter J. "Good Roads and the Automobile in the United States 1880 – 1929," *Geographical Review* 72 (1982): pp. 327 – 349.

Hussey, John. *Champoeg: Place of Transition; A Disputed History* (Portland: Oregon Historical Society, 1967).

Jacobs, Meg. *Panic at the Pump: The Energy Crisis and the Transformation of American Politics in the 1970s.* (New York: Hill and Wang, 2016).

Jetté, Melinda Marie. *At the Hearth of the Crossed Races: A French-Indian Community in Nineteenth-Century Oregon, 1812 – 1859.* (Corvallis: Oregon State University Press, 2015).

Kemery, Becky. *Yurts: Living in the Round.* (Salt Lake City: Gibbs Smith, 2006).

Krimsky, Paula Gibson. "Reading, Writing, and the Great Outdoors: Frederick Gunn's School Transforms Victorian-era Education," *Connecticut History* July 18, 2019.

Lansing, William A. *Camps and Calluses: The Civilian Conservation Corps in Southwestern Oregon* (North Bend, Ore.: Self-published, 2014).

Larson, Zeb. "Silver Falls State Park and the Early Environmental Movement," *Oregon Historical Quarterly* 112 (2011): pp. 34 – 57.

Leggett, Fannie. "A Short Historical Sketch of a Part of the Bristow Family," *Lane County Historian* 13:3 (Fall 1968): 63 – 68.

Lerner, Preston. "Innovations in Driving: Shock Absorbers," *Popular Science* Sept 19, 2012.

Lewis, David G. "The Kalapuya Village of Champoeg," *Quartux Journal* June 25, 2016.

Lewis, David G. "The Spirit of Colonization of Indian Country: Vista House and American Nationalism," *Quartux Journal* Sept 4, 2017.

Lewis, David. "Four Deaths: The Near Destruction of Western Oregon Tribes and Native Lifeways, Removal to Reservation, and Erasure from History," *Oregon Historical Quarterly* 115:3 (2014): pp. 414 – 437.

Lewis, Dylan. "Unpaid Protectors: Volunteerism and the Diminishing Role of Federal Responsibility in the National Park Service," in *Protected Areas in a Changing World: Proceedings of the 2013 George Wright Society Conference on Parks, Protected Areas, and Cultural sites.* Samantha Weber, ed. (Hancock, MI: George Wright Society, 2014): pp. 95 – 100.

Linhares, Tom. *Recent History of Oregon's Property Tax System, with an Emphasis On Its Impact On Multnomah County Local Governments*, ed. Elizabeth Provost (Self-published, 2011).

Lipin, Lawrence M. "'Cast Aside the Automobile Enthusiast': Class Conflict, Tax Policy, and the Preservation of Nature in Progressive-Era Oregon," *Oregon Historical Quarterly* 107:2 (2006): pp. 166 – 195.

Lipin, Lawrence M. and William Lunch. "Moralistic Direct Democracy: Political Insurgents, Religion, and the State in Twentieth-Century Oregon," *Oregon Historical Quarterly* 110:4 (2009): pp. 514 – 545.

Lipin, Lawrence M. *Workers and the Wild: Conservation, Consumerism, and Labor in Oregon, 1910 – 1930*. (Urbana: University of Illinois, 2007).

Lippke, Richard L. "Should States Be in the Gambling Business?" *Public Affairs Quarterly* 11:1 (1997): pp. 57 – 73.

Lo, Clarence Y. H. *Small Property versus Big Government: The Social Origins of the Property Tax Revolt*. (Berkeley: University of California Press, 2018).

Long, Reub and Ron Shay, "Interview: Reub Long on the Management of Central Oregon's Rangelands," *Oregon Historical Quarterly* 88:2 (1987): pp. 183 – 195.

Love, Matt. *The Far Out Story of Vortex I* (Nestucca Spit Press, 2004).

Lunch, William M. "Budgeting by Initiative: An Oxymoron," *Willamette Law Review* 34:663 (1998): pp. 663-674.

Lyman, H.S. "Reminiscences of F. X. Matthieu," *Quarterly of the Oregon Historical Society* 1:1 (1900): pp. 73 – 104.

Maher, Neil M. *Nature's New Deal: The Civilian Conservation Corps and the Roots of the American Environmental Movement* (New York: Oxford University Press, 2008).

Mangun, Kimberley. *A Force for Change: Beatrice Morrow Cannady and the Struggle for Civil Rights in Oregon, 1912 – 1936* (Corvallis: Oregon State University Press, 2010).

Mark, Stephen R. *Preserving the Living Past: John C. Merriam's Legacy in the State and National Parks* (Berkeley: University of California Press, 2005).

Marsh, Kevin R. *Drawing Lines in the Forest: Creating Wilderness Areas in the Pacific Northwest* (Seattle: University of Washington Press, 2009).

McCarthy, Patrick. "'Living History' as the 'Real Thing': A Comparative Analysis of the Modern Mountain Man Rendezvous, Renaissance Fairs, and Civil War Re-Enactments," *ETC: A Review of General Semantics* 71:2 (2014): pp. 106 – 123.

McClelland, Linda Flint. *Building the National Parks: Historic Landscape Design and Construction* (Baltimore: John Hopkins University Press, 1998).

McCoy, Robert R. "The Paradox of Oregon's Progressive Politics: The Political Career of Walter Marcus Pierce," *Oregon Historical Quarterly* 110:3 (2009): pp. 390 – 419.

Merriam, Jr., Lawrence C. *Oregon's Highway Park System, 1921 – 1989: An Administrative History* (Salem: Oregon Parks and Recreation Department, 1992).

Mikesell, John L. "The Path of the Tax Revolt: Statewide Expenditure and Tax Control Referenda since Proposition 13," *State and Local Government Review* 18:1 (1986): pp. 5 – 12.

Munro, Sarah Baker. "The Seventy-Fifth Anniversary of the New Deal: Oregon's Legacy," *Oregon Historical Quarterly* 109:2 (2008): pp. 304 – 311.

Nelson, Nancy J. "Tribes and the Oregon Parks and Recreation Department—Partnerships in Training, Repatriation, and Traditional Plant Gathering," in Dennis G. Griffin *et al*, "The State of Oregon and Nine Federally-Recognized Tribes Forge a Path Forward," *Journal of Northwest Anthropology* 55:1 (2021): pp. 173 – 184.

Nesbit, Virginia. "Sarah Helmick and Helmick Park," *Quarterly of the Oregon Historical Society* 26:4 (1925): pp. 444 – 447.

O'Leary, Pieter M. "A Walk in the Park: A Legal Overview of California's State and Federal Parks and the Laws Governing Their Use and Enjoyment," *Natural Resources Journal* 52:1 (Spring 2012),

O'Neill, William L. *American High: The Years of Confidence, 1945 – 1960* (New York: Simon and Schuster, 1986).

Owen, John D. "Workweeks and Leisure: An Analysis of Trends, 1948 – 75, *Monthly Labor Review* 99:8 (1976): 3 – 8.

Philips, Patty [Patricia] Whereat. "Revisiting Woahink and Cleawox," Shichil's Blog, July 10, 2015.

Phillips, Sarah. *This Land, This Nation: Conservation, Rural America, and the New Deal* (New York: Cambridge University Press, 2007).

Pomeroy, Earl. *In Search of the Golden West: The Tourist in Western America* (New York: Alfred A. Knopf, 1957).

Posner, Kenneth A. *Stalking the Black Swan: Research and Decision Making in a World of Extreme Volatility* (New York: Columbia University Press, 2010).

Post, Emily. *By Motor to the Golden Gate* (New York: D. Appleton, 1916).

Potter, Elisabeth Walton. "The National Historic Preservation Act at Fifty," *Oregon Historical Quarterly* 117:3 (Fall 2016): pp. 378 – 401.

Prentice, Deborah A. and Erica Carranza. "What Women and Men Should Be, Shouldn't Be, Are Allowed to Be, and Don't Have to Be: The Contents of Proscriptive Gender Stereotypes," *Psychology of Women Quarterly* 26:4 (2002): pp. 269 – 281.

Ramsey, Bill. "The Adventures of the 'Four Vagabonds'; 1921: Camping with the President," *Model T Times* July/August 2018, pp. 24 – 27.

Robbins, William G. "Town and Country in Oregon: A Conflicted Legacy," *Oregon Historical Quarterly* 110:1 (2009): pp. 52 – 73.

Robbins, William G. *Oregon: This Storied Land* (Portland: Oregon Historical Society Press, 2005).

Romero, Carol Jusenius. "The Economics of Volunteerism: A Review," in *America's Aging: Productive Roles in an Older Society* (Washington, D.C.: National Academy Press, 1986): pp. 23 – 50.

Rothman, Hal. *Devil's Bargains: Tourism in the Twentieth-Century American West* (Kansas: University of Kansas Press, 1998).

Russell, Jr. Robert D. "Unrealized Visions: Medford and the City Beautiful Movement," *Oregon Historical Quarterly* 102:2 (2001): pp. 196 – 209.

Scharff, Virginia. *Twenty Thousand Roads: Women, Movement, and the West* (Berkeley: University of California Press, 2003).

Smith, Gregory. "Living with Oregon's Measure 5: The Costs of Property Tax Relief in Two Suburban Elementary Schools," *Phi Delta Kappan* 76:6 (1995): pp. 4452 – 4461.

Snyder, Ann Virtu. "Location, Location, Location: Reflections of an Itinerant Practitioner," *NWSA Journal* 17:2 (2005), pp. 142 – 149.

Spanbauer, Mary Kay. "Kansas & The President's Commission On Americans Outdoors," *Kansas Wildlife & Parks* 45:6 (Nov/Dec 1988): pp. 39 – 43.

Special Issue: Remembering Celilo Falls, *Oregon Historical Quarterly* 108 (2007).

Sprague, John Francis. *Sprague's Journal of Maine History 1* (Dover, ME: John Francis Sprague, 1913).

Straton, Kathryn A. *Oregon's Beaches: A Birthright Preserved* (Salem: Oregon State Parks and Recreation Branch, 1977).

Thompson, Heather Ann. "Why Mass Incarceration Matters: Rethinking Crisis, Decline, and Transformation in Postwar American History," *Journal of American History* 97:3 (2010), pp. 703 – 734.

Toy Jr., Eckard V. "Oregon At War," *Oregon Historical Quarterly* 102:2 (2001): pp. 413 – 433.

Toy, Eckard V. "The Ku Klux Klan in Oregon," *Experiences in the Promised Land: Essays in Pacific Northwest History*, G. Thomas Edwards and Carlos A. Schwantes, eds. (Seattle: University of Washington, 1986): pp. 269 – 286.

Twitchell, James B. *Winnebago Nation: The RV in American Culture* (New York: Columbia University Press, 2014).

Tyler, Melissa et al. "California State Parks: Preserving Our Natural and Cultural Treasures," (Exhibit, California State Archives, 2014; digital adaptation by Jessica Herrick, 2016).

Uecker, Jeffry. "Picturing the Corps of Discovery: The Lewis and Clark Expedition in American Art," *Oregon Historical Quarterly* 103:4 (2002): pp. 452 – 479.

University of Oregon, *Oregana* (1956), ed. Sue French (Eugene: University of Oregon Student Publications Board, 1956).

Vaughn, Chelsea K. "'The Road That Won an Empire': Commemoration, Commercialization, and Auto Tourism at the 'Top o' Blue Mountains,'" *Oregon Historical Quarterly* 115 (2014): pp. 6 – 37.

Vogel, David. *California Greenin': How the Golden State Became an Environmental Leader.* (Princeton, N.J.: Princeton University Press, 2018).

Walsh, Megan K., Cathy Whitlock, and Patrick J. Bartlein. "1200 years of fire and vegetation history in the Willamette Valley, Oregon and Washington, reconstructed using high-resolution macroscopic charcoal and pollen analysis," *Palaeogeography, Palaeoclimatology, Palaeoecology* 297:2 (2010): pp. 273 – 289.

Walth, Brent. *Fire at Eden's Gate: Tom McCall and the Oregon Story* (Portland: Oregon Historical Society Press, 1994).

Walth, Brent. "No Deposit, No Return: Richard Chambers, Tom McCall, and the Oregon Bottle Bill," *Oregon Historical Quarterly* 95:3 (1994): 278 – 299.

Weis, Alec *et al.* "Applying a Lens of Racial Equity to Our Parks," *Parks & Recreation* 53 (2018), 36+.

Weiselberg, Erik. "He All but Made the Mountains: William Gladstone Steel, Mountain Climbing, and the Establishment of Crater Lake National Park," *Oregon Historical Quarterly* 103:1 (2002): pp. 50 – 75.

Woodzicka, Julie A. and Thomas E. Ford. "A Framework for Thinking About the (not-so-funny) Effect of Sexist Humor," *Europe's Journal of Psychology* 6:3 (2010): pp. 174 – 195.

Wyckoff, William with William Cronon. *How to Read the American West: A Field Guide.* (Seattle: University of Washington Press, 2014), pp. 296 – 297.

Young, Terence. "'Green and Shady Camps': E.P. Meinecke and the Restoration of America's Public Campgrounds," *George Wright Forum* 31:1 (2014): 69 – 76.

Young, Terence. *Heading Out: A History of American Camping* (Ithaca: Cornell University Press, 2017).